Belfast Met

3 7777 00176206 1

Belf

D1649625

HEALTH AND CARE IN
SOCIETIES

A new international approac

17   REPL 2014

HC

Liz Lloyd

First published in Great Britain in 2012 by

The Policy Press
University of Bristol
Fourth Floor
Beacon House
Queen's Road
Bristol BS8 1QU
UK
Tel +44 (0)117 331 4054
Fax +44 (0)117 331 4093
e-mail tpp-info@bristol.ac.uk
www.policypress.co.uk

North American office:

The Policy Press
c/o The University of Chicago Press
1427 East 60th Street
Chicago, IL 60637, USA
t: +1 773 702 7700
f: +1 773-702-9756
e:sales@press.uchicago.edu
www.press.uchicago.edu

© The Policy Press 2012

British Library Cataloguing in Publication Data
A catalogue record for this book is available from the British Library.

Library of Congress Cataloging-in-Publication Data
A catalog record for this book has been requested.

ISBN 978 1 86134 918 7 paperback
ISBN 978 1 86134 919 4 hardcover

The right of Liz Lloyd to be identified as author of this work has been asserted by her in accordance with the 1988 Copyright, Designs and Patents Act.

All rights reserved: no part of this publication may be reproduced, stored in a retrieval system, or transmitted in any form or by any means, electronic, mechanical, photocopying, recording, or otherwise without the prior permission of The Policy Press.

The statements and opinions contained within this publication are solely those of the author and not of The University of Bristol or The Policy Press. The University of Bristol and The Policy Press disclaim responsibility for any injury to persons or property resulting from any material published in this publication.

The Policy Press works to counter discrimination on grounds of gender, race, disability, age and sexuality.

Cover design by The Policy Press
Front cover: image kindly supplied by istock
Printed and bound in Great Britain by TJ International, Padstow
The Policy Press uses environmentally responsible print partners

Contents

List of abbreviations   iv

Foreword by Judith Phillips   v

Acknowledgements   vi

one   Introduction   1

two   Patterns and trends in ageing and health   11

three   Understanding health and care   27

four   The policy process in health and care   47

five   Healthy ageing: upstream actions to prevent illness   69

six   Medicine, ageing and healthcare   89

seven   Care for health in later life   111

eight   Conclusion   131

References   141

Index   161

List of abbreviations

ADL	Activity of Daily Living
DALY	Disability Adjusted Life Years
GBD	Global Burden of Disease
GDP	Gross Domestic Product
IADL	Instrumental Activity of Daily Living
IFI	international financial institution
IMF	International Monetary Fund
INGO	international non-governmental organisation
MDGs	Millennium Development Goals
MIPAA	Madrid International Plan of Action on Ageing
NGO	non-governmental organisation
OECD	Organisation for Economic and Social Development
UNRISD	United Nations Research Institute for Social Development
WHO	World Health Organization

Foreword

Judith Phillips

A global view of the complex relationship between health, care and ageing is provided in this refreshing approach to significant issues of later life. The book challenges a number of key assumptions of policy and practice, such as stereotypes of older people as a burden and drain on resources and society. It also questions the narrow and negative focus on healthcare in contrast to promoting positive health and well-being. Underpinning the discussion are frameworks to help the reader critique the processes involved in health and social care policies and the dominant discourses that have pervaded our thinking of how to address health and social care needs of an older population. An ethics of care approach and an understanding of the lifecourse are central to the reframing of these issues.

This book captures the essence of the 'Ageing and the Lifecourse' series, based on critical gerontology and lifecourse perspectives. With renewed interest in mid and later life, the series 'Ageing and the Lifecourse' bridges the gaps in the literature as well as provides cutting-edge debate on new and traditional areas of ageing within a lifecourse perspective, while focusing on the social rather than the medical aspects of ageing. Such an approach will appeal to professionals as well as academics engaged in these debates at local, regional, national and global levels. It has considerable relevance to policy makers in health and social care, particularly at a time when, in many parts of the world, economic considerations are in the forefront of the debate on how to provide health and social care in ageing societies.

Acknowledgements

Thanks are due to many people for the generous support they have given throughout the process of writing and producing this text. I am most grateful to Alison Shaw and the staff at The Policy Press, who provided excellent support and guidance throughout, to Judith Phillips for her advice on developing the book and to the anonymous reviewer whose constructive comments were very helpful at the completion stage. I am equally grateful to my colleagues at the School for Policy Studies as well as to my friends and family who have provided unstinting support and encouragement. Particular thanks are due to Ailsa Cameron, Marion Lovell-Jones, Randall Smith, and above all to Ed Cape.

ONE

Introduction

Ageing, health and care are complex and contentious concepts and have become inextricably linked in policy debates around the world. Apocalyptic 'time-bomb' messages continue to circulate, although they are now often accompanied by the more positive message that population ageing is a cause for celebration. The policy agenda on health and care in the context of ageing societies appears to have been settled and the task at hand is not to seek answers about the best way to respond so as much as to ensure compliance at local, national and international levels to a particular set of principles, consistent with a wider neoliberal economic agenda. Despite the economic crises of recent years, the neoliberal agenda remains firmly in place in the context of policies on health and care.

The World Health Organization estimates that by 2025, 63% of all deaths in the world will be among the over-65s. In high-income countries, the 20th century saw greater increases in life expectancy than in the whole of previous history. According to the Global Forum for Health Research (www.globalforumhealth. org) almost 85% of deaths in high-income countries now occur after the age of 60, compared with 45% in low- to middle-income countries. Trends such as these might be seen as a cause for either celebration or deep anxiety, but in any case warrant serious attention so as to understand their impact on social and cultural life. In countries with established welfare states these trends have taxed the minds of policy makers over recent decades and, allowing for some variations, an agenda for health and care has emerged which has two overarching principles. The first of these is that a focus on the gap between life expectancy and *healthy* life expectancy is crucial. Accordingly, policies should be focused on the promotion of healthy and active ageing so that independence can continue for as long as possible in later life. The second is that governments should keep a tight rein on spending in health and social care so that when older people begin to fail in their attempts to maintain self-reliance and become dependent on others, the costs of caring for them are contained. These two principles permeate a range of policies at all levels, from the local to the global, and both of them generate a host of questions as to their viability, necessity and applicability in different contexts. Consistent with neoliberal economic policies, the tight rein on spending is widely regarded as meaning that the private, for-profit sector should replace the state as the primary provider of services, because of its perceived greater efficiency. The private sector is also central to the related policy discourse of *consumerism*, which entails the individualisation of services and the promotion of choice for older people as service users. In the context of globalisation, debates in one country or region reverberate around the world. Thus, care for older people in the affluent 'global north' relies to a large extent on a supply of cheap labour from the countries of the 'global south'. As populations in the global south are also ageing very rapidly, ethical questions arise about the impact of the migration of health and care workers on the countries of origin that can ill afford to lose them.

One way of understanding how these principles became so firmly established in policy agendas is to analyse policies as *processes*, which are continuously taking place in the context of a globalised economy. A core focus of this book is on the ways in which conceptualisations of healthy ageing and the conditions of caring developed in high-income countries have found their way into global policies, despite socioeconomic inequalities and cultural and historical differences. There is a parallel policy discourse of *rights*, which is seen in the demands of older people for action on age discrimination and decent pensions, as well as in campaigns to improve healthcare and tackle global inequalities in health. There is an ongoing conflict between the idea of health as a human right and the idea of health as a commodity, with the latter currently in the ascendant but with the former being maintained by continuing strong commitment to the ideals of public health based on human rights (see, for example, Anderson 2006, Navarro 2007, Labonté 2008). Inequalities in health and in access to healthcare generate strong views and deeply held feelings. Sen (2004: 21), for example, commented: 'In any discussion of social equity and justice, illness and health must figure as a major concern', while Anand (2004) argued that health is directly constitutive of a person's well-being and that, as poor health constrains actions and choices, promoting good health is a matter of social justice. Indeed, some would argue that inequalities in health and healthcare are the ultimate expression of social injustice (Segall 2007).

The unequal distribution of the spectacular gains in life expectancy that have occurred through the 20th century both within and between countries is an evident measure of global injustice. Yet, inequalities persist in spite of years of global declarations and policies to tackle them. In dominant global policy discourses, the cost of population ageing is arguably an overriding agenda that overshadows that of action on the injustice of inequalities. The policy process reflects inequalities in power and in the capacity to influence how and to what purpose issues are defined as they are. Analysis of the *process* of policies highlights how such policy debates are 'framed' and how priorities for action are established through contestation, negotiation and compromise. Contemporary debates on long-term care policies exemplify all three: for example the rights of unpaid carers to recognition; the rights of paid carers to decent working conditions and wages; and the rights of people who are cared for to determine the conditions of caring. Being about rights and resources and the relationship between them, these debates are both *moral* and *political* and often entail deep divergences and unresolved conflicts of interest between groups.

Policies to promote healthy ageing are strongly individualistic and moral in tone, the personal responsibility of the individual to age in good health being ubiquitous in health promotion messages: to exercise more, to eat well and to cease smoking. There is nothing particularly new in this; these have been the stock-in-trade messages of health promotion for decades. However, linked with the rising *numbers* of older people and anxieties over containing the cost of care, the moral message of healthy ageing is sharpened, so that even though the outcomes of a healthy life might be the enjoyment of a longer life, the primary purpose is to ensure that older people make minimum claims on the public purse. It follows also that this message generates questions concerning the rights to healthcare for those who do not succeed in maintaining their health, and already in some contexts consideration is being given to whether treatment decisions should be conditional on life-style changes, which assumes greater significance in the context of the overarching message about the cost of population ageing.

The policy principle of containing the costs of care also generates questions concerning who should bear responsibility for meeting those costs, and once again the answer that emerges from policy circles is highly individualistic. Within developed welfare states, there has been a long-standing debate about whether long-term care costs should be pooled or borne by the individual, but in the context of population ageing at a time of dominant neoliberal economic policies the terms of the debate have been changed and the question increasingly is not whether but *how* and *to what extent* individuals should bear the cost. As Phillipson (2006) noted, the removal of the security of socialised forms of support has individualised risk so that ageing itself becomes a matter of risk. In turn, questions are raised about what will be the expectations on families to provide material and other forms of support. In contexts where little or no formal welfare state exists the costs of care have always been borne by the individuals and families, but there is increasing concern about the sustainability of these arrangements (Bedford 2010). Where nation-states have few or no resources the private sector is in a powerful position to dictate the terms of its involvement in health and social care. Looking after those who are unable to benefit is the job of the non-governmental organisations (NGOs).

These moral and political questions are unavoidable in a discussion of health and care in ageing societies and demand a deeper analysis of policies than one that is focused merely on the viability of strategies on healthy ageing or fiscal policies to contain welfare expenditure. It requires a critical analysis of why it is that the policy agenda has been framed in the way described above. For example, as discussed in this text, despite evidence to the contrary, a simplistic model of dependency ratios continues to be used in policy making. In fact, the negative characterisation of dependence is a crucial element of policies on health and care, reflecting the dominance of the policy agendas of high-income countries on the rest of the world. Without doubt, in Western cultures dependence on the care of others entails a loss of citizen rights and heightens the risk of marginalisation from mainstream society. Yet, as is increasingly acknowledged in gerontology, the lifecourse usually ends in conditions of sickness and dependency, however successful individuals are at compressing the period of illness into as short a time as possible (Gilleard and Higgs 2000, Twigg 2006). Attention to our embodied selves calls into question the sustainability of policies that characterise the citizen as a disembodied, independent subject (Kittay et al 2005).

In this text, which draws on literature from a range of disciplines, the critical analysis of these complex issues is framed by the theoretical frameworks on care developed by feminist ethicists (Tronto 1993, Sevenhuijsen 1998, Kittay et al 2005, Held 2006). There are variations within this school of thought, but all take it as a fundamental principle that dependence and a need for care must be understood as characteristics inherent within the human condition, not as aberrations. Feminist ethicists argue that in Western cultures the *social* nature of human life has been eclipsed by a preoccupation with individual autonomy and independence. Rejection of the characterisation of humans as essentially self-sufficient and independent underpins the whole body of work in the ethics of care and is encapsulated in the observation that in order to achieve independence and autonomy human beings must first be cared for. At the heart of this perspective and in common with other philosophical schools of thought is the emphasis placed on the centrality of human beings' *social* nature. It is argued that this is not the *outcome of* relationships between individuals but that, on the contrary, what connects us to others is *prior to* our individuality, not consequent upon it. For example, Mahon and Robinson (2011a) argued that an emphasis on the isolated, self-reliant, autonomous individual does not adequately reflect the social realities in most communities around the world. Instead, they proposed a 'relational autonomy', which holds that ultimately autonomy is achieved in and through relationships. It is important to stress that feminist ethicists argue not *against* the idea of individual autonomy, but for recognition that it is mutually constitutive (Mahon and Robinson 2011b:181). The focus on autonomy is particularly relevant in the context of ageing. The loss of autonomy, in the sense of individual rational thought and behaviour, is associated with cognitive impairment; but at a broader level a loss of autonomy, in the sense of individual self-sufficiency, frequently goes hand-in-hand with declining health and an increase in reliance on others for support and care. The value of an ethics of care perspective is that it does not differentiate between old (dependent) and young (independent) but sees dependency as inherent within the entire lifecourse and thus overcomes the tendency to regard older people as 'the other'.

A second fundamental principle within the feminist ethics of care is the critique of the dichotomy between public and private domains of life and the place of care. Feminist ethicists argue that care has been devalued and, being antithetical to the dominant model of autonomy, has been excluded from the public sphere and confined to the private sphere. Indeed, Tronto (1993) argues that it is the very centrality of care to human life that has led to its devaluation within contemporary political life and its containment behind doors in the private sphere of the family or institution because it poses such a threat to contemporary ideas about autonomy. It would be reasonable to ask at this point why, if care has been confined to the private sphere, it holds such a central place in the global policy agenda in relation to ageing populations. From a feminist ethics of care perspective, the answer to this question is evident in the way that policies are framed by dichotomous thinking about public and private spheres of care. The preoccupation of policy makers is

—

with the economics of care provision and the organisation and management of care services. What is less evident in policy debates is attention to the *practices* of care, which are regarded as the business of the private domain, preferably within the family, where care is assumed to come naturally. The privacy surrounding family care practices extends to institutional and home-based care practices also, and there is an evident lack of public awareness or regulation of care practices in most parts of the world. Indeed, it is often when a scandal emerges about cruel or inhuman behaviour that public attention turns to institutional care practices, and even then it is usually short lived. There is an especially serious lack of understanding of how practices of care are perceived from the point of view of those older people who are on the receiving end. Even where a 'service-user perspective' is sought, there is a tendency to engage in discussion with proxies, in the form of representative organisations and carers' groups. As Kittay et al (2005) argued, the private–public distinction can itself be seen as a product of denial about the inevitability of human dependency.

The ethics of care is central to international perspectives on ageing health and care for a number of interrelated reasons. The first of these concerns the core principle concerning the interdependence of human beings. This insight opens up a different way of understanding health and well-being as the outcome of social relationships. This applies not only at the micro-level of care relationships but also at the global level. Global patterns of interdependency, as explored further in Chapter Seven, are shaped by gender relations, colonial histories and contemporary socioeconomic inequalities. For example, the idea of 'global care chains' (Yeates 2004) describes the way in which migration patterns have developed to meet the need for care workers in relatively affluent countries, with far-reaching consequences for labour relations and ideas about citizenship rights. The migration of mainly women care workers from poorer parts of the world to more affluent countries of North America and Europe to take up low-paid jobs in health and social services has, as Mahon and Robinson argued, 'translated the unequal relations of personal interdependency into the unequal relations of transnational interdependency' (2011a: 25).

Second, the ethics of care exposes the limitations of liberal individualism seen in marketised models of health and welfare at a global level. Its challenge is based on its rejection of the currently dominant idealised version of the autonomous rational individual. Held (2006) argued that while individualism is relevant to citizenship, it is not all that citizenship is about. The extension of markets into health and welfare services has reinforced the idea that contractual relationships between self-interested strangers of equal standing are *the* desired form within public services. However, Held raised the question of what this means in services such as healthcare, where people who are ill may be far removed from the assumptions that underlie the contractual model of relationships. As argued, old age commonly entails a loss of self-reliance and increased dependency on others, and this places older people in a particularly invidious position within markets. Held's observation also reflects the principle that ethics should be grounded in people's experiences – the 'real world', as opposed to the abstract world of market relations.

Third, the ethics of care offers a valuable critique of dichotomous thinking between justice and care. In the context of social policies, justice is widely regarded as the moral framework for public life, while care is seen as the moral framework of private life. How these two relate to each other is the subject of much debate and, as pointed out above, the divide between public and private domains is problematic. There is now more widespread acceptance of the need for the principles of justice to apply in the private world of family relationships. For example, the abuse of older people within the family is, at least in principle, regarded as unacceptable. An ethic of justice demands that the rights of people enshrined in the UN Declaration of Human Rights, to a life that is free of cruel, inhuman or degrading treatment, must be upheld and that public bodies have a responsibility to attend to this. Indeed, the World Health Organization supported the Toronto Declaration on the Global Prevention of Elder Abuse (WHO 2002c). Yet it is known that the abuse of older people continues to be prevalent throughout the world and that authorities fail to pay adequate attention to it. To understand why this is so draws attention to the need for an ethic of care to apply to the public domain. Feminist ethicists argue that the encapsulation of rights in abstract form – such as in the Toronto Declaration – runs the risk that they end up remaining as lofty ideals with little impact in practice. The reason for this is that the moral agenda of rights and justice is conceptualised as separate from and above the world of politics (Tronto 1993) and this conceptual differentiation obfuscates the way in which political considerations influence and shape the moral agenda, both in the abstract and in reality. The exercise of power within the political sphere has a profound influence on the setting of moral agendas and statements concerning the rights of individuals. Hence, the *language* of policies is highly moral in tone, but policies *in practice* become subsumed into political agendas where the management of resources is the primary rationale.

It follows that rights are not immutable but are always contingent and always to be defended. Thus, while declarations and overarching policy aims are valuable for articulating public standards they cannot be relied upon as a basis for tackling the abuse of power. An ethics of care approach to dealing with the abuse of older people would start not from a reliance on declarations (although these might be strategically invoked) but first and foremost from an understanding of the experiences of people involved in abusive relationships – both the abused and the abuser – so that political action and choices about appropriate interventions and resource allocation could be better informed. The ethics of care is thus a form of *political* ethics, in which an enriched notion of social justice can be achieved through awareness of social practices and the ways in which these are influenced by power. To paraphrase Held: the justice motive is about fairness and equity; the care motive sees that needs are met.

A final reason why the ethics of care is of central importance to this text concerns its epistemological insights that are of particular relevance to understanding how

–

care is conceptualised within policy processes, at national and international levels. In Chapter Four of this text is a discussion of the way in which concerns are taken up by governments and international bodies in the first place, what happens to these issues once they are on the agenda and, importantly, what difference is made by policy actions. The models of health and care that have come to dominate the policy process are woefully inadequate as a knowledge base, to the detriment of older people. To take just one example, the presentation of 'dependency ratios' and the impact of ageing populations on these gives no recognition at all of the value of unpaid care, which in all contexts constitutes the majority of care provided and in many contexts is all the care there is. The crucially important level of care provided by grandparents to children orphaned by HIV/AIDS in sub-Saharan Africa is just one example. Nevertheless, despite their major role as care providers, older people are characterised as a drain on resources by reference to chronological age in a rather rough and ready way. There is a pressing need for a fuller understanding of people's experiences of ageing to be articulated within policies.

How the book is organised

Within the confines of this book, the approach taken is to critically analyse the policy developments that flow from the overarching principles set out above and to focus on their implications for the interrelationship between ageing, health and care. As an interdisciplinary endeavour, the book is informed by a broad literature and the next three chapters explore a range of important strands in the knowledge base. Chapter Two looks at the contemporary patterns and trends in population ageing, life expectancy, mortality and morbidity. This discussion highlights significant issues at the level of individual ageing, including the extension of the lifecourse. It provides a discussion of the range of perspectives on the difference between life expectancy and healthy life expectancy, which has come to be such a powerful discourse in policies. It also focuses on the nature of ageing at the population level and the contentious issue of dependency ratios. Important within this discussion also is the significance of global inequalities in health, how these are perceived in the context of ageing populations worldwide and how they influence policy agendas.

In Chapter Three different conceptualisations of health and care are examined by reference to social and epidemiological research. The critique developed throughout this text, that policies reflect an over-narrow perspective on both health and care, is underlined by this discussion. The richness and variety of ways of understanding health, illness and care set out in this chapter stands in stark contrast to the impoverished view of all three found in policies. Of crucial importance to debates on health and care is an understanding of the lifecourse, as analysed in both epidemiology and gerontology, and the relationship between the third and fourth ages. A brief explanation of these terms would be helpful at this point: the idea of the third age, generally ascribed to Laslett (1989), is that during the latter part of the 20th century a new stage in the lifecourse emerged, which offered opportunities for independence and personal development for the relatively healthy and financially secure cohorts of people in the years following retirement from paid employment. These opportunities can be understood as consequent on prevailing social conditions, such as retirement pensions and the availability of leisure and educational opportunities. However, at the point where older people's health begins to decline and they become dependent on others, the third age gives way to a fourth age, when the stark reality of mortality is evident.

Chapter Four goes on to examine in more detail the policy process. In this chapter the focus turns again to global concerns, as it is at the global level that the inconnectedness of policies and practices on health and care can be best appreciated. Policy is presented as a process, involving the exercise of power by different 'actors' in the form of national, international and transnational organisations. Of central importance is the relationship between different levels of policy making. This chapter also focuses on the point raised above concerning the tensions between the moral and political agendas. In the context of global health concerns, the roles of the World Health Organization (WHO) and the World Bank and the relationship between these provide a means of understanding how policy agendas become established. Policies reflect cultural values, and discussion of values within policies on health and care in the context of ageing societies inevitably raises questions concerning the distribution of resources. The capabilities approach, which has influenced policies at a global level, is examined critically in relation to its implications for ageing.

The following three chapters are organised around different aspects of health and care and how these feature in policies. They follow a model of health promotion that has been in circulation for some years, known as the 'tertiary prevention model' (Ashton and Seymour 1988). In its original form the model held that illness could be prevented at three levels: primary, secondary and tertiary. It is also used in a more positive sense to argue that health can be promoted at these three levels and that is the approach taken.

At the primary level, which is the focus of Chapter Five, are actions to promote health 'upstream'. That is, actions to prevent illness from occurring and to promote positive health and well-being. At the primary level, policy actions are the business of health promotion. These include a whole raft of measures, including those on environmental health, income security and education that pay attention to the socioeconomic determinants of health. However, as is discussed, although upstream actions have a strong ethical base and are widely regarded as the way to tackle inequalities in health, in practice the approach of health promotion has been the subject of criticism for failing to uphold the principles on which it was founded, having become preoccupied with individual behaviour rather than socioeconomic determinants of health. In the context of ageing, health-promoting practices at the primary level tend to reflect third age interests and identities, and here the focus is on promoting active ageing at the individual level. However, policies on active ageing are open to criticism for the way in which they have become shaped by broader economic imperatives to reduce demand on healthcare, which have led to a narrow and limited understanding of health and activity in old age.

At the secondary level, as discussed in Chapter Six, are actions to *restore* health through healthcare interventions. The secondary level of health promotion is arguably more important in later life than at other periods of the lifecourse. This is illustrated by reference to particular health conditions that are associated with later life and the growth in prevalence of long-term illness. The growth in long-term conditions poses a challenge to politicians and healthcare providers as well as to the traditional relationship between doctor and patient, all of which have implications for older people as users of healthcare services. The role of medicine in later life is strongly influenced by globalisation and the practices of transnational pharmaceutical and healthcare corporations, which have influenced international agendas in healthcare as well as the provision of healthcare at the local level. A discussion of secondary-level prevention also inevitably entails a focus on debates concerning the medicalisation of old age and the role of medicine in shaping experiences of ageing and in extending life expectancy.

At the tertiary level are actions that promote health even in the context of incurable and terminal illness. These are the subject of Chapter Seven. The relevance of this level to later life is obvious: not only are chronic diseases more prevalent in later life, but the picture of mortality described at the beginning of this chapter highlights how death is more and more concentrated in old age. The tertiary level is not only about *maintaining* health. As Bernard (2000) argued, the word 'maintain' can be seen to have negative connotations, suggesting that all that can be done is to prevent unnecessary complications, but a broader perspective on health demonstrates the potential for health promotion, including in the context of life-threatening disease, when palliative care is needed. Palliative care can be health promoting, by paying attention to physical, psychological, social and spiritual needs. This chapter also examines the ways in which care has been developed in the context of policies for older people who might be regarded as in the fourth age, with associated loss of capacity for self-care. The development of care services once again draws attention to the significance of global agendas and the ways in which policies on care provision overlap with policies on employment, migration and trade.

The three levels should be understood as interacting. For example, health is valued more highly when under threat, since it is the onset of illness conditions that frequently prompts people to make the changes in their life-styles that promote better health. Hence people receiving secondary-level interventions are likely to be more receptive to primary-level prevention messages. The model is useful in pointing to the potential of health-promotion messages for all – not only the not-yet-sick or the recently recovered. It therefore helps to overcome the tendency to take a polarised view of prevention, treatment and care.

Care is frequently assumed to be of relevance only as action to relieve the suffering, discomfort and disabilities associated with disease, and particularly so in the context of chronic, long-standing and incurable disease. But there are compelling reasons for understanding the ethics of care as relevant to the whole range of health-related policies and practices. It is hoped that this book provides a contribution to developing such an understanding.

TWO

Patterns and trends in ageing and health

Introduction

The UN World Population Ageing Report for 2009 stressed the implications of population ageing for the viability of intergenerational support systems and the sustainability of social security and healthcare systems (UN 2010a). These concerns are amplified in countries where the *speed* at which population ageing occurs is greatest, many of which are countries where social security and healthcare systems are least well developed. The significance of the trends is enormous. In this chapter the focus is on the data on life expectancy and on mortality and morbidity rates, and on the implications of these as a basis for policy making on health and care. It sets the scene for the discussion in subsequent chapters. Since policies both influence and are influenced by the data, a critical approach is necessary which questions approaches to information gathering and interpretation as well as analysing the basis on which policy priorities are established.

The production of information on ageing, health and care is influenced by a range of factors: practical, methodological, conceptual and political. Studies of global inequalities in health, for example, are often based on comparisons between regional groupings of countries, which have traditionally been organised in these ways, based on preconceived ideas about their comparability that are derived in part from colonial histories (Day et al 2008). Within these regional groupings there are significant variations between countries in patterns of health, which highlight the important of political and cultural contexts as well as broad measures of socioeconomic status. International comparisons are open to question also because of the scale of difference in population size, which, as pointed out by Lloyd-Sherlock (2010), presents a distorted picture. National-level data also obscures inequalities within countries and, in some cases, the extent of inequalities calls into question the value of the national data. For example, in India, as Mini (2009) pointed out, between different states the patterns and trends in mortality and morbidity vary enormously. In the state of Kerala the figures are more comparable to those in high-income countries than to other Indian states. Inequalities in health between ethnic groups are also masked by national-level data. Another example is Australia, where the health and life expectancy of the Aboriginal people is more akin to that found in low-income countries than to the non-Aboriginal Australian population.

Further challenges emerge over the multiple meanings of age. As discussed, crude calculations of dependency ratios based on a population's age structure have long been the subject of criticism within gerontology. Dependency ratios present a distorted picture because chronological age alone is not a reliable indicator of health and independence. Lutz et al (2008) observed that population projections do not take into account what it means to be 'old' and how this might change over time. To develop effective policies, more complex measures are needed that take account of levels of health. Meanings of disability and functional health are also wide open to interpretation. For example, measures of functional health such as Activities of Daily Living (ADLs) and Instrumental Activities of Daily Living (IADLs) are used widely and yet, as Victor (2010) pointed out, cultural complexities call into question whether data gathered are based on shared understandings of the terms.

The Global Burden of Disease (GBD) Project was set up in 1993 with a view to understanding the impacts of different diseases (Mathers et al 2001). The data produced are widely used in the development of policies on health, being regarded as a reliable and comprehensive source of information. One of their outputs – the Disability Adjusted Life Years (DALY) measure – has proved highly contentious and was criticised for the underlying assumption that a disabled life is worth less than a fully non-disabled life (Anand and Hanson 2006, Hyder and Morrow 2006). Anand and Hanson (2006) set out a range of arguments in their critique of DALYs. The first concerns the idea of burden itself. They argued that what DALYs actually measure is the aggregate quantity of illness, rather than the levels of dependency on society that follow from this. There is no attempt to identify the range of factors affecting the circumstances of living with an illness or impairment, such as the amount of support given by a family or the level of support demanded from public health and social care services. A second argument is that an inadequate information set is used in calculating the burden. The DALY measure draws on information about the individual – age, sex, disability status and time period – and incorporates this into a resource-allocation strategy as though all health outcomes were alike. Third, as DALYs do not distinguish between people of different income level or socioeconomic status but treat whole populations the same, the DALY measure runs counter to the principle of equity in health. Lastly, the variables that are included differ as between the measurement of the burden of disease and the allocation of resources. For example, a person with a pre-existing health condition ranks lower for resources than a person who was healthy and then became disabled. This is arguably the opposite of what should be the case. Wimo et al (2007) examined the impact of health economic assessments on dementia in particular and argued that perspectives on the 'cost' of the disease will differ according to the perspective of the person calculating the cost. The GBD approach does not tell us about how costs are distributed among different players – the person with dementia, the carer, the health service provider or society more generally.

A critique of the GBD project by Buvinić et al (2006) focused on gender inequalities in health and the factors that affect both differentials between men and women, including their risk of disease, their labour force participation and consequent access to health benefits, and their unequal utilisation of healthcare. They pointed to the evidence from a range of low- and middle-income countries that shows how, although women tend to have more illness, they also have less healthcare. The factors that influence this imbalance include the affordability of healthcare and related social constraints arising from women's financial disadvantage. In addition, the extent and range of their caring responsibilities can act as a disincentive to seek help. Institutional factors, including men's control over health budgets and facilities, add to women's disadvantaged position. The approach to age-weighting in the GBD project has come under fire also for portraying older people as unproductive, although the counter-argument to this is that the calculation of DALYs is based on the whole lifecourse, which means that everyone is treated equally in terms of how the productive and dependent elements of their lives are measured. This is a reasonable point to take into account in terms of how the data are produced, but it does not overcome the problem associated with how the data are presented, interpreted and acted upon. The presentation of groups of people by age alone as either productive or dependent inevitably disadvantages older people as a group, even if there is recognition that, as individuals, their levels of dependency fluctuate over the lifecourse. In the context of the discussion in this text, a point made by Hyder and Morrow (2006) is highly pertinent. They argued that perceptions about the value of a life are often implicit in priorities for the allocation of resources, but that such perceptions and the decisions that flow from these should be made explicit. Thus, if the intention is to place a value on a life according to economic and social productivity, it would be better to factor this in explicitly for all age groups rather than to subsume productivity under an age weighting. These debates underline the importance of a critical perspective on the production of data on health and care and on the use to which they are put.

Life expectancy and mortality rates

Much has been written about the dramatic changes in life expectancy that have occurred over the past 100 years around the world. At a global level, since 1950 almost 20 years has been added to average life expectancy at birth (WHO 2003a) and it is predicted that a further 8 years will be added by 2045–50, making average global life expectancy 75.5 years. However, persistent inequalities in life expectancy are equally dramatic. Figure 2.1 shows life expectancy in later life at world levels at ages 60, 65 and 80 in three regions of the world: more developed, less developed and least developed (UN 2009).[1]

---

[1] The terminology used to denote different levels of wealth and development between parts of the World is contentious. In this text, for the sake of simplicity, the terminology used by the sources of data is adhered to.

Figure 2.1: Life expectancy at ages 60, 65 and 80 in 2005–10, world and development regions

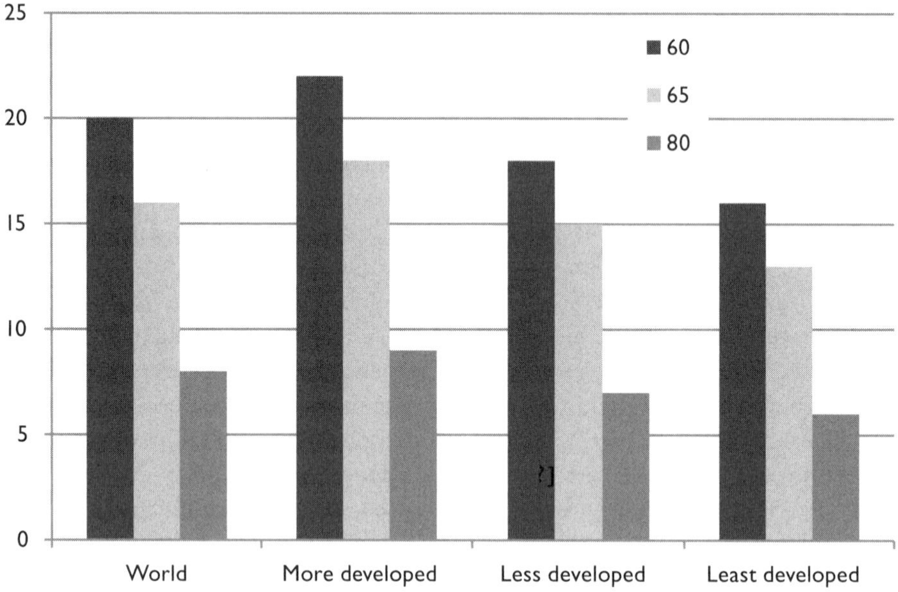

Source: UN (2010a: 9)

The 2008 World Health report (WHO 2008a) identified three patterns of relationships between economic growth and life expectancy at birth over the past three decades. First, in high-income countries almost 85% of deaths occur in the over-60s, in contrast to 45% in low- and middle-income countries. However, the WHO report also points out that future life expectancy could be affected by contrary factors. For example, increased wealth is also associated with increased levels of obesity and related diseases, such as diabetes, and the impact of these on life expectancy is not yet known. In the second grouping, which includes the Russian Federation and newly independent states of Eastern Europe, gains in per capita GDP were not consistently accompanied by gains in life expectancy. In these countries, widespread poverty, the decline in public spending on health and other public services, together with violence and unhealthy life-styles, led to a period of stagnation in life expectancy for women and a reduction for men (Lutz et al 2008). In China, gains in life expectancy had already occurred before the 1980s, and subsequent economic reforms led to greater wealth in the form of an overall increase in GDP, but this was accompanied by only modest improvements in life expectancy. These are attributed to improved living conditions, which have not applied uniformly.

The third grouping consists of low-income countries – mainly in sub-Saharan Africa – that make up 10% of the world's population, and which, as the 2008 WHO report (WHO 2008a) comments, are 'under stress'. What these countries have had in common over the past three decades is a combination of stagnating economic growth, debt and political instability together with factors associated with lack of education – particularly for girls. There has also been greater exposure to environmental hazards as well as to war and conflict, and there are also inadequate infrastructures for communication. In sub-Saharan African countries with the lowest life expectancy, high levels of HIV/AIDS and under-funded healthcare systems place older people in a vulnerable position, not only in terms of their own healthcare needs but also in the demands placed on them as carers for their adult children and their grandchildren.

Causes of death

Current trends in mortality have been analysed at length by the Global Burden of Disease (GBD) project (Lopez et al 2006). Figures from this project identify the top 20 causes of death in the world at all ages for the year 2004, shown in Table 2.1. Non-communicable (especially cardio-vascular) diseases now dominate worldwide in the ranking of causes of death. According to the GBD project, in 2002 almost

Table 2.1: Leading causes of death for all ages, worldwide (2004)

	Cause	Number of deaths (millions)	Percentage
1	Ischaemic heart disease	7.2	12.2
2	Cerebrovascular disease	5.7	9.7
3	Lower respiratory infections	4.2	7.1
4	COPD*	3.0	3.0
5	Diarrhoeal diseases	2.2	3.7
6	HIV/AIDS	2.0	3.5
7	Tuberculosis	1.5	2.5
8	Trachea, bronchus, lung cancers	1.3	2.3
8	Road traffic accidents	1.3	2.2
10	Prematurity and low birth weight	1.2	2.0
11	Neonatal infections	1.1	1.9
12	Diabetes mellitus	1.1	1.9
13	Hypertensive heart disease	1.0	1.7
14	Malaria	0.9	1.5
15	Birth asphyxia and birth trauma	0.9	1.5
16	Self-inflicted injuries	0.8	1.4
17	Stomach cancer	0.8	1.4
18	Cirrhosis of the liver	0.8	1.3
19	Nephritis and nephrosis	0.7	1.3
20	Colon and rectum cancers	0.6	1.1

Note: *COPD: chronic obstructive pulmonary disease
Source: Adapted from WHO (2008b)

half of all deaths in high-income countries were from non-communicable diseases, including cardio-vascular diseases, diabetes, chronic lung disease and four cancers. In contrast, in low- and middle-income countries communicable diseases – including respiratory infections, HIV/AIDS, diarrhoea, TB and malaria – still cause significant numbers of deaths. An epidemiological transition is occurring, in which the causes of death that predominated at the beginning of the 20th century, such as tuberculosis, are being replaced by non-communicable diseases, such as heart disease. It is described by Omran as 'the complex change in patterns of health and disease *and* on the interactions between these patterns and their demographic, economic and sociologic determinants and consequences' (Omran 2005:732). According to Omran, the epidemiologic transition has three successive stages. First is the 'Age of Pestilence and Famine', when life expectancy is low and there is no sustained population growth. Second is the 'Age of Receding Pandemics', when life expectancy at birth begins to rise as mortality rates decline and disease epidemics become less frequent. This stage is marked by significant population growth. Third is the 'Age of Degenerative and Man-made Diseases', when mortality declines and reaches a stable level, average life expectancy at birth rises and fertility becomes the crucial factor in population growth. Omran's model has been refined and developed to include two additional stages. The fourth stage, the 'Age of Delayed Degenerative Diseases' describes the situation common currently in the richest countries, in which people live for longer with diseases such as cardio-vascular diseases and cancer before eventually succumbing to them. Omran argues that there is ample evidence of this stage taking place currently. The fifth stage is speculative and refers to the 'Age of Emergent and Re-emergent Infections', which predicts a resurgence of infectious diseases, associated with globalisation.

Kinsella and Velkoff (2001) highlighted East and South-East Asia as a region where epidemiologic change has been particularly rapid. In the second half of the 20th century in Taiwan, for example, infectious and parasitic diseases gave way to chronic and degenerative diseases as primary causes of death, with tuberculosis dropping out of the 10 leading causes of death completely by 1996. However, the epidemiologic transition thesis is open to debate and Omran's model has been subjected to some criticism because its sequential stages do not accurately reflect the conditions that exist in some countries and regions. Caselli et al (2002), for example, argued that sub-Saharan African countries have yet to complete the transition to the third stage, although communicable diseases account for more than half of all deaths, while some Eastern European countries have yet to enter the fourth, as a result of the patterns of morbidity and mortality that have occurred there since the end of the communist era.

A further point is that countries with broadly similar socioeconomic status differ in their stage of transition, while at the same time there are similarities between countries of different economic status. In Mexico – a country that would be in the UN's 'less developed' category – the picture of causes of death is comparable to that in high-income countries. Palloni and McEniry (2007) analysed mortality and morbidity data from Latin America and the Caribbean and found considerable variability between the countries studied in levels of self-reported diabetes. This region is currently experiencing an epidemic of diabetes and obesity and overall prevalence levels are as high as if not higher than those found in the US, and affect women in particular. However, differences within the region were significant. Cuba, for example, had the lowest levels of obesity and self-reported diabetes. The adoption of sedentary life-styles and of diets rich in saturated fats and sugars in all countries studied except Cuba goes some way to explain this, but differences between the other countries suggest that there are yet other factors at play, such as malnutrition at earlier stages of the lifecourse, pointing to the importance of lifecourse factors for health in later life.

The 'double burden'

In the rapidly ageing low-income countries, high mortality rates from communicable diseases have combined with high levels of deaths from accidents and non-communicable disease to create a double burden. Long-term or chronic diseases are often referred to as the diseases of affluence, but this view ignores the extent of risk to people in low- and middle-income countries. As the 2008 World Health Report commented: 'It is insufficiently appreciated that the shift to chronic diseases for adult health has come on top of an unfinished agenda related to communicable diseases and maternal, newborn and child health' (WHO 2008a: 9). Not only that, but exposure to a wider range of risk factors among the world's poorest children renders them more vulnerable to chronic diseases in adulthood. Yach and Beaglehole (2004) pointed out that, with the exception of Africa (because of the impact of HIV), chronic diseases are more frequent as causes of death than are communicable diseases, and contribute to health inequalities within and between countries at all levels of development. Yach and Beaglehole also argued that global trade and marketing exacerbate the growth of chronic disease and encourage its entrenchment in all regions. This is seen in the uptake of diets rich in saturated fats and sugars, in raised tobacco consumption and more sedentary life-styles, which create the conditions for chronic diseases. China provides a clear example of this, with a rise in levels of cardio-vascular disease death rates as well as childhood obesity and Type 2 diabetes. Aggressive marketing by food, tobacco and alcohol companies increases risk levels, and the risk is exacerbated by low levels of investment in health education programmes or other policy interventions to provide messages about the harmful effects of products. Chronic and long-term diseases are often characterised as 'life-style' diseases, and socioeconomic and political factors such as those identified in China are overlooked.

It should not be assumed from looking at mortality rates that the 'double burden' does not apply in Africa. Infectious diseases continue to dominate the mortality figures – largely due to the prevalence of HIV – but there is a concurrent rise in chronic and non-communicable diseases. In short, wealthier populations face an increasing risk of chronic diseases such as diabetes and hypertension but poorer populations are at risk of these diseases *as well as* infectious diseases. An exacerbating factor is that over many years health policies have focused on combating infectious diseases to the detriment of efforts to tackle rising chronic disease. Agyei-Mensah and de-Graft Aikins (2010) examined the double burden as it affected the population there and they referred to conditions in Accra as a reflection of the 'protracted polarized model' of epidemiologic transition first described by Frenk et al (1989) in the context of Latin America. This term describes the continued co-existence of chronic and non-communicable diseases on the one hand and persistent infectious diseases on the other. The 'polarized' element of the model describes the ways in which socioeconomic inequalities determine the level of people's risk to both communicable and non-communicable disease. The poor are more likely than the rich to develop chronic diseases, to develop them earlier in the lifecourse (affecting their ability to earn an income) and to have less access to healthcare. These are the conditions that give rise to the 'protracted' element of the model, seen in a downward spiral leading to greater poverty and therefore further risk of ill-health.

Figures on the relationship between the ageing of societies and disease prevalence can generate an over-simplistic picture in which communicable diseases are associated with childhood and younger adulthood and non-communicable diseases with older age. In reality the patterns are much more complex. For example, older people are included among the most vulnerable groups when an outbreak of influenza occurs and in the context of poverty younger people are made more vulnerable to developing chronic diseases. In addition, there is a strong relationship between infectious disease and long-term disability over the lifecourse, as pointed out above. For example, hearing and sight loss as a result of infectious diseases in childhood will shape experiences of ageing in many and complex ways, not least because of increased vulnerability to poverty and unemployment.

The magnitude of the growth in morbidity and mortality from non-communicable diseases is emphasised by Nolte and McKee (2008), who argued that the current trends are leading to unprecedented suffering and premature deaths. The determinants of non-communicable diseases are a combination of life-style and socioeconomic factors. Poor diet, lack of physical activity and smoking have all led to high incidence of obesity, diabetes and vascular disease. At the same time, countries where under-nutrition used to be a major problem are now experiencing high levels of obesity and the speed at which this change has occurred highlights the importance of socioeconomic and cultural factors. As Nolte and McKee pointed out the as the prevalence of non-communicable diseases is likely to continue growing, the consequences for social development and for health systems need to be factored into policy agendas.

Morbidity and disability

The growing prevalence of non-fatal chronic and long-term conditions was set out in the 2004 GBD Report (WHO 2008b), and this emphasised the importance of these trends for health policy priorities and planning health systems. The 2001 UK Census revealed that over 50% of the population aged over 75 had a limiting long-standing illness, and in the European Union an estimated two-thirds of people who have reached pensionable age have at least two (Nolte and McKee 2008). Examination of the data on non-fatal conditions goes some way towards developing a better understanding of the health problems faced by older people and provides some indication of the relationship between the kind of large-scale data discussed above and the individual person's experience. Key questions concern the kinds of health problems that are likely to be encountered and how levels of health and illness will impact on individual experiences of ageing, especially bearing in mind that individuals might have multiple morbidities.

At the population level, disability prevalence increases with age but the interrelationship of age and socioeconomic factors presents a more complex picture of disability. Table 2.2 highlights the inequalities that exist between different regions of the world in relation to chronic illness. This shows the prevalence of moderate and severe disability in different parts of the world by age. It is evident that some of the diseases prevalent in old age in high-income countries are also prevalent among younger people in low- and middle-income countries. For example, hearing loss and refractive errors (sight problems) are more prevalent among the 60+ age group than younger people in high-income countries, but the reverse is the case in low- and middle-income countries. It is also the case that while older people constitute a higher proportion of the population in high-income countries they do not have such high levels of disability as do older people in low- and middle-income countries (WHO 2008b). To explain these differences the factors that lead to the development of chronic disease and disability need to be taken into account

The extent to which higher prevalence of disease in later life is attributable to age per se is the subject of a wider debate. According to Margrain and Boulton, sensory impairment is 'the characteristic feature of old age', the medical term 'presbyopia' literally meaning 'old eye' (2005: 121). Visual acuity declines with age, cataracts become more prevalent from middle age to old age, and macular degeneration is commonly 'age-related' (Fletcher 2007). However, many other diseases, including dementia and arthritis, are not age related in the strict sense, as they are also experienced at earlier stages of the lifecourse. Data on prevalence and incidence of dementia in different countries are very variable, for many of the reasons outlined above, including the interpretation of symptoms, decisions about whether to consult and diagnostic practices. Ferri et al (2005) estimated that in 2006 at a global level 24 million people had dementia and that this figure would double every 20 years, to 42 million in 2020 and 81 million in 2040.

Table 2.2: Estimated prevalence of moderate and severe disability (millions) for leading disabling conditions by age for high-income and low- and middle-income countries

	Disabling condition	High-income countries		Low- and middle-income countries		World
		0–59 years	60 years and over	0–59 years	60 years and over	All ages
1	Hearing loss	7.4	18.5	54.3	43.9	124.2
2	Refractive errors	7.7	6.4	68.1	39.8	121.9
3	Depression	15.8	0.5	77.6	4.8	98.7
4	Cataracts	0.5	1.1	20.8	31.4	53.8
5	Unintentional injuries	2.8	1.1	35.4	5.7	45.0
6	Osteoarthritis	1.9	8.1	14.1	19.4	43.4
7	Alcohol dependence and problem use	7.3	0.4	31.0	1.8	40.5
8	Infertility due unsafe abortion and maternal sepsis	0.8	0.0	32.5	0.0	33.4
9	Macular degeneration	1.8	6.0	9.0	15.1	31.9
10	Chronic obstructive pulmonary disease	3.2	4.5	10.9	8.0	26.6
11	Ischaemic heart disease	1.0	2.2	8.1	11.9	23.2
12	Bipolar disorder	3.3	0.4	17.6	0.8	22.2
13	Asthma	2.9	0.5	15.1	0.9	19.4
14	Schizophrenia	2.2	0.4	13.1	1.0	16.7
15	Glaucoma	0.4	1.5	5.7	7.9	15.5
16	Alzheimer's disease and other dementias	0.4	6.2	1.3	7.0	14.9
17	Panic disorder	1.9	0.1	11.4	0.3	13.8
18	Cerebrovascular disease	1.4	2.2	5.9	3.0	11.9
19	Rheumatoid arthritis	1.3	1.7	5.9	3.0	11.9
20	Drug dependence and problem use	3.7	0.1	8.0	0.1	11.8

Source: Adapted from WHO (2008b: 35)

The gross inequalities that exist at a global level between the richest and poorest parts of the world are shown in stark relief in the figures on mortality, life expectancy and morbidity. Marmot (2005) highlighted the widespread nature of the social gradient in health as an indication of how sensitive health is to social and economic factors. As has already been pointed out, differences within regions of the world and countries reinforce this message. Continued refinement of knowledge of social inequalities in health has produced stronger evidence of the importance of socioeconomic and environmental determinants. Marmot (2005) argued that social determinants of health inequalities in old age claim attention alongside those of health at younger ages. The extent to which this has occurred is a moot point. Lloyd-Sherlock (2010), for example, argued that older people's health needs are consistently overlooked in debates about health development.

Gender inequalities

At a global level women represent the majority of the population aged 60 or over. Gender differences in life expectancy are well established, with the exception of very few countries (men outnumber women aged 60 or over in, for example, Kuwait, Qatar and the United Arab Emirates). The gender gap is set to decrease in more developed regions but to widen in the least developed regions, bringing women in least developed regions closer to the world average than their male counterparts. There are several reasons why gender matters in terms of health policies. Apart from the conditions that are specific to women, often associated with reproduction, there are also conditions related to women's greater longevity, which increase their risk of developing Alzheimer's disease and other dementias, osteoarthritis and osteoporosis (Buvinić et al 2006). There are also health problems that can be attributed at least in part to gender relations, including domestic violence and genital mutilation. These are difficult to enumerate because familial and social pressures discourage women from seeking help. Widowhood is a known cause of mental health problems and women are more likely than men to be widowed. It is estimated that at a global level 48% of older women are married, compared with 80% of men. In the least developed countries the difference is greater, with 41% of women married compared with 81% of men (WHO 2009, UN 2010a). This in turn raises questions about who will care for them when their health declines.

Chronic illness, disability and the compression of morbidity thesis

Increased life expectancy generates questions about levels of health and illness experienced in the additional years. Are the extra years of life that have been gained over the past century spent in good or bad health, and are there differences and inequalities between people or does ageing have a 'levelling' effect on health? Policy makers need answers to these questions so as to enable them to plan for health and social care services, but the evidence is unclear and contradictory and the availability of data varies considerably between countries.

Mortality rates, morbidity rates and disability rates are apparently not moving in the same direction. According to Kinsella and Velkoff (2001), while mortality rates drop, morbidity and disability rates tend to rise, and questions arise about whether living longer is necessarily an unqualified benefit. The distinction between morbidity and disability is important here, as it highlights that not all illness necessarily leads to disability. Crimmins (2004) pointed out that in the US, while disease prevalence among the over-60s increased during the 1990s, the prevalence of loss of function and disability decreased.

The compression of morbidity thesis, proposed by Fries (1980), offers one explanation for these complex figures. First, there have been delays in the onset of chronic disease and second, evidence suggests that, in the US at least, there has been a slowing in the rate of increase in life expectancy. The picture Fries developed was that, as humans would reach the natural limit of the life span and remain in good health for more years, there would inevitably be a compression of morbidity. He argued that the compression of mortality inevitably leads to the compression of morbidity because individuals born over same time period are likely to die within the same 5- to 15-year period and, since there can be no mortality without disease, morbidity must also be compressed into those years.

Subsequently, however, evidence showed that the main cause of the increase in the maximum achieved life span was the decline in mortality among people over age 70. This posed a challenge to Fries' original thesis: the argument that there must be compression of mortality could not be sustained because, although mortality at younger ages decreased, there was evidently *decompression* at the oldest ages and, because the added years are spent with disease, there is arguably a decompression of morbidity.

Not surprisingly, the compression of morbidity thesis has been of great interest to policy makers, service planners and health professionals. Westendorp and Kirkwood (2007), for example, argued that because 'under current conditions we are going to live longer with more years spent in poor health' (p 33) the aim of healthcare should be to continue interventions that enable us to increasingly overcome the complications of disease. The distinction between chronic illness and disability is important here, because a major concern would be to increase years of life lived without functional limitation and disability despite the presence of disease. However, developing a shared understanding of the potential for improving health at the oldest ages is a problem, Westendorp and Kirkwood argue, because disease among older people is occurring within a 'knowledge shadow'. It is simply not known whether the health of older people in the future will follow a predictable pattern. Health status at earlier stages of the lifecourse is an important factor and there is a cumulative advantage gained in old age by individuals who have socioeconomic advantages earlier in the lifecourse, which leads to a compression of morbidity. However, there are many other factors to take into account, including the rise in obesity levels associated with higher living standards discussed above, which could lead to an expansion of morbidity in later life (Prus 2003).

Howse (2006) argued that although the compression of morbidity thesis is unsustainable in its original form, it is possible for compression of morbidity to occur without compression of mortality, as long as healthy life expectancy increases at a faster rate than life expectancy. He presented three alternative scenarios: the *expansion of morbidity*, *compression of morbidity* and *dynamic equilibrium*. Expansion of morbidity would be the outcome where medical advances prevent fatal outcomes from age-related degenerative diseases but the incidence and the pattern of increasing disability from those diseases remain stable. Objections to this scenario are that medical advances have done more than improve mortality rates, not least because of secondary prevention – the availability of medical treatment and care that slows down the progress of a disease and prevents secondary or associated health problems. Howse also pointed to the body of evidence against the expansion of morbidity thesis. This shows inequalities in late life morbidity and disability, which are explained by reference to environmental rather than individual factors. However, Howse pointed out that the possibility remains that there could be an absolute expansion of morbidity even though people stay healthier for longer, if life expectancy increases faster than healthy or disability-free life expectancy (see also Batljan and Lagergren 2005).

In exploring the idea of dynamic equilibrium, Howse made reference to the role of primary, secondary and tertiary prevention. The expansion of morbidity thesis looks to secondary prevention to extend the period of life spent with disease; the compression of morbidity thesis looks to primary prevention to delay the onset of disease. The dynamic equilibrium thesis, however, highlights the significance of delay in the *intermediate stages* of disease – the period at which the progression of a disease shifts from being less severe to more severe and disabling. It is possible that people with chronic degenerative disease are living longer because of improved secondary prevention and also because primary prevention factors have led to better underlying health. This would lead to an increase in overall prevalence of mild/less disabling disease, but also to largely stable rates of severe disease. Secondary prevention therefore increases in importance as a health promotion strategy as people age – as is discussed at greater length in Chapter Six.

Population ageing and social support

The rate of ageing of populations has major implications for social support in later life. The growth rate of older populations is currently twice that of the population generally. Again, differences between the development regions are striking. In Europe, currently the area with the highest proportion of older people, 22% of the population is aged 60 years or over – projected to rise to almost 35% by 2050, as compared to 11% in Africa. However, the rate of change, coupled with numbers of older people living in developing countries presents a more complex picture. As Harper (2006) pointed out, it is developing countries that face extreme rapidity of ageing. For example, the percentage of populations aged over 65 in Latin American countries is predicted to rise within 20 years to the levels currently seen in Japan and in Western Europe. Harper also pointed to the challenge related to absolute numbers of older people in developing countries, which, she argued, gives the lie to the widely held view that population ageing is a challenge primarily to the developed world. Two-thirds of the world's older population (aged 60 or over) live in developing countries, and the absolute numbers are set to double, to reach 1 billion by 2030. The challenge arises from the lack of infrastructure available to support people as they age – either economically or in terms of public institutions or welfare regimes. People in developing countries are therefore compelled to continue paid employment past the age when their counterparts in the developed regions will have retired. This trend is reinforced by the institution of retirement and the provision of retirement pensions more common in the formal employment regimes associated with developed countries rather than with the informal employment and self-employment patterns associated with less developed countries. The UN figures show that in Burundi, Malawi and Mozambique over three-quarters of people aged over 65 are still working, as compared with less than 1.5% in France, Luxembourg and Malta. Figures in high-income countries are likely to change as the age at which people can claim pensions rises.

The association between labour force participation and health in later life is complex and cannot be separated from factors such as conditions of work and levels of income, as well as questions of compulsion and choice. Work is often associated with better health, but this positive association depends on the kind of work involved (Cameron et al 2010). Recent changes in the labour force participation rates of older people in some European countries are associated with policy efforts to secure the sustainability of pension schemes and are not primarily about the health of workers, nor do they take account of the differential impacts on health of different kinds of work.

Social support in the context of population ageing is characterised as a nightmare scenario for policy makers and, as argued, this scenario has underpinned the development of policies on health and care. While crude measures of proportions of age groups within populations can easily be translated into a 'time bomb' thesis, in which the proportion of over-65s to the middle 'working age' group shifts to an unsustainable point, closer analysis reveals a more complex picture. As discussed, there are numerous critiques of dependency ratios. Apart from the unpredictability of future demand for healthcare, there is also the fluctuating nature of demographic trends in line with birth-rates and the movement of cohorts through the lifecourse. In the UK, for example, the baby-boomer 'bulge' is likely to lead to a temporary peak in demand for services around 2030. A further important point is that it has been demonstrated over a number of years that at all ages individual demand for healthcare is highest in the period immediately prior to death (Dixon et al 2004). The growing concentration of mortality in old age that occurred throughout the 20th century has led to a concentration of health expenditure on older people, not simply because of age per se, but because of proximity to death – a form of redistribution of expenditures that would have been made anyway. Kinsella and Velkoff (2001) also pointed to evidence from OECD countries (generally the most aged) that among older people living in the community demand for healthcare tends to peak between the ages of 75 to 79 and then to tail off thereafter. This evidence also suggests that although the *numbers* of older people using services are higher the *cost per service* is less for older than for younger people. While the ageing of populations, particularly in the context of low- and middle-income countries, presents a major challenge to policy makers, such evidence points to the need for more sophisticated understanding of demographic trends and their implications for demand and cost in healthcare. There are obviously good reasons to consider the impact of the changing age structure on the capacity of any population to provide support where it is needed, but the socially constructed nature of age gradations blurs the picture, and the historical contexts of systems of support need to be given more attention. In contexts where care for older people is entirely in the hands of families, the pressures of population ageing are very different from those pressures experienced in countries that have had a system of welfare in place over decades. It is because both the need for and provision of care for older people is so variable that it is not possible to predict demand on the basis of chronological age alone. Referring to the policy expectation that the demand for long-term care and the costs associated with it are likely to increase dramatically, Saltman et al (2006) remarked that recent studies both confirm and moderate these predictions.

A crucially important point, as raised in the introductory chapter, is that economically productive activities are many and varied at all ages, including among those aged over 65, including paid employment, but also many other forms of work that are not counted. Examples include the contribution to childcare made by grandparents, which enables adult children to take up paid employment, and voluntary and community work. Nevertheless, the concept of dependency ratios, despite its rather rough and ready nature remains highly influential within policy circles. It can be seen to have influenced changes in retirement and pension policies in the UK and other Western countries, for example, as well as changes in global policies on preventing illness in later life. A core theme here is that dominant discourses on the unsustainable nature of population ageing need to be understood for their influence on health and social care policy, the priorities that are established, the strategies adopted and the attitudes and practices of people working in health and care services.

Summary

The broad picture outlined above raises a number of points to be explored at greater length in subsequent chapters. The demographic trends and patterns considered have an undoubted effect on the way in which ageing, health and care are understood. However, ways of understanding are shaped by the knowledge base, and the use of this knowledge base as a foundation for developing policies provokes a critical response. Variations in the patterns of demographic transition highlight the ways in which socioeconomic and political factors shape life expectancy and mortality patterns. The double burden of morbidity experienced by low- and middle-income countries belies the perception that population ageing is primarily a Western phenomenon, although it is the experiences of Western, high-income countries that have shaped ideas about the nature of global population ageing and its implications for policies. The discussion of the compression of morbidity highlights that it is by no means a certainty, yet as an ideal it occupies a central place in policies on health in later life. The evidence also demonstrates the central importance of understanding more fully the ways in which socioeconomic determinants of health interact with behavioural and cultural factors throughout the lifecourse to produce such high levels of inequality in life expectancy and health. These inequalities stimulate ethical questions about equity and justice in healthcare. At the same time, the need for a better understanding of dependency across the lifecourse is needed that does not rely on crude age-based calculations. All in all, the data stimulate more questions than answers, which in subsequent chapters will be discussed at greater length.

THREE

Understanding health and care

Introduction

In this chapter the focus is on ways of conceptualising health, care and the lifecourse. Health has been a major focus in the social sciences since the middle of the 20th century, and disciplinary differences as well as changes and developments within disciplines can be traced in a range of conceptualisations and models of health. Social research on non-medical perceptions of health and illness has generated interest in the *meaning* of health. Until recently, relatively little attention has been paid to the significance of age as an influencing factor in the construction of the meaning of health. As Higgs and Rees-Jones (2009) argued, until recently most medical sociologists have tended to treat age as a homogenised category, have neglected inequalities in health in old age and have failed to engage with older people's individual experiences of chronic illness. The ageing of societies and the extension of life expectancy have stimulated more interest in ageing, and in epidemiology there has been a growth of interest in lifecourse perspectives (Kuh and Ben Schlomo 2004). Care has been an important focus of feminist research over the decades. In 1978 Hilary Land (1978) argued that social policies on family care neglected inequalities between men and women, and in the years since then feminist researchers have focused on the complex relationship between women's position in the labour market and their responsibilities for care. More than 30 years on, the same debate continues in the context of globalisation and the internationalisation of care work (Williams 2010). At the same time the perspectives of disability rights researchers have focused attention on the negative dimensions of care (Thomas 2004, Shakespeare 2006).

The centrality of health and care to old age is unquestionable. Victor (2010) identified the determinants of health in old age as individual genetic make-up, individual behaviour, exposure to environmental and occupational hazards and the availability and quality of healthcare, as well as social factors such as gender, ethnicity and class, which impact on health status, health behaviour and access to healthcare. From a lifecourse perspective the determinants of health must also include care, since it is only through being cared for in infancy that an individual survives to reach old age. There is also an increasing realisation of the crucial importance to health of social relationships throughout life, as argued by Ryff and Singer (1998) and discussed below.

Biomedical approaches to health

There is a fundamental distinction between negative and positive conceptualisations of health. The biomedical model is negative in that it regards health as the absence of disease and its focus is on disease and its cure. Within this definition, health is understood only as a state of being where no abnormalities in physical functioning are evident. It is only when there is an abnormality, as defined and measured against accepted norms and standards of bodily functions, that an intervention is required to restore health. Within the biomedical model disease is understood as an entity with a specific aetiology which is responsive to expert diagnosis and treatment. Critiques of the biomedical model are plentiful, many having been developed in the latter part of the 20th century. From within the discipline of medicine is the public health critique that the biomedical model neglects broader social determinants of health and illness (Marmot 2005). Critiques of biomedicine have particular resonance in later life, when health is at greater risk of compromise. Indeed, critical gerontologists endorse the public health critique, to argue that biomedicine has played a determining role in the individualisation and medicalisation of old age. Estes et al (2003), for example, argued that biomedicine reduces ageing to a set of individual complaints and ignores the needs of older people for public health, housing, nutrition, preventive care and chronic and long-term care. Their critical perspective goes further, to argue also that biomedicine legitimises the discourses of professional helpers and that the ideological power of biomedicine is such that it comes to 'stand for everything that ageing might be about' (2003: 80). Thus, for Estes et al, while medical solutions are needed to the health problems that occur through the process of ageing, they exact a price. As evidence, they point to the increasing number of human experiences that have become defined as medical conditions and to the associated substantial profits made by the biomedical industry and health insurance market. Looked at from this perspective, the conclusion is easily drawn that the price exacted by biomedicine is unacceptably high.

The critique presented by Estes et al (2003) is important in highlighting the negative impacts of biomedicine. Biomedical definitions of the physiological effects of ageing as 'disease symptoms' are wide open to question. For example, challenges to the biomedical model of the menopause as a form of dysfunction and deficiency have pointed to the ways in which these accounts have been constructed and the cultural variations in how the menopause is understood. While menopausal women in Western cultures consult doctors over symptoms, in other cultures the menopause is not regarded as a medical matter but is welcomed as a time of life free from childbearing responsibilities (Wray 2007).

However, it is also arguable that the practice of biomedicine is not monolithic but has within it a range of perspectives and emphases, some of which are to do with the social, political, economic and cultural contexts in which it operates. Importantly, as discussed further in Chapter Six, evidence suggests that the increasing levels of chronic disease are contributing towards changes in perspective, as the central focus on a cure gives way to a focus on symptom management. Medical practice also varies in terms of degrees of cooperation with other professional groups and, in the context of disease that is not amenable to cure, biomedicine's power is less complete. It also needs to be borne in mind that the practice of medicine is shaped and influenced by policy contexts, including the different levels of state control over biomedical practices and the functioning of the pharmaceutical industry.

The capacity of biomedicine to drown out 'lay' voices in defining health is also open to question. Higgs and Rees-Jones (2009) argued that within Western cultures a significant feature of the past half-century has been the restructuring of social knowledge, so that 'the old certainties of science, technology and rationality bump up against experiential and lay knowledge', challenging hierarchical boundaries between professionals and lay people (p 12). The growing availability of information about health conditions and diseases has changed relationships between doctors and patients. Indeed, people living with chronic disease can develop a level of expertise that can exceed that of their general practitioner.

There is also greater awareness of the phenomenon of iatrogenetic disease. This is an issue of particular concern to older people whose complex health conditions can mean that the medications they are given for different disorders are incompatible. Polypharmacy – defined as the use of five or more medications in one individual – is particularly common among older people and is increasingly regarded as a negative consequence of biomedicine. Research highlights the potential hazards of polypharmacy, including falls, increased levels of hospitalisation and medication-induced illness (Gorard 2006). There is evidence, too, that older people are concerned about their medication intake. Lumme-Sandt et al (2000), for example, found that older people do not necessarily comply with their doctors' prescriptions but establish their own routines and dosages, with the aim of minimising the amount of medicines they take.

Biomedicine has been open to challenge from a range of interest groups, including disabled people and patients' associations and alternative and complementary health practitioners. In many Western societies there has been a rise in the use of complementary therapies. This trend is very much in keeping with contemporary cultural values of individual choice and control. When compared with mainstream medical consultations, complementary healthcare offers a more holistic approach, with more time and attention being given to individual consultations. Patients have an opportunity to talk through their health history and life-style, rather than focusing on specific symptoms. Some therapies are more suited to a 'complementary' role than are others, and are more acceptable in particular contexts of healthcare. For example, therapies such as acupuncture, massage and aromatherapy are increasingly part of the management of long-term and terminal illness, which can be of particular benefit to older people.

Critiques of biomedicine tend to portray its practitioners as oppressive and coercive, and characterise patients as somewhat helpless and passive victims. This point was argued by Lupton (1995), who called for a less black-and-white portrayal ofWestern medicine and a better understanding of the role played by patients in the context of medical care. Research by McFarlane and Kelleher (2002) identified generally positive views of medical practice in a group of Irish people born in the 1920s, despite instances of poor treatment. These views are explicable at least in part by reference to the lifecourse of this cohort. As McFarlane and Kelleher explained, the health services were developed during the lifetimes of this group of research participants. They had experienced at first hand significant reductions in the diseases that were widespread in their childhoods, as well as vast improvements in access to health and medical services. For them, biomedicine was a positive influence on the quality of life of their communities.

At the individual level, a biomedical interpretation of a patient's account of symptoms might be welcomed because it provides an objectively defined explanation for what is experienced. Blaxter (1983), for example, identified how Scottish working-class women regarded illness as weakness, whereas disease as defined by a medical doctor was not. Similarly, Williams (1990) found that older research respondents in Aberdeen thought that unless illness could be validated as disease, it was devalued. The importance of a diagnosis is widely recognised in many of the illnesses associated with old age, including dementia (Innes 2009).

It is therefore important to recognise variations in the role, status and power of biomedicine across different contexts and at different points in history. In addition, as Blaxter (2004) concluded, biomedicine now admits multiple and interactive causes of disease and illness, and it would be foolish to present a medical model of health as entirely separate from and in opposition to a social model.

Health as the absence of illness

Like the biomedical model, the conceptualisation of health as the absence of illness is also a negative definition of health, but there is a distinction between 'disease' and 'illness' where illness is a subjective state – 'how one feels' – rather than an objectively defined entity. The distinction between illness and disease goes some way to explain the often-cited experience of older people who say they feel well despite having identifiable diseases. The evident discrepancies between objective measures of health, on the one hand, and individual perspectives, on the other, have been well documented (see, for example, Bardage et al 2005, Bowling 2005, Staehelin 2005) and these findings lend support to Lupton's point about biomedicine and the role of patients. In practice with older people, when the focus is on managing chronic and long-term illness, a doctor is often not confined to the scientifically based treatment of diagnosed conditions but is necessarily focused on the relief of the symptoms that older people describe. Of course, how one feels or interprets symptoms (or, indeed, perceives what is being experienced as a 'symptom') will determine whether or not to consult a doctor or healer in the first place. Citing Mechanic (1968), Blaxter outlined 10 processes relevant to 'illness behaviour':

- The 'visibility, recognisability or perceptual salience of the symptoms
- Their perceived seriousness
- The extent to which they disrupt family, work and other social activities
- Their frequency or persistence
- The tolerance threshold of those who are exposed to and evaluate them, including self and others
- Available information, knowledge and cultural assumptions and understandings
- Psychological processes such as denial or fear
- Other needs or motives competing with the response to illness
- Competing possible interpretations of the symptoms
- The availability of treatment resources and the costs (monetary or other) of taking action.' (Blaxter 2004: 73)

This list reflects the complex interplay of individual, social and cultural factors that influence behaviour related to healthcare. The illness model also introduces a *moral* dimension to the conceptualisation of health, and perceptions of whether symptoms warrant professional consultation will also be influenced by the perceived cost of obtaining help. In the study by McFarlane and Kelleher (2002) referred to above it was found that older people were critical of what they regarded as excessive and unnecessary use of doctors' time by younger people. The moral dimension of healthcare usage is particularly important in relation to ageing, in the context of widespread alarm about the cost of population ageing. If the overarching message about ageing populations is that older people are a burden on resources, what impact does this have on older people's decisions about seeking help for health problems?

Decisions about whether to consult a professional reflect cultural assumptions about what is regarded as 'normal' health (Biswas et al 2006). As Blaxter (2004) pointed out, there is a great range of 'normal' variability, and age is a crucial factor in this range, with generally higher expectations of illness and disability in old age. There is a distinction to be drawn between the idea of normal as 'usual' and normal as 'non-pathological' (Higgs and Rees-Jones 2009). It is known that older people engage in comparisons with others concerning their health and that they form judgements about what they might expect as they age. Whether a condition is regarded as pathological is grounded in human judgement rather than in scientific fact. As Bond and Cabrero argued, 'whether we attribute ill-health to our own experience of ageing will depend on the culture, time and place in which we live and our own personality' (2007: 117). A related point concerns the prevailing context of support and care available and how this is perceived. Where there are no formal social care services, older people might resist seeking help because they wish to avoid being seen as a burden on their family. On the other hand, in the context of institutional welfare regimes an older person might resist seeking help because of fears about the consequences of being seen to be going downhill.

The availability of services is an issue that will be explored at greater length in Chapter Six, but should be noted at this stage as an important factor that influences people's perspectives on their health and their decisions about whether to seek help with health problems. This applies equally to modern biomedicine, complementary and alternative therapies, as well as 'traditional medicines' – those medical practices that are indigenous to different cultures (WHO 2002a, 2004a).

Functional or instrumental models of health: health as a means to an end

Health is also frequently conceptualised in functional terms, focused on an individual's ability or inability to carry out their normal everyday roles and functions. Functional conceptualisations of health can be both biomedical and non-biomedical, but from either perspective health is important in terms of what it enables an individual to do, rather than how an individual feels or whether they have an identifiable disease. The WHO's International Classification of Functioning, Disability and Health conceptualises disability and functioning as the outcomes of the interaction between health conditions and contextual factors (WHO 2001). In functional definitions, health is a means to an end, and vitally important to the maintenance of independence and the achievement of goals (Bowling 2005). Standard measures of ADLs or IADLs are used widely as screening tools to identify levels of disability within populations (Craig and Mindell 2005). As discussed further in Chapter Seven, these have been criticised for being too narrowly drawn, the term 'functioning' being not adequate as a description of the richness of human life, activities and relationships (Ryff and Singer 1998). In policy terms there is an increased emphasis on a functional conceptualisation of health, which is compatible with a managerialist approach to the provision of health and care services.

Functioning, in the sense of being active or 'keeping going' is also about maintaining strength. Williams (1990), for example, identified that having the strength to continue to function in the context of constitutional weakness was a source of pride among the older Aberdonians he interviewed. He identified a perception of health as a source of strength to resist illness or disease, or as a source of power of recovery. Weakness, in contrast, represented debility or having little in reserve. This might be specific weaknesses, such as a 'weak chest', but might also be more general, entailing a total and permanent collapse of strength and loss of the power of recovery. A broader perspective on functional health links it with confidence and a sense of mastery and control over everyday decisions. In this sense, even in the context of physical illness or disease one can feel health if one has control over events or decisions. Again, this conceptualisation of health has particular resonance for later life, because older people's control over events and decisions is frequently compromised by poor health.

Context is essential to understanding a functional view of health (Victor 2010). Nettleton (2006) pointed to research findings that suggest working-class women from a range of ethnic groups are likely to hold functional views of health, and that these are linked with their social obligations. Similarly, from an individual point of view, functional definitions of health are relative: as Blaxter (2004) argued, it all depends what one wants or needs to do. Again, age is a consideration, as age-appropriateness is a factor in decisions about what one wants to do or how hampered one might feel if unable to do it. Hence 'super-fit' older people who run marathons or climb mountains achieve heroic status because they go beyond what is regarded as normal for their age. In policy terms, a functional view of health is strongly associated with self-reliance and independence, which is of particular significance to older people. Katz (2006) argued that since the late 20th century *functional* notions of age, constructed through professionally applied tests and measurements (such as ADLS and IADLs), have become dominant, to the point of displacing ideas about chronological ageing. On the other hand, Blane et al (2008) argued that more attention should be given to functional health in older people, since many of the functional limitations experienced by older people (such as falls, urinary incontinence and arthritic pain) are often avoidable. In healthcare, functional ageing is increasingly regarded as a more accurate predictor of remaining life expectancy, and in this sense as of great value in the task of managing demands on health and long-term care. As Katz (2006) argued, this is also of great value to neoliberal agendas for health policy. The key issue, therefore, is how information about functional ageing is used and whether this usage is to the benefit of older people or merely as a means of controlling demand for services.

Positive conceptualisations of health: the salutogenic approach

The WHO (1978) described as a paradigm shift the declaration by the 1977 Alma Ata conference that health is

> a state of complete physical, mental and social well being, and not merely the absence of disease or infirmity, is a fundamental human right and that the attainment of the highest possible level of health is a most important world-wide social goal whose realization requires the action of many other social and economic sectors in addition to the health sector.

This declaration conceptualised health in positive rather than negative terms and pointed to the importance of non-bodily dimensions of health. It also linked health to ideals of human rights and social justice. The Alma Ata declaration has been much criticised for its idealistic and unrealistic tone but has nevertheless been influential in shaping the way in which health promotion has developed subsequently – discussed further in subsequent chapters. Within the WHO, ideas about the nature of health have been strongly influenced by the work of Antonovsky (1979). Antonovsky took as his starting-point the question of why it is that people with similar opportunities and in similar socioeconomic circumstances appear to have very different health outcomes. The explanation he identified took into account how people's earlier life experience can instil in them the confidence to perceive meaning in the world, and the resources to cope with the normal stressors and challenges of life. This he developed into the concept of salutogenesis. Within this concept is the understanding that the conceptual dichotomy between health and disease is misleading, since most people are neither healthy nor diseased but occupy a position somewhere on a continuum between the two.

For Antonovsky it was evident that the upstream approach alone was not enough to secure health and that, in addition to securing salutogenic environments, it is also necessary to teach people to swim in the stream. He identified an interaction between, on the one hand, '*generalised resistance resources*' – typically money, social support, knowledge, experience, intelligence and traditions – and, on the other hand, a '*sense of coherence*' – the ability to make use of these. A salutogenic environment is one which promotes a sense of coherence and makes it easier for people to deal with the challenges of life. At the same time, assisting people to develop the resources to cope with the challenges of everyday life can help to move them along the health–disease continuum towards better health. The salutogenic view of health is therefore the opposite of the pathogenic view. In the years since the concept was first defined, it has been refined and developed and has found its way into international debates on health promotion and community development (Morgan and Ziglio 2007, Billings and Hashem 2009).

An aspect of salutogenic health that has not been given a great deal of attention in gerontology is that of spiritual health. In some traditions, spiritual health is regarded as inseparable from other forms of health, with many, including Ayurvedic and Chinese traditions, holding to the principles of health as a form of balance and harmony. Prior et al (2002) identified a belief among older Chinese research participants in the UK that health was fundamentally related to spiritual happiness and inner contentment. While the importance of spiritual health is increasingly recognised, there are obstacles to putting it into practice within modern scientific and secular healthcare systems and bureaucratic organisational structures. Coleman (2011) makes the additional point that one of the consequences of globalisation and migration is that it is becoming increasingly impossible to make assumptions about older people's spiritual or religious lives, which poses a challenge for health systems. There are spheres of practice where there is a stronger emphasis on spiritual health, notably in palliative care. Significantly, this is an approach to healthcare that originated within religious organisations as an alternative to prevailing scientific biomedical practice.

Ryff and Singer (1998) and Ryff, Singer and Love (2004) pointed to the persistence of the *idea* of positive health but a lack of progress in carrying out the idea in practice, so that – as discussed in Chapter Two – typical indices of health focus on the negative, mortality and morbidity rates being the meat and drink of public health. Ryff and Singer identified three important principles for understanding positive health: the first is that it is fundamentally a philosophical, not a medical phenomenon, the second that it is about the interconnections of mind and body and the third that it is a multidimensional dynamic process, rather than a discrete state. Ultimately, they argued, human well-being is 'an issue of engagement in living, involving expression of a broad range of human potentialities: intellectual, social, emotional and physical' (1998: 2). Ryff and Singer also pointed out that while there are significant cultural differences to consider in the way that well-being (or 'the good life') is perceived, there are also key elements that transcend cultural boundaries. From their assessment of a wide range of philosophical, ethical, psychological and sociological accounts of positive human health they highlight two features that are present universally, both of which are dynamic processes and come from 'invested, committed living', rather than being obtained effortlessly. These are:

- *purpose in life*: the sense that one's life is meaningful
- *quality connections to others*: possessing rich and fulfilling bonds with others.

These two features are what Ryff and Singer termed the primary features of positive human health. Also frequently evident in accounts of positive health are the concepts of *positive self-regard* and *a sense of mastery* or control over life. Taken together, these four are the features that Ryff and Singer argued can be linked to bodily health and functioning. They point to the importance of *emotion* as the nexus between mind and body and to the physiological mechanisms entailed in stress, the effects of emotions on the immune system and on healing and recovery from disease to support this view. The analysis by Ryff and Singer is unusual in its attempt to bridge the different conceptualisations of health and make the links between broad public health concerns and individual health and illness. Its value to the study of ageing is that it provides a way of understanding better older people's experiences of changing health and the emotional significance of these experiences.

Health and identity

James and Hockey (2007) explored the links between concepts of health and illness, on the one hand, and social identity, on the other. They argue that individuals are actively engaged in constructing meaning related to their experiences of being ill or being well. Their agency in this task means that their identity as 'ill' or 'well' individuals is not thrust upon them but negotiated with their participation. Importantly for the discussion in this text, James and Hockey make the salient point that the idea of social construction needs to accommodate the physical reality of the body and changes in the body through the lifecourse. They coin the term 'the negotiated body' to describe the process through which changes in the body are interpreted at the subjective level and how individual interpretations and adjustments to physical changes are mediated by cultural norms and expectations. As they argue:

> while biological changes in the body *do* occur, the ways in which these changes are incorporated, ignored, championed, dismissed, embraced, or rejected by any individual are not necessarily predetermined – either by the biological processes which have taken place or by the social context within which the individual, embodied self is positioned. (p 17)

A related argument is developed by Twigg (2006). Drawing on Foucauldian theory, Twigg argued that the ageing body should not be seen as primarily biological, but as cultural. She cited the example of incontinence, which is a low priority for attention and is therefore often ignored by health practitioners, with serious and often unnecessary consequences for older people's physical, mental and social health. On the other hand, Twigg argued, while the cultural critiques of biomedicine provide important insights, cultural theories have fed a desire among gerontologists to disassociate old age from biomedical accounts of ill-health and decline. Within post-modernist and post-structuralist thinking there is therefore an overemphasis on old-age identities that lacks attention to the ageing body and runs the risk of age-denial and reinforcing ageist attitudes. Like Hockey and James (2003), Twigg argued that a better understanding is needed of how the body and the self are formed and reformed in a dialectical relationship.

Twigg's insights can be linked to the lay perspectives of health discussed above. As she pointed out, people's understanding of health emerges from the concrete realities of their everyday lives and experiences, which are informed by prevailing norms, values and beliefs. With ageing comes the increasing likelihood that these experiences will include a loss of self-reliance and growing dependency on others, whether families or formal care services or both. From the UK context, Twigg argued that the biomedical paradigm is still dominant within healthcare and that this is often at odds with patients' own experiences of their bodies. At the same time, policies on *social* care exhibit a very underdeveloped understanding of the body, which may be seen as an irrelevance in that context, and of concern only to health professionals. Higgs and Rees-Jones (2009) discussed three important aspects of bodily ageing which also highlight the relationship between body and culture: bodily *appearance* (cultural practices that shape and control age-associated changes in appearance), bodily *functioning* (the 'machinery' of the body) and bodily *control* (capacity for self-care).

Appearance is highly relevant to the discussion of health as identity. For older people, the emphasis on the visual, a characteristic of Western consumer cultures, places them in an invidious position, as they fall short of cultural expectations which are centred on youthfulness (Twigg 2006). In age-stratified consumer cultures the expectation is that people will make efforts to remain looking young, and there has been a vast growth in the range of techniques and products designed to enable them to do this (Vincent 2006b). However, as Higgs et al (2009) pointed out, being a consumer of anti-ageing products is not guaranteed to satisfy, since the effects of anti-ageing are temporary. Higgs et al also point out how the public differentiates between those products that are merely cosmetic and those that have health benefits. Special diets, vitamin supplements and 'nutraceuticals' are part of the aesthetic of contemporary consumer culture which has been increasingly absorbed into public health discourses of fitness and vitality. Improving and maintaining bodily fitness and a healthy appearance has become an individual responsibility, for which self-discipline is essential. Higgs and Rees-Jones argued that consumer society 'rests on an increasing focus on the self as constructed through regimes of the body ranging from plastic surgery and body maintenance to health, fitness and diet regimes' (2009: 85).

These various conceptualisations of health are not mutually exclusive and their significance varies according to context. Ideas about health are inextricably linked to prevailing cultural ideologies, norms and values. Clearly, the preoccupation with appearance discussed above is more relevant to consumerist cultures. However, as will be further explored, the fluctuations and changes in cultural contexts are reflected in ideas about ageing and health. Apt (1996: 73), for example, described how the long-held traditional view that ageing increases social esteem has been challenged within the contemporary Ghanaian cultural context. Younger people in Ghana now regard old age as defined by failing health and increased disability, particularly inability to walk unimpaired, to see and hear clearly. Such changes need to be examined for their relationship to developments in the socioeconomic and policy contexts and changing discourses about the citizenship of older people.

Conceptualising care

Multiple meanings of care have developed over the past decades, particularly within feminist writing, with distinctions drawn between caring about and caring for, between care as work and care as emotion and care as practice and care as disposition. From the disabled people's movement has come a challenge to the very idea of care because of its connotations of dependency and a lack of autonomy. Disabled writers have argued that a focus on care contributes to the objectification of disabled people. Beresford (2008), for example, argued that the concept of care frames disabled people as dependent and is 'inherently unequal and controlling' (p 13). This perspective is important in relation to contemporary struggles by disabled people to achieve full citizen rights. However, the counter-argument is not to ignore conditions of dependency that lead to a need for care but to see these as applicable to everyone, not just to particular categories of people who are then objectified. To be framed as dependent is a problem when seen in the context of a culture that regards independence as the norm. Regarding a need for care as inherent in the human condition means that ideas about citizenship also need to change.

The view in this text is that, fundamentally, care is a necessity of life, albeit a complex and hard-to-define concept. Fisher and Tronto (1990: 40) gave a broad definition of caring as:

> a species activity that includes everything that we do to maintain, continue and repair our 'world' so that we can live in it as well as possible.

A similarly broad definition is given by Kofman and Raghuram (2009: 3), for whom care is:

> the work of looking after the physical, psychological, emotional and developmental needs of one or more people [as well as] a range of human experiences and relationships of obligation, trust, loyalty and commitment concerned with the well-being of others.

The breadth of these definitions has generated the criticism that they are too all-encompassing and that it becomes difficult to distinguish care from other activities. In Bowden's view, the complexity and diversity of the ethical possibilities of care defy definition. In her view, it is through examining the *practices* of care that a better understanding can be developed of 'what can be known but cannot be defined'. For Bowden, practices of care entail 'a range of ethical priorities, commitments, attitudes and beliefs that are central to the well being of the person' (1997: 184). In this sense, care is a prerequisite for the holistic health model of the WHO and not only relevant in the context of illness and disease.

In cultures that value independence and individual autonomy, care has become a highly contentious issue for policy and practice. The characterisation of care as a quantifiable, measurable set of activities has been open to criticism from feminists in particular, who point to the complexity of care as a practice that is embedded within relationships and which is shaped by social and cultural contexts, including the institution of the family as well as the organisation of formal support services (Sevenhuijsen 1998).

As outlined in Chapter One, the feminist ethics of care is based on the understanding that vulnerability and frailty – and therefore the need for care – are inherent within the human condition. Kittay (1999) refers to 'inevitable dependencies', which are a facet of human life and give rise to a need for care. The need for care exists throughout the lifecourse, but is greater at some times than at others. The giving and receiving of care necessarily entails a consideration of ethics, since the need for care places people in a position of relative powerlessness, and without an ethical framework being 'cared for' would exacerbate an individual's vulnerability rather than ease it. The relational nature of care means that the perspectives of all involved need to be taken into account. Kittay developed the concept of 'nested dependencies' to explain that the needs of those who provide care require attention as well as the needs of those on the receiving end. Feminist ethicists have also stressed that in modern societies care is antithetical to the prevailing culture of independence and self-reliance that underpins the dominant model of the citizen as consumer. As discussed in Chapter Ones, the devaluation of care as a practice can be seen in its absence from public debate. Twigg (2002), for example, argued that the practices of care are absent from policies that are ostensibly all about the care of older people. Instead, these focus almost exclusively on the demand and supply of services and the costs and funding of these, and pay little attention to what kind of care is needed or how it is experienced by those who receive it.

Tronto (1993) conceptualised care as a process with five stages: *attentiveness, responsibility, competence, responsiveness* and *integrity. Attentiveness* means noticing what is going on, realising that there is a need. Lack of awareness of older people's health and care needs is a major concern. In the context of the increased policy emphasis on keeping down the cost of care, less attentiveness to the needs of older people and their families is highly likely. As Lloyd–Sherlock (2010) argued, there is a lack of attention to older people's needs for care in most countries of the world. However, to maintain an ethic of care it would be necessary to ensure that attentiveness did not become over-intrusive or a form of surveillance – an aspect of care that is highly contentious. For example, the use of technological devices to monitor the movements of disabled or frail older people is done in the name of safety and enabling older people to remain in their homes, as they wish. It could therefore be regarded as being attentive to their needs and wishes. Alternatively, it could be regarded as the antithesis of care because it substitutes machines for human contact and places conditions on enabling older people to remain at home. Home thus becomes a site of surveillance rather than a place of privacy.

The second stage of care is *responsibility*, either taking on the role of care provider or seeing that the need for care is attended to. A sense of responsibility might come from a range of sources, such as familial obligations, adherence to marriage vows or feelings of love and affection, a sense of indebtedness or a combination of motivations. This element of the model raises many questions concerning the qualitative nature of care within families and in formal settings. At a broader level, questions about responsibility are at the heart of debates about the balance of individual and collective responsibilities for personal welfare. The key questions in these debates are who provides care, who is entitled to receive it, and who pays for it.

The third stage of an ethic of care is *competence*. This aspect of Tronto's model is important in relation to the tensions described above between the moral and political agendas and the way that the perceived implications of population ageing for the cost of care have overshadowed action on tackling inequalities in health. Competence does not mean merely ensuring that individual carers are well educated and trained to practice practise effectively; it also means ensuring that the necessary resources are allocated to ensure that well-educated carers can carry out their role to a high standard.

The fourth stage of Tronto's model is *responsiveness*. This requires that we start from the standpoint of the one needing care. This element is in tune with the ideals of 'person-centredness' that have emerged in social care in countries with relatively well-developed welfare states. Person-centredness in dementia care is a good example (Kitwood 1997). However, the prioritisation of efficiency and cost containment in welfare has led to increased managerial controls over resources and these often prove a stumbling-block to responsiveness in formal services. As Land and Himmelweit (2010) argued, the less tangible aspects of good care that arise from warm relationships between care provider and recipient are the very things that fall by the wayside in the name of market efficiency.

For Held (2006), care is both a *practice* and a *value*. Regarding care as a practice entails an ethical responsibility to have an appreciation of the conditions of care work. Regarding care as a value entails understanding care as something more than simply meeting the needs of those who are dependent. It provides a basis for normative evaluation of practices at both micro- and macro-level. Hence, feminists point to the low status of both care providers and recipients and see the explanation for this in the patriarchal conditions under which services have developed.

The micro-level work of care – *caring for* – is often separated conceptually from the macro-level, formal organisation of care. However, these two levels are inextricably linked. The capacity of families to provide care, in the sense of tending for members who are unable to care for themselves, is part of the landscape of policy making, determining whether alternative forms of care are needed to compensate or substitute, and such policies will be influenced by a combination of cultural, social and economic factors. In Singapore, for example, despite major problems in sustaining family care because of demographic trends and changes to women's position in the labour market, the government still insists that institutional care should be 'the last resort' because family care provides warmth, companionship and emotional support in ways that other forms of care do not (Yeoh and Huang 2010). Rozario and Hong (2011) argue that the Confucian ethics that underpin policies on the care of older people and the ideology of familism are inextricably linked with neoconservative policies on welfare. This perspective on family care is often associated with East Asian traditions of filial piety, but it also has deep roots in other cultural settings. The values that underpin the promotion of non-institutionalised care services in modern welfare states encompass the view that a care home should be the last resort (Heywood et al 2002).

The centrality of care to health pertains to the health both of the care recipient and of the carer. The ethics of care perspective holds that the need *to* care, as well as the need *for* care, is fundamental to well-being. However, as has been argued by feminist commentators, the relationship between caring for others and the health of the carer is negative when the conditions are not right. Mackintosh and Tibandebage (2006) argued that the scale of the HIV/AIDS crisis in sub-Saharan Africa has highlighted how assumptions about older women's caring capacity have placed an unmanageable burden on their shoulders and have exacerbated health problems that were already severe in the context of extreme poverty and a lack of material resources.

Conceptualisations of care are thus many and varied, and this review of perspectives upholds Bowden's observation about its complexity and its centrality to health and well-being. The different levels at which care practices occur should be understood not as dichotomous but as deeply entwined. Care policies have the capacity to enable relationships of care to flourish or to struggle. The importance of taking into account the needs of all concerned in practices of care cannot be overestimated, since a lack of support for one person will inevitably affect others.

A lifecourse approach to health and care

The conceptualisations of health and care discussed above highlight the value of a lifecourse perspective. Both negative and positive conceptualisations of health and the centrality of care to life draw attention to the factors that have throughout life affected the process of ageing and the conditions of life in old age. But there is more to the lifecourse than a means for seeking retrospective explanations of conditions of life in old age. The concept of the lifecourse provides a *dynamic* model for analysing the relationships between health, care and ageing.

In epidemiology there has been a significant growth of interest in developing knowledge concerning the lifecourse factors that lead to chronic disease in old age. The controversial 'Barker hypothesis', that health and illness in later life have their origins in foetal development, has generated a long debate concerning the relative influences of genetic and biological factors, on the one hand, and socioeconomic factors, on the other (Kuh and Ben Shlomo 2004). Barker's work, published in the 1990s, was criticised for its tendency to overlook the influence of social and economic factors in later life, and subsequent epidemiological studies have adopted a broader perspective on lifecourse determinants that include the socioeconomic and the policy-related (Aboderin et al 2002, Blane 2006). Zhang et al (2010), for example, researched the links between childhood nutritional deprivation and the development of cognitive impairment in later life, and made the salient point that attention to poor nutrition in children worldwide could, in addition to the obvious benefits to children in the short term, also have benefits over the long term by reducing levels of cognitive decline in old age.

The methodological challenges in this field of research are significant, particularly when seeking to establish the nature of the interrelationship between the biological, psychological and social dimensions of health *and* their role as determinants of health and disease in later life. Kuh and Ben-Shlomo (2004) pointed to four models of lifecourse epidemiology, which are not mutually exclusive. The first two of these are described as '*critical period models*', in which the body is biologically programmed to disease in later life as a result of exposure to risk factors at a particular time in the development of the body, the results of which might or might not be modified at a later time. An example of this is the study of cardio-vascular mortality in the Boy-Orr Carnegie cohort study, which identified how socioeconomic factors generally had an effect on particular cardio-vascular diseases in later life, but that the effects varied according to the age at which these influences were experienced. The second two are variations on the idea of the *accumulation of risk* across the lifecourse, either through the clustering of risk factors or through the sequencing of risks in a chain reaction. These models point to the ways in which exposure to adverse socioeconomic conditions over the lifecourse result in disability arising from chronic illness in old age. The mechanisms through which this process occurs are a priority for epidemiological research. It is known that individuals vary in their capacity to adapt to different risks and hazards to health throughout the lifecourse and that intrinsic and extrinsic factors are implicated in this. Kuh and Ben-Shlomo (2004), for example, identify the pathways along which exposure to a range of interrelated biological, environmental and psycho-social factors in infancy and childhood can lead to poor lung function in later life. Westendorp and Kirkwood (2007) described ageing as a gradual, lifelong accumulation of subtle 'faults' in the body's cells and organs, and not as a phase of development that begins in mid-life. Genetic factors combine with nutrition, life-style, environment and chance to produce individual experiences of ageing. For example, loss of bone density is normal as part of the process of ageing. However, whether or not an individual will develop osteoporosis will depend on the original state of bone density and the rate of loss, both of which can be related to nutritional and environmental factors which start at the prenatal stage of life.

Despite its inclusion of socioeconomic factors, the epidemiological approach to the lifecourse is still primarily disease focused. In social gerontology the lifecourse is also seen as a model for understanding the conditions of ageing and of old age through attention to the cumulative effects of earlier life experiences. However, there are key differences in how these cumulative experiences are analysed, and to what end. In social gerontology, the lifecourse approach is concerned not so much with establishing causal links between earlier and later periods of the lifecourse, as with understanding the dialectical nature of the relationship between individual and social factors across the lifecourse. As Dannefer and Settersten expressed it, a lifecourse perspective points towards an understanding of ageing as an 'experientially contingent reality, involving continuous interactions between body, psyche and social world' (2010: 4). It is the linkage between the individual experience of ageing, on the one hand, and the social and historical contexts within which individual ageing occurs, on the other hand, that also differentiates the lifecourse approach from the individual-level 'life-cycle' or 'life-span' approach. Dannefer (2003) argued that evidence of cumulative advantage and/or disadvantage (CAD) over the lifecourse has demonstrated consistently how ageing is a collective and not just an individual process. Bengston et al (2005) conceptualised the lifecourse as 'a sequence of age-linked transitions that are embedded in social institutions and history'. They identified five key principles:

1. *Linked lives*: the interconnectedness of lives, especially across the generations.
2. *Historical time and place*: the social and historical contexts that shape individual lives and the lives of particular birth cohorts.
3. *Transitions and timing*: the synchronicity of individual changes and changes in the wider social and economic contexts that might be advantageous or disadvantageous.
4. *Agency*: the interrelationship between the individual and the context of their life, where the individual has the capacity to plan and make decisions within the constraints and opportunities that exist.
5. *Human development as life-long processes*: learning and development can continue into the last stages of the lifecourse, including at the end of life.

The cultural turn in social gerontology has generated questions about the value within contemporary Western societies of the concept of the lifecourse as an explanatory model, given the growing importance of individual identities. From this perspective, the concept of the lifecourse, with its references to standardised, age-linked patterns of behaviour and roles, might be regarded as more applicable to an earlier period of the 20th century. Contemporary cultural trends, such as are seen in patterns of marriage and childbearing, work and retirement, stand in contrast to these standardised age-linked patterns, and suggest that the diversity of life-styles, with the growth of personal choice and autonomy have made the lifecourse less predictable (Gilleard and Higgs 2000, Higgs and Rees-Jones 2009). From this perspective, ageing itself has become a much more reflexive project than it used to be and individuals have considerable agency in determining the path of their own ageing, including through the adoption of a healthy lifestyle.

Harper (2006) questioned the value of the lifecourse perspectives developed within Western cultures, which she argued are not always applicable to the study of ageing in other parts of the world, where the transitions from one stage of the lifecourse to another are not necessarily linked to chronological age per se but to the alignments and realignment of roles and social relationships, which vary according to context. The concept of the lifecourse must therefore be approached critically, with a view to the historical and cultural contexts in which it is being applied.

The third age–fourth age dichotomy

The idea of the third age emphasises the opportunities for freedom and growth in post-employment life. Laslett (1989) argued that the third age was itself a stage in the lifecourse that was both personally chosen and the product of collective circumstances. A publication by the then Age Concern England, entitled *Older, Richer, Fitter* (Metz and Underwood 2005), illustrates this point well. This publication focuses on the potential of the 'mature market' of an ageing society and the growth in demand for 'cosmaceutical' and 'nutraceutical' products, specifically targeted at older people. Higgs et al (2009) referred to the technologies of human individuality, which, they argue, have not only created a distinction between 'natural' and 'normal' ageing but have also placed health at the centre of the frame. What they refer to as the 'will to health' (p 689) is central to the pursuit of an agentic third-age life-style is typical of late modernity. This has created a distinction between natural ageing (coming to terms with a process of physical and mental decline) and normal ageing (maintaining the norms of self-care aimed at delaying such a decline). As Gilleard and Higgs argued: 'most, if not all life-style cultural practices are institutionalized "anti-ageing" strategies' (2000: 83). To be engaged in these practices maintains one's position as a 'third-ager'. The third-age identity is that of the active and healthy individual, living a productive life and participating in market consumption. It is the responsibility of the third-ager to stave off the fourth-age identity – that of the physically frail and dependent old person who lacks the skills of self-care.

It is essential to bear in mind the importance of socioeconomic determinants of health in this discussion of the third-age/fourth-age dichotomy. Health in the sense of fitness goes hand-in-hand with a higher standard of living. Being richer and fitter enables older individuals to make the necessary choices and decisions that are denied to poorer people who are effectively excluded from the agenda. As discussed further in Chapter Five, the discourse of self-care and active ageing associated with the third age fails to take socioeconomic determinants of health into consideration. Hence the message of active ageing is applied globally, including in contexts where it is irrelevant to the point of insult. For example, campaigns to abolish the statutory retirement age stress the positive benefits to health of paid employment but overlook the position of vast numbers of older people in the world who have no access to a retirement pension and are compelled to continue working even when it is evidently damaging to their health.

According to Twigg (2006), optimistic accounts of the third age are possible only 'by projecting into a dark Fourth Age all the problems and difficulties' associated with ageing. Gilleard and Higgs (2010) developed the idea of the fourth age as a 'social imaginary', meaning 'a place where our greatest fears reside but which can only be addressed by allusion and metaphor' (2010: 126). Twigg pointed to the closeness of the fourth age to death as one reason why this period of the lifecourse lacks meaning. Since death lacks meaning in modern secular societies, the period prior to death is also emptied of meaning and understood simply as a period of decline. Lawton (2000) referred to the extended period of 'liminality' experienced by older people in contemporary Western societies as a form of social death that is experienced prior to physical death. These themes will be explored further in Chapter Seven.

The process of progression from third to fourth age is a subject of increasing interest in gerontology. Higgs and Rees-Jones (2009: 86) referred to this as a process of gradual withdrawal from successful body maintenance and acceptance of bodily limits, which they termed the 'arc of acquiescence'. The arc varies in shape and length according to available social, cultural and economic capital and the nature of interactions between self and society. In medical research, attempts to establish the age at which the third age ends and the fourth age starts have focused on the prevention of age-related health problems (Staehelin 2005). Predictors of morbidity and mortality are inextricably linked with policy concerns over dependency ratios, the emphasis being on the compression of morbidity. This reinforces the points discussed above concerning functional health and how what Katz (2006) termed 'functional age' has become the dominant discourse in ageing and health. Progression from the third to the fourth age is evidently not a neat chronological transition, but in policy-making the emphasis on functional health reflects a desire for predictability and manageability in meeting demand for healthcare.

Summary

The complexity of concepts such as health and care discussed in this chapter stand in sharp contrast with the narrow functionalist perspectives portrayed in the global patterns and trends discussed in Chapter Two and this has significant implications for policy making. Of course, policy makers need to take action and cannot forever be on hold while striving to understand the complexity and diversity of older people's health and their experiences of care. However, the overview of different perspectives on health and care highlights how particular discourses have become dominant in policy debates. Key points to highlight include the importance of conceptualising health in old age as more than the absence of disease and as more than the sum of individual capacity for self-care. Of equal importance is the perception of supportive social relationships as a prerequisite for health and well-being throughout the lifecourse. The concept of salutogenesis draws attention to the social dimensions of health and to the value of health-promoting social and physical environments. The dynamic concept of the lifecourse highlights how relationships between individual health and social factors are not static but are subject to flux and change. In the next chapter, these themes are explored further in the particular context of policies for health and care.

FOUR

The policy process in health and care

Introduction

The discussions in the previous chapters have made a number of references to the role of policy in shaping the concepts of ageing, health and care. The aim of this chapter is to focus more specifically on policies as *processes* which are continuous, characterised by conflicts of interests and shaped through the exercise of power. An important aspect of the exercise of power is the production of knowledge to inform policy agendas. In health and social care policies, discourses surrounding demographic trends play a crucial role. As is argued, older people are frequently characterised *en masse* as an economic problem, and changes in dependency ratios within ageing societies as a threat to the intergenerational contract. Paradoxically, while ageing populations are firmly established on policy agendas everywhere as a policy maker's headache, it still remains the case that policy success is measured by reference to increased life expectancy and the prevention of premature deaths. 'League tables' of life expectancy are produced regularly as a record of national success or failure, with Japan currently in the position of world record-holder.

Gross inequalities in health have provided and continue to provide a strong moral imperative for policy action, but demographic trends are influencing ideas about what kind of action is needed. As discussed, health systems in low-income countries are experiencing a double burden because the need to address the growth of chronic diseases combines with an unfinished agenda of tackling communicable diseases, and it is increasingly recognised that addressing this double burden will require global rather than national policies and strategies. Age is an increasingly important element in the debate concerning the moral case for policy action on health. Beaglehole and Bonita (2009), for example, drew attention to the need for a new approach in public health which is more aware of the effects of demographic trends. Demographic trends raise questions concerning distributive justice, including whether the claims of different age groups for healthcare are in competition. The question of whether the age of an individual should have a bearing on their entitlement to resources and their eligibility for services is often perceived to apply at the micro-level of professional decision making, such as making renal therapies available to older people. At the macro-level, age emerges also as a central issue in debates surrounding the moral basis of resource allocation in health (Daniels 2008). Hence both socioeconomic inequalities in health and age-related inequalities in access to healthcare provoke debate about equity.

Concerning the role of policies, an important question to consider at the outset is *what the evidence is that policies make a difference to health*. Debates on health inequalities have for many years reflected differences of view about whether policy action should target health inequalities or should simply rely on economic growth to improve living standards and – as a consequence – health, but the argument that economic growth and not policy action will improve health is less prevalent now. The World Bank now acknowledges the value of social policies. Its 2010 Global Monitoring Report noted that without effective policy responses the social impact of the economic crisis of the 1990s in low-income countries would have been far worse and that, although the outcomes of the 2008 crisis are not yet fully understood, the hope is that social policy action will have the effect of dampening the worst effects (World Bank 2010). A further twist to the debate about this relationship between economic growth, policies and health is that there is increasing acceptance of the view that policies on health and welfare have a positive impact on economic growth (Mkandawire 2001). Evidence on the social determinants of health demonstrates that, in order to have an impact on health, policy action would need to go far wider than health policy per se, to include a range of measures, including on income security, housing and environmental health (Marmot 2005). Another argument, from Wilkinson and Pickett (2009), is that in the context of high-income countries the relationship between income and health is more a function of inequality, with social position and *relative* income being determining factors, rather than differences in living standards per se. From this perspective, material living standards need to be understood for what they signify in terms of social position. Social life, social networks and social support are strongly associated with health and have a bearing on policy decisions. The discussion in this chapter focuses, in turn, on the idea of policies as process; the *context* of policy making, including the impact of globalisation; *ideological* factors that influence policy agendas and priorities; *political and organisational* factors that reflect the exercise of power and the governance of health and welfare; *implementation* issues; and the processes of *bargaining and compromise* that occur within the policy process. In the final section of the chapter the discussion is of *values and ethics* in relation to equity, with particular attention drawn to the capabilities approach.

Policy as process

The idea of policy as a *process* underpins the discussion in this chapter (Hill and Hupe 2009). The aim is to elaborate on key features of this process and to provide a framework for understanding the themes of prevention, treatment and care that are picked up in subsequent chapters. An ideal-type of the policy process would be that a social phenomenon is identified as a problem requiring attention. It then gets on to the agenda of policy makers, who design a remedy that is produced as a policy on paper, which in turn is given to appropriate bodies to implement in practice. However, this neatly sequential ideal-type bears little resemblance to the reality. Instead, the policy process is better understood as a patchwork of actions and non-actions by a range of governmental and non-governmental organisations which is influenced by material resources, cultural values and political power. Particular socioeconomic, political, historical and environmental contexts will shape and influence decisions that are made. Issues do not emerge uninfluenced by political concerns, and individual policy actions are influenced by wider policy agendas and what are understood to be the most pressing problems.

The context of the policy process: the impacts of globalisation

The impacts of globalisation on health and care have been subjected to far broader debate than is possible to cover in this text. Of particular concern here are the global-level liberalisation of markets and production and the consequences of these, which affect national-level policies on health, social security and care in the context of population ageing. From a critical gerontology perspective, Phillipson (2006) identified three aspects of globalisation that are of particular relevance to ageing. The first is its influence on the *ideological* terrain: that is, ageing has been socially constructed as a new form of risk. The influence on the ideological terrain, from Phillipson's perspective, is that global-level interactions and the intensification of global ties have contributed to a politicisation of ageing as well as a strengthening of the perception that population ageing is a worldwide problem. The dominance of neoliberal economics, he argued, is reinforced through these global ties and affects profoundly the ways in which national governments set their own policy priorities, including those relating to old age.

The second aspect identified by Phillipson concerns the *new forms of risk* that have emerged in conjunction with globalisation. These have removed the securities of social institutions like pensions and other social support for old age and placed responsibility on the shoulders of individuals. Ageing itself thus becomes a matter of individual, not pooled or collective risk. The third impact identified by Phillipson is the role played by globalisation in the creation of *new structures* for the control and management of ageing. People's rights have become more fragmented and the spread of powerful global organisations has generated new social and political forms. Phillipson argued that globalisation has also exacerbated socioeconomic inequalities in later life. The globalisation of financial markets has particular effects, as highlighted in a study of pension-fund capitalism by Vincent (2006a). As Vincent pointed out, the concerns of the wealthy about the security of their pension funds are very different from the concerns of the poor, and these inequalities are played out at a global level. Hence, risk is 'exported' to developing countries, where insecurity is borne by the rural poor, particularly the old and women, in order to sustain the pension funds of the richer nations. Within developing countries, pension policies are often modelled on those in high-income countries, so that those in pensionable employment enjoy benefits in retirement that are denied to the majority (Lloyd-Sherlock 2006). The banking crisis of 2008 has exacerbated this divergence of interests and generated greater insecurity among the poorest, and greater inequalities. These themes – ideological, political and organisational – are echoed in a range of debates about globalisation that are of relevance to this discussion.

The ideological terrain: the development of dominant policy discourses on ageing

The processes by which particular concepts and ideas come to dominate policy processes represent power struggles between interested parties. Bozorgmehr observed that what have come to be understood as 'common goals' are better understood as 'successes in the battle of theories' (2010: 12). The policy process inevitably entails the shaping of ideas so that they fit overarching policy agendas. Hence, the ageing of populations is seen as a policy problem. Why particular issues come to dominate the policy process as problems is a matter of debate. Indeed, Colebatch (2005) argued that that the policy process is to a large extent about negotiation and the creation of shared meaning and the questions: 'what requires attention and what is the nature of this problem' are wide open to interpretation. This point is highly relevant to the issue of how demographic trends are interpreted and what policy actions are pursued as a consequence. The UN's 2007 World Economic and Social Survey showed that increases in healthcare expenditure in a number of countries over recent decades can be attributed only in part to ageing populations. In spite of this, changes in dependency ratios push concerns about care to the top of policy agendas and frame these in over-simplistic ways.

There is a high degree of consensus over the ideological impact of globalisation on welfare. Yeates (2005), for example, made the pertinent point that in the global debates and struggles over the future of welfare, the dominant themes that emerge are all variants of liberalism. She identified these themes as the increasing emphasis on individual responsibility and choice; a restricted role for the public sector in both financing and welfare service provision; a more substantial role for the commercial sector; and minimum regulation of the commercial sector. She also noted that there are no international governmental organisations advancing a democratic or redistributive agenda for welfare, of the kind that exists in Nordic countries. The underlying assumption about the superiority of the commercial sector is open to question. Leaving older people's health and care to the market has evidently had negative effects. For example, in the UK in 2011 the collapse of Southern Cross, one of the largest for-profit care companies in the care-homes business, raised serious questions about the role of the commercial sector, particularly private equity firms, in providing care. Nevertheless the view that the private sector is preferable to the state has come to dominate at a global level and, as Baars (2006) argued, has provided a convenient rationale for national governments to overlook older people's welfare needs.

A related point is the way in which particular discourses dominate and eclipse others. In the previous chapter it was argued that policy makers often fail to grasp the realities of life for those who need or provide care. As an example, the United Nations Research Institute for Social Development (UNRISD) programme on

Gender and Development pointed to the invisibility of unpaid care within global economic policies (Razavi 2007, Abe 2010). As a consequence, a whole raft of activities that have demonstrable economic benefit to societies is completely overlooked when it comes to establishing policies. This is to the detriment of people involved in care relationships because the conditions of their lives are not seen and understood and therefore not supported. However, it is also to the detriment of societies more generally because the value of evidently productive activities is not recognised and counted. As discussed in the previous chapter, the development of health and social care policies would be enhanced immeasurably by a fuller understanding of the extent and nature of unpaid care. It is because the *practices* of care do not fit underlying assumptions about what are suitable subjects for policy makers that they are absent from public policy discourses. Instead, policies have tended to adopt a narrow, commoditised view of care that focuses on processes of commissioning and trade between government agencies and commercial corporations and the regulations that govern these, which offer only a partial picture. It is important to emphasise that, although unpaid care work has been all but invisible in global economic policies, there is ample evidence to show how these policies affect the giving and receiving of care. This evidence is discussed further in Chapter Seven.

The political and organisational terrain

Phillipson's point about the increased power and influence of global non-governmental organisations has also been analysed at length by a range of commentators, again with broad agreement about their rising importance. An important aspect of these debates concerns the shifting levels of power of different global organisations in the sphere of health and care. Deacon (2007) identified what he termed 'global policy advocate coalitions' which represent widely divergent interests. These include the UN, the WHO, the World Bank, a range of international corporations, pharmaceutical companies, healthcare providers, social and political movements and international non-governmental organisations (INGOs). He pointed to the increased influence of the World Bank through the funding of national projects, the development of public–private partnerships and the direct provision of goods and services. The increased influence over health and welfare systems of international financial institutions (IFIs) such as the International Monetary Fund and the World Bank is regarded as a matter of concern by many commentators. Hein and Kohlmorgen, for example, argued that there is 'hardly any other field of global politics where new institutional forms have gained comparable significance as in global public health, particularly in relation to financing' (2008: 84). Evidence that economic growth facilitated by IFIs has been followed by increased social inequalities, higher unemployment, more insecure forms of employment and environmental degradation has amassed over the years (Soubbotina 2004, Hassim and Razavi 2006). Relationships between governmental and non-governmental bodies in health and care services have been particularly contentious in recent decades. The WHO's 2008 World Health Report acknowledged that 'the blurring of boundaries between private enterprise and public institutions' has transformed relations between citizens, professionals and politicians in different parts of the world (WHO 2008a: xiii).

The role of the World Bank in relation to healthcare policies and practices has received a great deal of attention. As the single biggest donor of money for health projects, the World Bank has had direct influence on national health and welfare policies. Gorman (2002) argued that the World Bank virtually monopolised debates in the 1990s over pension reform, while others have argued that the actions of the World Bank systematically undermined the ideals of Alma Ata as the aim of equity in healthcare was overtaken by the drive for economic efficiency, with little attention to the wider determinants of health. The World Bank has been in competition with the WHO over the conceptual underpinnings of global health politics, although within the World Bank itself the conceptualisation of health has also been hotly contested (Hein and Kohlmorgen 2008). The 1993 World Bank report *Investing in Health* and the 1994 report *Averting the Old Age Crisis* were both highly instrumental in the restructuring of health and welfare services. The 'time-bomb' thesis contained within the 1994 report gave legitimacy to neoliberal, 'safety-net' models of health and welfare services and to the promotion of the private sector as the most efficient provider of services to older people.

The World Bank was in the mainstream of economic thinking at the time, taking a similar line to that of the International Monetary Fund (IMF) and playing a major role in the entrenchment of neoliberal political values. Lloyd-Sherlock (2010) made the point that in many developing countries the health sector reforms shaped by the World Bank have resulted in a dramatic expansion of private healthcare services, with INGOs seeking to compensate for declining state capacity. Without such voluntary interventions, he commented, there would be no healthcare at all for the poorest groups who are unable to pay for services in the private, commercial sector. Navarro (2008) regarded the relative weakness of the WHO in comparison with the World Bank as a problem, but he was also deeply critical of the WHO, which he argued had shown an underlying commitment to the very political and economic systems that have proved so counter-productive to its aims at Alma Ata and Ottawa.

The contest within the World Bank over its economic strategies highlights the centrality of values to policy actions. In its 2002 report *The Policy Roots of Economic Crisis and Poverty* the World Bank acknowledged that the very structural adjustment policies it had so enthusiastically promoted in the 1990s had in fact exacerbated socioeconomic inequalities and contributed to further impoverishment and marginalisation of the poor. This report signalled a major shift in the World Bank's policies, which changed to prioritise poverty reduction. Its 2006 World Development Report, *Equity and Development*, was explicit in its support for human rights as a basic policy principle. It argued for public health reforms, better sanitation, clean water supplies and immunisation programmes for the benefit of the many rather than the privileged elite – policies that were entirely in line with those of the WHO and INGOs.

It would be a gross oversimplification to conclude that differences of opinion over policy priorities for health and welfare were resolved by this change of tune. As Anderson (2006) argued, deeply entrenched problems caused by structural adjustment programmes had lasting effects which persisted long after these programmes were replaced with poverty-reduction strategies. Furthermore, while the aims have changed, the underlying economic models have not and the World Bank remains committed to the private sector as the best option for service provision, albeit in partnership with public and voluntary sectors. A recent World Bank publication still claims that a shift of resources away from public to private sector organisations is the best approach to tackling chronic and non-communicable disease in developing countries (Adeyi et al 2007). Neoliberal economics still permeate global policies, including, for example, the 'pro-poor' policies of the OECD, which are deeply compromised by neoliberal assumptions and corrupted by conflicts of interest (Anderson 2006).

The *governance* of health and social care is a crucial point which draws attention to the relationship between global institutions and national governments. Deacon (2007) argued that the relative power and influence of global policy actors and nation-states is a matter of debate and in any case differs between policy areas. There are particular concerns in relation to healthcare, the governance of which has been weak in the context of a rapidly growing market. Lee et al (2009) identified four particular consequences of this: first, globalisation changes the distribution of power and authority, causing national governments (and hence their regulatory regimes) to be weakened. Second, globalisation is strengthening the connections across different spheres of policy. For example, policies on trade and migration have knock-on effects on healthcare systems in relation to both healthcare provision and staffing. Third, the proliferation of institutions, particularly those that are market-based, has a negative effect on governance. Transnational corporations, civic and social organisations, as well as 'hybrid' organisations such as public-private partnerships, have radically altered traditional lines of accountability. A fourth effect is the shift in power and authority that can be seen in the rise in influence of the World Bank through its activities in lending to the health sector since the 1980s and the parallel loss of power by the WHO. The rise in the World Bank's power and authority is evident in other spheres of welfare provision also, including over pension policies, where it has eclipsed the previously pre-eminent authority of the International Labour Organisation (Yeates 2005). An analysis of pensions policies by Orenstein (2005) highlighted how transnational non-governmental policy actors are often responsible for their formulation and transfer to individual countries – what he termed a form of 'governance without government' at the global level.

The pressures faced by governments from transnational corporations can be seen in relation to public health measures, such as policies to tax products and industrial production methods where these are known to be harmful to health but are also associated with economic growth and job creation. For example, the Framework Convention on Tobacco Control still has not been fully implemented and tobacco companies continue to resist attempts to deter smoking. At the time of writing, the tobacco company Philip Morris has threatened to sue the Australian government over a plan to introduce plain packaging on cigarettes (Guardian 2011). These pressures are hard in any context, but in low-income countries the capacity for action is more restricted and policy strategies on health can be frustrated. Labonté et al (2011) analysed the nature of the impact of global trade treaties and pointed to the policy *space* and policy *capacity* of national governments to take effective action on chronic diseases. Policy space refers to the freedom and scope of governments to choose the policies that meet their particular aims, while policy capacity refers to their fiscal ability to enact those policies or regulations. Trade treaties can enhance or erode national governments' space and capacity. With reference to food, tobacco and alcohol in particular, Labonté et al concluded that the liberalisation of trade and finance has increased 'the global diffusion of risk factors for chronic disease' (2011: 18).

On the other hand, it is also argued that the nation–state remains an important actor and the relative importance of the role played by global institutions in the erosion of welfare systems at the national level is a matter of debate (Palier and Sykes 2001). National governments have always been able to facilitate or restrict opportunities for private healthcare provision through measures such as subsidies or tax relief for private health insurance schemes. Moreover, nation–states remain a significant force not only in making decisions about whether or not to advance international practices but also in the way these practices are adapted in different national settings (Labonté 2008, Nolte and McKee 2008b). As Gough pointed out, the implementation of neoliberal models at the local level will inevitably be 'refracted through domestic regimes' (2001: 185). The concept of policy transfer encapsulates this process. Ideas about how policies, practices and institutions in health and social care *should be* developed have had remarkable success in becoming dominant discourses, but there are discernible differences between nations in the extent and nature of their impact. For example, Yeates (2005) argued that differences in impact on welfare systems can be understood by reference to political and economic contexts and historical traditions. These include how well-established and well-resourced a welfare system is and what local priorities are for social protection. Local priorities were also emphasised by Silva et al (2011), who argued that while neoliberal policies had a profound and lasting effect on the healthcare system in Bolivia, this effect cannot be attributed entirely to the World Bank because the national governments in power at the time were receptive to the Structural Adjustment Programmes. They also suggested that left–wing governments tend to separate control over action on the social determinants of health, on the one hand, and provision of curative healthcare, on the other, the former being in the public sector and the latter in private hands.

Governmental action can also support the transfer of ideas. For example, in 2004 the European Union instituted the Open Method of Co-ordination in social protection and social inclusion, including in the fields of healthcare and long-term care, in order to enable member states to identify practices that could be transferable between them (Glendinning and Moran 2009). Nolte and McKee (2008b) observed that while there is a high degree of consensus about how to respond effectively to the treatment and care of chronic disease, there are wide variations between countries in the ways that they adapt and develop their responses (Zhan and Montgomery 2003, Wilson 2006). The concept of 'path dependency' in the policy process provides an explanation for these variations, highlighting how innovations in policies and practices are shaped by existing policies and practices. Izuhara (2010), for example, discussed the cultural context of intergenerational relations in East Asia and the way in which care has become socialised and marketised. The concept of 'filial piety' describes the long-standing framework that has defined family obligations in East Asian cultures. The effect of socialisation and marketisation has changed traditional boundaries between families and the state, and affected ideas about family loyalties and obligations. However, individual countries are changing in different ways. In China, a market in institutional care has opened up, paralleled by a gradual change of view about institutional care as a source of family pride rather than shame. This is because the willingness of one's children to bear the high cost of institutional care has increasingly come to be interpreted as a form of filial piety. In Japan, as in China, the expectation that long-term care is a family obligation has changed, but there change has occurred over a longer period than in China and has included the introduction of social insurance for older people and home-centred care services. In this context, family support has increasingly meant emotional support and the organisation and management of community-based resources.

Policy implementation: fine on paper but poor in practice?

Much has been written about the gap between the rhetoric and the realities of policies – the implementation gap that seems to dog progressive policies – and many explanations have been developed (see, for example, Hill and Hupe 2002). Policy-making on poverty reduction is a case in point. In the year 2000 the Millennium Development Goals (MDGs) – to eradicate extreme poverty and improve the health and welfare of the world's poorest people by 2015 – replaced the 'Health for All by the Year 2000' declaration of the 1977 World Health Assembly. Since the two policies are so similar, questions are raised about why, in 23 years, so little progress was made on the first. According to Global Health Watch (2005), the answer lies in the macro-economic contexts and the economic crises that occurred soon after the 1977 conference. The Structural Adjustment Programmes introduced by the IMF and the World Bank at the time were regarded as being of primary importance, although, as discussed, these exacerbated rather than addressed the health problems of the world's poor

Fast-forward to the present day, and the impact of the 2008 banking crisis on the MDGs has been significant, as people's disposable income in low- and middle-income countries is reduced. Access to healthcare is one of the areas badly affected. In middle-income countries such as Turkey, for example, spending on healthcare and medicines was one of the areas where people reported that they had been forced to cut back. Of course, access to healthcare that is free at the point of delivery ameliorates the impact of a drop in disposable income – a point that reinforces the relevance of local context. More generally, the observation of the Global Health Watch team concerning the overriding impact of the macro-economic context coincides precisely with Tronto's argument raised in Chapter One, that the moral agenda of rights (as in the Health For All programme) is easily eclipsed by more pressing political concerns because it is conceptualised separately from the political agenda of resources (Tronto 1993).

In the context of this discussion on implementation, an important point concerns whether policies are too vague and idealistic to have practical application. For example, since the Second World War the WHO and others have campaigned for intersectoral action to promote health and for a broad-based primary healthcare system. In its 1978 conference in Alma Ata the WHO called for primary healthcare to be the main focus of healthcare systems and an integral part of the overall social and economic development of societies. Again, in 1986, the WHO's Ottawa Charter proposed a framework for action by policy makers on primary healthcare which recommended a reorientation of health services beyond clinical and curative functions, to multisectoral preventive work (WHO 1986). Over the succeeding decades numerous criticisms of the Alma Ata declaration have emerged, frequently targeted at its idealistic, rhetorical and impractical nature.

From this history emerge questions about the value of policies that have only symbolic strength. Arguably, the ideals of the Alma Ata declaration still hold out a model for a possible alternative to contemporary health policies, even though the commitment to equity and justice in health that it encapsulated is evidently hobbled by more dominant political agendas. Its influence is significant as a focus for organising for equity in global health, but the lack of progress in achieving its aims draws attention to the compromise of its ideals over the years. For example, in 2008 the World Health Report drew a distinction between the broad-based model of *primary healthcare* (multisectoral and 'upstream') and *primary care*, which is specifically focused on the practices of health services. Primary care in its newly defined form has had evident practical application: Kickbusch (2010), for example, pointed to its direct influence on the South Australian government's Strategic Plan for health. From this perspective, compromise can pave the way for change, albeit slow and partial. Katz (2009), on the other hand, was critical of the way in which the 2008 World Health Report neglected any reference to health as a right (as defined in the Alma Ata declaration), but sought instead to prioritise the *economic* case for primary healthcare. Katz contrasted this report with the report of the Commission on Social Determinants of Health, published the same year (CSDH 2008). He argued that the CSDH provides clear evidence of social policies and programmes as among the determinants of marked health inequalities, and that the case for a rights-based approach to health still stands.

In 1982, between the Alma Ata conference and the Ottawa Declaration, the UN's Vienna International Plan of Action on Ageing – the first international policy on ageing – was passed (UN 1983). This drew attention to demographic trends and the envisaged ageing of societies, and argued in favour of urgent policy action at a global level. It also considered issues of equity across age groups both in relation to the *distribution of the benefits* of development and in *the potential for conflict* between age groups arising from changes in dependency ratios. Like the Ottawa Charter, the Vienna Plan maintained that the way to promote older people's health and well-being was necessarily intersectoral in nature, encompassing health promotion throughout the lifecourse in order to combat the detrimental effects of premature ageing. The evidence on the outcomes of the Vienna Plan is not resoundingly positive. Sidorenko and Walker (2004) identified that when asked about its impact on their policies, governments responded that it had been 'useful' but several issues were raised that still needed to be addressed, including concerns about violence and neglect experienced by older people and the welfare needs of older people in rural areas of developing countries, in particular. Gorman (2002) was critical of the Vienna Plan, noting that its aims were far beyond the means of many governments in the developing world and that it accorded little or no role to NGOs in its implementation. From this perspective, the problems of implementation lie in lack of attention to the practical relevance of policies and to the potential for ideals to be translated into action.

The Madrid International Plan of Action on Ageing (MIPAA) attempted to by-pass the problems that had limited the effectiveness of the Vienna Plan. Two primary principles underpin the MIPAA. The first is a 'development approach to population ageing', which entailed mainstreaming into plans and policies the concerns of age. The second is a 'lifecourse intergenerational approach' to policy, which stresses equity and reciprocity between age groups. The MIPAA is, as Sidorenko and Walker (2004) commented, comprehensive in its coverage. Thus, the developmental focus was intended to incorporate the concerns of older people into existing strategies for national development and poverty eradication. The mainstreaming approach committed signatory governments to incorporating a perspective on ageing into their policies as a first step towards the implementation of the Plan. This was seen as a relatively cost-neutral way of making progress on raising awareness of older people's concerns and of the effects of societal ageing on social development.

A review of progress on the MIPAA, however, noted major shortcomings in progress towards the mainstreaming of ageing, which was a particularly disappointing finding, given that this was acknowledged to be the approach of choice for developing countries with limited resources (UN 2008). The global financial crises that have occurred since the MIPAA was passed will doubtless have played a part in downgrading the importance of policies on ageing within the broader political agendas of national governments. However, shortcomings in the implementation of the MIPAA cannot be explained entirely by reference to a lack of resources. As Harper (2006) argued, ageing is not a pressing issue in many developing countries and the MIPAA will not have been seen as a policy priority. Lloyd-Sherlock argued that there is 'a failure of most policies in most countries to promote financially sustainable interventions that maximise well being for all in later life' (2010: 235). From this perspective, the inadequacy of policies in relation to age is deeply embedded, in all contexts, including at a global level. It is deeply ironic that, despite its strong official support for the MIPAA, the UN's own 2011 summit on non-communicable diseases omitted Alzheimer's disease and other dementias from its planned programme.

Engagement in the policy process: struggle and compromise

The discussion so far has highlighted how the policy process is never tidy and straightforward but always reflects a struggle between diverse interest groups with more or less muscle to flex. Kickbusch (2010) represents a highly pragmatic approach to involvement in this process, as pointed out above. She took the high level of political interest in health issues as an indication that health has moved from being a vertical, 'sectoral' issue to being a horizontal issue of relevance to a wide range of societal goals. For Kickbusch, this has provided a good reason for groups interested in promoting health to organise, develop ideas and get involved with the policy process. Policy agendas, she argued, are 'actions triggered by windows of opportunity which can be opened by policy entrepreneurs' (2010: 263). Kickbusch suggested that it is the convergence of 'problems, policy alternatives and politics' that makes policy. When issues are defined as problems, policy makers need to address them by reference to alternative strategies, informed by current knowledge and experience. The trickiest aspect of this process is political. The skills of bargaining, compromise and negotiation are not easy to sustain by those unused to involvement in the policy process.

As discussed, the WHO's 2008 World Health Report, *Primary Healthcare: Now More than Ever*, presented a more pragmatic and context-specific form of primary healthcare than that espoused within the Alma Ata declaration. This report sees the reduction of inequalities in health, universal coverage of healthcare and intersectoral action on health as important ongoing aims for the WHO. However, it highlights that three 'worrisome trends' put these at risk:

- health systems that focus disproportionately on a narrow offer of curative care
- health systems where a command-and-control approach to disease control focused on short-term results is fragmenting service delivery
- health systems where a hands-off or laissez-faire approach to governance has allowed unregulated commercialisation of health to flourish. (WHO 2008a: xiii)

The combined effect of these trends is the lack of a comprehensive and balanced approach to healthcare, inequitable access, impoverishing costs to individuals and an erosion of trust in healthcare systems as regulatory regimes are undermined. Certainly these trends do not bode well for older people who have incurable chronic health conditions that require integrated services to support them. The lack of effective regulation of private sector services and care homes is a significant problem (Lloyd-Sherlock 2010). Even within this non-contentious approach to primary care, there are evident problems, and the report itself has been criticised roundly. In a scathing commentary Katz (2009) argued that its presentation of primary healthcare is a 'lite' version that makes no reference to the broader economic structures that exacerbate the very inequalities and injustices that primary healthcare has been grappling with for decades, nor to the social determinants of health; nor does it recognise the power differentials that exist between the 'stakeholders' involved in the policy dialogues that the WHO envisages regarding the governance of primary care.

The WHO's plans to develop *age-friendliness* in different settings might appear somewhat naïve and insignificant, compared with the scale of the 'worrisome trends'. The concept of age-friendliness is difficult to pin down, as it is associated with such a wide range of activities (Kalache 2009). It can also be regarded as a compromise of the principle of a rights-based approach to healthcare and of action against age discrimination. Indeed, following Katz (2009), it could be seen as a 'lite' form of campaigns to abolish age discrimination in healthcare. WHO guidelines on Age-friendly Primary Healthcare (WHO 2004b), for example, focus on healthcare staff, aiming to improve attitudes as well as knowledge and skills in treating the diseases of old age. At the same time, age-friendliness also entails a focus on the management of primary healthcare so as to raise awareness of how to make services more approachable, and easy to access physically. Age-friendly primary care centres are seen as models for promoting social inclusion, providing inspiration to other sectors such as transport and housing. Age-friendly primary care is also about the empowerment of older people, giving them information about healthy living so as to prevent or delay the onset of chronic diseases and disabilities. In this sense it is very individualistic and entirely compatible with a neoliberal agenda.

Global Age-friendly Cities (WHO 2007b) take a more 'upstream' approach, emphasising the importance of preventive healthcare, salutogenic environments and physically accessible buildings, spaces and transport systems. In the context of other global trends that are apparently antithetical to the ideas underpinning age-friendliness, the question arises: are age-friendly cities likely to be implemented in practice? The evidence from the Age-friendly Cities movement suggests that it can provide a platform for local actions that are of benefit to older people. In addition, it can play a part in the development of what the WHO is calling an 'age-friendly movement' (WHO 2007b), promoting the possibilities for networks between older people's groups in different parts of the world and of bottom-up approaches to the development of policies and practices that affect older people. This suggests that the benefits are relatively small scale rather than signalling a fundamental shift in attitudes towards older people, although the benefits to the particular groups participating should not be overlooked.

Bottom-up influences are frequently associated with NGOs. As noted by Klein and Kohlmorgen (2008), during the 1990s NGOs assumed a more prominent position in the policy process and through their combined political weight achieved results in influencing international discourses on health and pushing a view of health as social justice. However, NGOs vary in terms of their power and influence. In the field of ageing there are large NGOs in areas where the demographic transition is advanced, but in the developing world the picture is less positive and a negative view of ageing prevails (Gorman 2002). Here, there are fewer organisations working with older people and those that exist are more charitable than political in nature. Gorman called for NGOs in ageing to move beyond the immediacy of service provision, to make the links between their experiences of working with older people at the community level and the wider policy agendas.

A problem for NGOs is that even where they succeed in getting involved in the policy process and expanding their sphere of influence they run the risk of becoming co-opted by those who have greater power and influence within global health governance circles. NGOs act where they can and take advantage of windows of opportunity – as Kickbusch (2010) suggested; but, as already discussed, wider policy priorities limit their influence. For example, in the field of public health the tendency has been to opt for 'vertical' strategies, focused on particular infectious diseases such as HIV, tuberculosis and malaria rather than on general public health measures. McIntyre (2004), for example, pointed to the role of the World Bank in restricting the scope of African health policies to actions, in this way. The major philanthropic foundations in the global health governance field have reinforced the disease-specific focus of health policies, thus tying NGOs to this policy agenda. Hein and Kohlmorgen (2008) noted how NGOs have been successful in improving access to medicines and how their successes were in part due to the convergence of interests of national governments who wished to make progress in tackling diseases such as HIV/AIDS, and of pharmaceutical companies who stood to gain from increased activity on disease-specific programmes. As Kickbusch argued, 'in health it seems easier to address vertical, disease-based problems with medical solutions rather than systemic issues and approaches' (2010: 263). Thus, while NGOs can benefit as participants in the policy process, they run the risk that their critical stance will be muted.

Values and ethics in health and care policies for ageing societies

This part of the chapter will analyse in greater depth particular underlying philosophical and ethical debates on health concerned with equity in health and healthcare. There are particular implications within these debates for ageing, and it is crucially important to explore them within the overall discussion in this text. Policy actions to promote equity in health have been influenced by different philosophical and ethical traditions. Labonté (2008) identified five discourses of health, which he analysed for their potential to generate action towards health equity. These are: health as *security*; health as *development*; health as a *global public good*; health as a *commodity*; and health as a *human right*.

Health as security concerns action to address global-level risks of infection, such as SARS, as well as risks related to political and economic instability. Health as security can be used to distort policy priorities and shift attention from equity concerns. On the other hand, security is a prerequisite for health and should, arguably, be a key feature of public health policy. Health as development is also a prominent discourse, which influenced the MDGs, but, as Labonté argued, it has been narrowly focused on economic performance and not enough on human potential. Health as development, arguably, could be a core feature of policies to promote equity through a focus on strengthening solidarity and social cohesion. Thus, in principle both health as security and health as development have potential to inform policies to promote equity, but in practice have not proved to be effective in this way.

The idea of health as global public good refers to an ethic that places collective benefit over individual gain. Its collective potential is not confined to individual nations, and from this perspective the actions of one country should not have negative 'spill-over' effects on another. The idea of health as a public good is in direct competition with the idea of health as a commodity. Hence, Labonté argues, cross-border flows of pharmaceuticals, new technologies and services such as insurance and health and care facilities have been designed to maximise profit and not promote health. In addition, international regulations developed through the World Trade Organisation, such as Trade Related Aspects of Intellectual Property Rights (TRIPS) and the General Agreement on Trade in Services (GATS), mean that elite groups and private companies benefit from the privatisation of health and care services and this is to the detriment of those who are unable to pay the costs.

Labonté regarded the health as a human right discourse as having great potential for equity in health. He argued that the rights discourse is one of the most highly globalised political values of our time. The WHO's own Commission on the Social Determinants of Health (CSDH 2008) provided clear evidence of the need to reassert a rights-based approach. In the context of health it is the most widely shared language of opposition to the idea of health as a commodity, although, as Labonté observed, it remains relatively weak in practice. This last point is a strong reminder of the frequently observed weakness inherent within moral agendas related to health discussed above.

Labonté's typology provides a useful basis for a discussion of values and ethics and their roles in the policy process at a global level. From the perspective of the ethics of care, the emphasis on rights would need to be assessed by reference to the limitations of the ethic of justice discussed in the introductory chapter. Health as a human right has undoubtedly been important as an alternative discourse to neoliberalism (Shrecker et al 2010), but the danger is that it will remain an abstract discourse while the health-as-commodity discourse continues to dominate political and economic actions. Since health cannot be separated from consideration of social well-being and the need for caring relationships, the aim of promoting equity must go further than the conferring of rights to individuals.

Age-related equity and the development of policies to combat age discrimination have featured strongly in the campaigning activities of older people's organisations in parts of the developed world, and at the UN the rights of older people have been given specific consideration since the General Assembly in 2010, when a working group on strengthening the human rights of older people was established. Initial reports to this group have identified, for example, that the abuse and neglect of older people (particularly older women) is a widespread problem not limited to any particular context or region (UN 2009). It remains to be seen if this action by the UN has greater impact than the WHO's 2002 Toronto Declaration on elder abuse referred to in Chapter One, but an ethics of care perspective would suggest that the human rights agenda will continue to be overshadowed by the wider political agenda of resources.

Equity in health: the capabilities approach

The capabilities approach, first developed by Amartya Sen (Sen 1999), has had significant impact within the UN, as is evident in its Human Development Reports (UN 2010b), and in the European Union's social policy agenda (Carpenter 2009). The capabilities approach was a reaction to the dominant economistic measures of social development, which Sen regarded as inadequate to the task of measuring well-being because they overlooked non-material values. The capabilities approach holds that what is important is *equity in the distribution of capabilities*, capabilities being the things that a person can effectively do or be. In Sen's view, following Aristotle, capabilities are positive freedoms, the freedom to do or be something, together with the means of exercising those freedoms. The capabilities approach ascribes a strong role to human agency also, as it includes what a person *chooses* to be or to do in line with his or her own values (Sen 1999, 2004).

Sen's ideas were developed by Nussbaum (2000) into a universal rights-based approach to capabilities which, she argues, should be relevant in any cultural setting. Unlike Sen, who resisted consolidating the idea of capabilities into defined universal measures, Nussbaum produced a list of 'central human capabilities'. These include life; bodily health; bodily integrity and mobility; senses, imagination and thought; emotions; practical reason; affiliation; awareness and concern for nature; play; and control over one's political and material environment. Nussbaum emphasised that this list is best understood as an integrated body of capabilities, but at the same time she also argued that the loss of any individual element would lead to a loss of human dignity.

The capabilities approach is highly regarded among international NGOs as applicable to the promotion of both material well-being and human rights. Barrientos (2010), for example, applied the capabilities approach to a study of pensions in Chile. He defended its value in policy making on social protection because, he argued, it provides a basis for a better understanding of vulnerability than is the case with straightforward 'welfarist' economics. Also he argued that the emphasis on individual agency is important because, while welfarist economics focus on generally available material goods, they do not differentiate between people in terms of the variability of their needs or how they would choose to spend their pensions.

There are, however, several critiques of the capabilities approach. A 'critical but sympathetic' view was given by Carpenter (2009), who argued that it has potential for the development of new models of citizenship which incorporate economic and social rights as well as civil and political rights. However, he argued that because growth-oriented global capitalism is embedded within it, there are limitations to its value as a basis for citizenship. Nevertheless he claimed that it is important because it 'asserts the essential similarity of our human needs and potentialities' and because it values social activities, including caring work (2009: 355). Lloyd-Sherlock (2002) is a similarly critical supporter. He argued that the capabilities approach lacks attention to the complexity and dynamics of the *lifecourse*. He maintained that Nussbaum's view of capabilities is too linear, failing to grasp the ways in which capabilities fluctuate through life and may diminish with ageing. Thus, while Nussbaum recognises that health in later life will be affected by earlier lifecourse experiences, she tends to see earlier experiences as external constraints rather than as inherent aspects of human experiences. For Lloyd-Sherlock, a more dynamic lifecourse model would also take better account of individuals' capacity to mitigate the disadvantages of structural constraints. In policy terms this would entail a better understanding of older people's values and preferences and the extent and variety of older people's internal capabilities, as well as a commitment to reducing structural constraints.

A more fundamental critique of the capabilities approach is that it is essentially individualistic rather than recognising the fundamental importance of relationships between people (Held 2006, Lewis and Giullari 2006, Dean 2009). The capabilities approach acknowledges that human beings are at times dependent on others and that sympathy with those who lack independence is important. However, it regards dependency as a deviation from the norm rather than a basic human characteristic. In this sense, the capabilities approach stands in contrast to the ethics of care – indeed, Nussbaum was critical of the ethics of care, which she regarded as disadvantageous to women who might become locked into caring roles. Lewis and Giullari (2006) made the point that a person's freedom to be and to do what he or she has reason to value will depend to a large extent on the needs and actions of others. Thus, the capabilities approach sees individuals as independent first, while the ethics of care conceptualises the individual as dependent on others in order to achieve independence and autonomy.

A post-colonialist critique of Nussbaum's approach by Charusheela (2009) argued that, despite Nussbaum's claim that her list of capabilities stands up in any cultural context, it in fact represents a colonialist perspective with modernist assumptions embedded within it. She gives as her example the identification of literacy, which is linked to the list of capabilities in several ways and has emerged as a key indicator of development. Drawing on Nzegwu (1995), Charusheela argued that within developing countries literacy has become institutionalised as a filter for access to a range of opportunities and that this leaves those who are illiterate further disadvantaged, whereas, in pre-colonial times literacy was not a prerequisite for a good quality of life or good standard of living. This is an important consideration in the context of international policy priorities for health that are linked to development strategies. It draws attention to the need to take account of local contexts, cultures and priorities.

Capabilities and healthcare policies

The capabilities approach is of particular relevance to policies on health because of its close association with social development. Ruger (2010) developed what she has termed a 'health capabilities paradigm', which places at its foundation the idea of *health as capabilities*. This idea embraces both function and agency. Function refers to what an individual is able to *do* or to *be*, while agency refers to the *freedom to achieve this*. In Ruger's paradigm, some capabilities are more central than others: disease, disability and malnutrition, for example, are central. In common with the public health approaches discussed above, this paradigm emphasises that *policies for health*, rather than health policies per se, are important for health equity. Hence, good health policies are a part of what is needed, rather than the whole picture, although achieving equity in capabilities is a key role of health policy specifically. Therefore the allocation of resources in health policies should be calculated so as to advance equity. Since measures of life expectancy represent one of the indicators of health capabilities, a core task of policy is to prioritise the avoidance of premature death and enable people to achieve the life expectancy that is known to be achievable. This priority inevitably means that resources should be targeted where life expectancy is lowest, which means that Ruger's paradigm is congruent with global movements for justice and equity that seek a redistribution of resources away from the wealthiest to the poorest.

However, by using life expectancy as an indicator of inequality and a basis for setting priorities, Ruger's paradigm also highlights ethical questions related to age. Ruger maintained that her approach 'provides the basis for prioritizing health goods and services to individuals below the average life expectancy rather than to those above that level'. Ruger equivocates somewhat on the question of whether this actually constitutes age-based rationing. She argues that:

> if a choice must be made due to resource constraints, efforts to extend life up to the maximum average life expectancy for all societies should be prioritised over extending life beyond that threshold level, but many societies will have the resources to devote to health beyond the threshold and should invest in extending the threshold further. (Ruger 2010: 201)

Not age-based rationing per se, perhaps, in that age is not regarded as a basis for rationing in general, but her argument opens an ethical can of worms, since extending the threshold of life expectancy would inevitably draw resources away from efforts to reduce global inequalities in life expectancy and could have the effect of increasing them. Ruger pointed to evidence on inequalities in life expectancy between low-, middle- and high-income countries and argued that any society should aim to reach the maximum average life expectancy that is known anywhere (currently the average of almost 83 years in Japan would be the goal). How this would be achieved is a moot point. Should more resources go into life extension in affluent countries when global inequalities in life expectancy are so great? If resources are diverted from affluent to low-income countries, how would that square with older people's campaigns in those countries against age discrimination in healthcare? And what kind of actions would be seen to constitute life extension? Would it be confined to developments such as artificial organs or include more run-of-the-mill procedures such as pace-makers for people aged over 83? How would procedures (such as the removal of cataracts) that are primarily about improving quality of life but that can also have the effect of extending life expectancy be regarded? Ruger's line of reasoning demonstrates that even where a health policy framework can lay claim to moral legitimacy through its focus on justice and equity, there remain thorny ethical questions related to age. General principles for setting priorities for resource allocation cannot be separated from contemporary political and economic contexts which place limits on the resources available for healthcare.

A related set of questions is raised by Daniels (2008). Daniels developed what he termed a 'prudential life-span account', which he claims overcomes some of the moral questions associated with a view of rationing at a particular point in time between different age-groups. A life span account would mean that any individual would have equal access to healthcare throughout life but that this might mean reduced access in later life. He denied that his approach to justice in healthcare is a form of age-based rationing but claimed that it is a means of identifying how resources for health can be allocated to secure opportunities across the life span, while recognising that these differ at different stages.

There are several arguments against the approach taken by Daniels, summarised by Macnicol (2006) as follows. First is the argument that the individual rights of patients to treatment should be based on clinical need irrespective of age. Second, setting an age as the point at which an individual's rights to healthcare are reduced is arbitrary, given the differences in health between people of the same age. Third, it is morally and politically unacceptable to withhold treatment from anyone because that group has a poorer-than-average health outcome. Such a decision would not be made in respect of gender, ethnicity or class and therefore should not be made in respect of age.

Daniels protested that his approach does not make assumptions about the value of a life at different ages, nor does it judge that more social benefit would be derived from saving the young than the old, or that the old have a duty to the young (or vice versa). He claimed that he was not arguing for age-based rationing as a *general* policy but saw his life-span approach as morally permissible in certain *specific circumstances*, when no alternative can be found. His conclusion is therefore similar to Ruger's, although Ruger argues that because there are sufficient resources in high-income countries to cover the cost of healthcare for all age-groups, such theoretical questions are unlikely to arise.

However, Daniels regards his 'life-span approach' as more urgent now than before because of the challenge of global ageing, which he suggested may be the 'greatest public health problem of this century' (2008: 165). This puts things into a somewhat different perspective because a global perspective on ageing calls for a global rather than national response. Hence, contrary to Ruger's conclusion, these are not theoretical but actual questions concerning the equitable distribution of global resources for health care. Daniels also questioned whether it would be prudent to trade off some acute services that might produce a short life extension, for care services that would improve the quality of life rather than extend it. From this perspective, age should be treated differently from other forms of discrimination, and it is quite possible that many older people would prefer not to have life extended if the quality of that life were poor. A crucial point is who has control over such decisions.

Summary

This chapter has taken a broad view of policies, considering the importance of policy action on health because of the moral imperative for action and because evidence demonstrates that policies make a difference to health in later life. Globalisation has generated new challenges that have affected national systems of healthcare and have contributed toward the consolidation of dominant discourses on health and care that are compatible with neoliberal policies. The global reach of neoliberal policies has exacerbated inequalities and these are experienced in old age in particular ways, including health and access to healthcare in later life. Differentials in power between actors in the policy process have resulted in a framing of older people's needs in particular ways and in establishing policy priorities that privilege economic interests over public health and well-being. Global policy debates reflect the difficulties of asserting the interests of relatively powerless groups and of pursuing the moral case for healthcare as a human right. The capabilities approach offers an alternative to the dominant economistic approach of global bodies such as the World Bank, but also presents age-related ethical questions that also highlight the relatively low social status of older people. Ethical debates frequently occur in the abstract, but the discussion of age-related resource allocation draws attention to policies and practices in the here and now. In relation to health equity, two points need to be emphasised: the first is that socioeconomic inequalities are not all about the poor but also about the rich and about the extent and nature of inequalities between rich and poor. The second point that flows from this is that arguments concerning age-related rationing in healthcare actually focus not on older people in general but on those who cannot afford to pay for healthcare and rely on public provision. These ethical questions are as much about socioeconomic inequalities as they are about age.

Throughout this chapter, the policy process has been identified as a patchwork of actions and non-actions, a process of negotiation that creates a shared understanding and perspective on phenomena such as health and care. The next three chapters focus on the ways that these shared understandings apply in particular contexts of health and care.

FIVE

Healthy ageing: upstream actions to prevent illness

Introduction

In this chapter the aim is to explore in greater depth the idea of primary prevention in health, often referred to as 'upstream' action. In the context of health, the idea of prevention is complicated by the different ways of conceptualising health. The key focus of upstream interventions to promote health in *later* life is on the gap between life expectancy and healthy life expectancy. The idea of the compression of morbidity has generated a plethora of studies designed to identify more accurately appropriate interventions that will delay the onset, or at least the progression, of disease so as to maximise functional health. Interventions to prevent disease are of interest for economic as well as health reasons. In their report published by the World Bank, Adeyi et al (2007) comment:

> if preventive interventions are successful, the need for treatment to address an NCD [non-communicable disease] could be delayed until old age, after a healthy and productive life has been lived. (p 24)

We can infer from this that it is individual productivity that matters, as well as individual health.

Evidence of the wide range of determinants of health has also influenced lifecourse perspectives in epidemiology and there is increasing interest in public health in the interactions between different upstream factors, including social and environmental as well as genetic and physiological factors. Better understanding of the interactions between these can inform action to prevent disease in later life (Kuh and Ben-Shlomo 2004).

However, prevention also encompasses a range of 'upstream' measures that are about the maximisation of good health rather than merely the prevention of disease. Salutogenic perspectives on health in old age can be seen as a riposte to negative perceptions of ageing as being all about loss, decline and death. The salutogenic concept of health, reflected in the often-quoted adage 'adding life to years not merely years to life', is an approach that has wide appeal and is reflected in the ideas of 'positive' and 'active' ageing. However, in common with other public health concepts, these ideas are open to question and some of the criticisms that have emerged reflect the points raised in the previous chapter concerning the policy process and the creation of shared meaning. As will be discussed, the meanings of prevention that have become dominant are not always to the benefit of older people.

Public health and health promotion

A broad definition of public health in its early days is provided by Winslow (1920):

> The science and art of preventing disease, prolonging life and promoting physical health and efficiency through organized community efforts for the sanitation of the environment, the control of community infections, the education of the individual in the principles of personal hygiene, the organization of medical and nursing service for the early diagnosis and preventive treatment of disease, and the development of the social machinery which will ensure to every individual in the community a standard of living adequate for the maintenance of health. (Winslow 1920: 23 cited in Birn et al 2009: 4)

As Birn et al argued, this definition could be adopted today as a basis for international actions and cooperation for health. Yet, over time, the broad approach to public health that it encapsulates has been hotly contested within health policy and practice, and differing disciplinary strands in public health have emerged. At a global level, these have had varying degrees of success. Thus, clinical epidemiology has achieved a much more secure place within health systems, as compared with other, non-clinical disciplines, such as health promotion. As discussed in Chapter Three, the lifecourse approach that developed in clinical epidemiology aims through scientific research to identify the causes of disease, establishing links between the determinants of health at earlier stages of the lifecourse and the occurrence of disease in later life. Health promotion, by contrast, has its roots in community development, being aimed at the empowerment of local communities and with a view to improving health as an outcome of this. An example is the 'Age-Friendly Cities' programme of the WHO, referred to in Chapter Three. This regards healthy urban environments as necessary to enable people to age well, and the participation of older people in decision making as an essential aspect of promoting health in old age (WHO 2007b).

With its roots in the sanitary movement of the 19th century, during the period of industrialisation and urbanisation in Europe, public health emerged as an important strategy for preventing contagion. Many of the debates that occurred in the 19th century remain relevant today and then, as now, the relative responsibilities of individuals, professionals and society for promoting health were hotly debated. As a multidisciplinary endeavour 'ranging from the surveillance of health and disease in populations, through to the provision of health advice and information' (Earle 2007: 1), public health is a broad and controversial sphere of practice. The breadth of its focus can be seen as both its strength and its weakness. While there is incontrovertible evidence of the multifactorial nature of the determinants of health, it is hard to articulate a clear line of policy when health is regarded as the outcome of everything that is done. Within public health, epidemiological surveys developed as a vital tool for public health services, drawing attention to gross inequalities in health and life expectancy and providing a rational basis for decisions about the allocation of resources and intersectoral policy action. Yet, as discussed in the previous chapter, policy action on this evidence has been weak.

Debates about the role and remit of public health shape and are shaped by policies, which reflect broader contemporary social, cultural and political concerns. For example, after the Second World War, reflecting the priorities of the time, a broad consensus developed around the idea of health as a human right, with responsibility for securing good health being primarily on governments. It was amid growing awareness of the glaring inequalities in health at a global level and the need for action to tackle these that the World Health Organization was formed. As discussed in Chapter Three, the WHO adopted a positive and holistic definition of health, but at the time of its inception saw healthcare *services* as the means of promoting health and raising the levels of health of the poorest in particular. Services organised and funded through compulsory insurance schemes were established across Western Europe and other parts of the world in the 20 years from 1945. In the UK it was expected that people would become healthier because of having the National Health Service and that their need for health services would diminish over time, thus reducing its cost. With the benefit of hindsight, this expectation is easily dismissed as hopelessly naïve. In the years since the Second World War the populations of relatively affluent countries have continued to demand healthcare in line with new developments, including life-extending medical innovations. In this period also, there were some successes in tackling infant and childhood mortality in less developed countries, but healthcare services tended to be concentrated in urban areas, based in hospitals and available only to those who could afford to pay (Rifkin and Walt 1986). Healthcare services proved not to be an effective vehicle for promoting public health.

The publication of the Lalonde Report in 1974 marked a discernible shift in thinking about health promotion. Lalonde argued that healthcare services were little more than a 'catchment net' for those who had become sick, and that they could not be relied upon as the sole or even the main policy measure to promote *health*. His 'health field concept' placed health services as one field within a four-field model of health:

1. Genetic predisposition
2. Physical and social environment
3. Health services
4. Individual life-style and behaviour.

Lalonde argued that promoting health would be best served by concentrating on the environment and life-style. Ashton and Seymour regard this report as marking the beginning of the 'New Public Health' stage, which brought together 'environmental change and personal preventive measures with appropriate therapeutic interventions, especially for the elderly and disabled' (1988: 21). The WHO took up Lalonde's ideas and in the 1970s adopted an intersectoral approach to health which acknowledged the relationship between individual health and the domains affecting it.

This approach took into account the constraints that prevented the full implementation of Western-style healthcare systems within less developed countries, including the cost of medicines and the realisation that it was the rich in the developing world that were benefiting while the poor – particularly those in rural areas – were left with no services at all. The intersectoral approach offered a way of ensuring that the development of healthcare would be in line with the broader social and cultural contexts. Rifkin and Walt (1986) referred to the debate that ensued between those who supported comprehensive primary healthcare and health development, on the one hand, and those who supported selective primary healthcare focused on specific interventions to reduce disease, on the other.

The WHO's policy of 'Health for All by the Year 2000' was published following the Alma Ata conference in 1978 (WHO 1981). This conference is widely regarded as a watershed in thinking about health and health promotion, with its emphasis on intersectoral action. Comprehensive primary healthcare services were identified as the most appropriate vehicle through which intersectoral action could be implemented and inequalities in health tackled. Primary healthcare was regarded as flexible enough to be socially and culturally acceptable and, being located within communities, easily accessible and affordable to all.

As discussed in the previous chapter, in 1986 the first international conference on health promotion at Ottawa produced the Ottawa Charter, which proposed a framework for action by policy makers and reinforced the message about the need to reorient health services beyond clinical and curative functions, to multisectoral preventive work (WHO 1986) The Ottawa international conference is regarded as a key point in the history of health promotion, generating what subsequently became known as the New Public Health Movement (McMichael and Beaglehole 2009). This envisaged health promotion as an activity that should take place further upstream from primary healthcare to create the *prerequisites* for a good life, rather than relying on health education or health services (Lindström and Eriksson 2006). The key prerequisites identified were peace, shelter, education, food, income, a stable eco-system, sustainable resources, social justice and equity. Taken up by the WHO, the Ottawa Charter generated new thinking about health promotion.

> Health promotion is the process of enabling people to increase control over, and to improve their health. To reach a state of complete physical, mental and social well-being, an individual or group must be able to identify and to realize aspirations, to satisfy needs, and to change or cope with the environment. Health is, therefore, seen as a resource for everyday life, not the objective of living. Health is a positive concept

> emphasizing social and personal resources, as well as physical capacities. Therefore, health promotion is not just the responsibility of the health sector, but goes beyond healthy life-styles to well-being. (WHO 1986)

The Charter also proposed a framework for intersectoral action on health. It was envisaged that policy makers across the board would consider the health impacts of policy measures, including, for example, those on work, leisure and the conservation of natural resources. For example, education was seen as a relevant site for health promotion because it had the capacity to prepare individuals for all stages of life, including the resilience to cope with chronic illness and injuries. The Charter also sought to strengthen community action in which people would be given greater control over decisions and supported in developing grass-roots community activities. In short, the holistic view of health that was developed encompassed every area of life, so that all actions at individual, community and societal level were relevant to health and the prevention of illness.

The Ottawa Charter made a major contribution to promoting awareness of the idea of positive health. In this respect, Eriksson and Linström (2005) point to the influence of Antonovsky (1979, 1996). As discussed in Chapter Three, Antonovsky's concept of salutogenesis holds that people's earlier life experiences can instil in them capacities and resources to cope with the normal stressors of life and give them the confidence to perceive meaning in the world – what he termed a 'sense of coherence'. As a concept, it has been remarkably enduring, despite its somewhat limited influence in tackling health inequalities in practice. For example, Morgan and Ziglio (2007) drew on the concept of salutogensis to develop the 'health assets model' for public health as a means of tackling health inequalities. According to Morgan and Ziglio, health assets can mean any resources – social, financial, physical, environmental or human – that individuals and communities have at their disposal which protect against negative health outcomes and promote health. They see the assets model as relevant at the individual level, with the potential to raise individual self-esteem, and at the community level, with the potential to build on the strengths of communities, thereby unlocking some of the barriers to effective action on health inequalities. They regard the values and principles of the assets model as a reflection and re-articulation of the Ottawa Charter.

Arguably, with its inherent lifecourse perspective, salutogenesis is directly relevant to health in later life. Billings and Hashem (2009) conducted a review of the concept for a European initiative in order to assess its usefulness in the promotion of mental health in older people. This review focused on the four types of life experience identified by Antonovsky that shape a sense of coherence (SOC): *comprehensibility*, a degree of predictability about life; *manageability*, having the resources to meet demands; *meaningfulness*, seeing that life makes sense and problems are worth investing energy in; and finally *emotional closeness*, the extent to which an individual has emotional bonds with others in their family and community. The review drew the conclusion that while Antonovsky's insights are thought provoking and impelling, there is insufficient evidence available to show that they can be transferred into meaningful and measurable strategies for health promotion. It argued also that Antonovsky does not have a monopoly on explaining positive health and that other concepts such as resilience, hardiness and purpose in life are equally important. The insights provided by Ryff and Singer (1998) and discussed in Chapter Three are also relevant to this discussion. They identified 'purpose in life' and 'quality connections to others' as primary features of positive human health and these features bear a strong resemblance to Antonovsky's view of a sense of coherence and emotional closeness. At the same time, their analysis of positive health, which highlights its broad philosophical nature, goes some way to explain the difficulty of encapsulating it into strategic health promotion measures.

Critiques of the New Public Health and health promotion

Since the Ottawa Charter, criticisms have continued concerning the gap between the policy rhetoric of intersectoral action on preventive measures and the reality of disease-focused practice. For example, Ryff and Singer commented on the persistence of negative definitions of health, arguing that even those efforts that aimed to measure multidimensional aspects of health and quality of life tended to focus on negative outcomes. They also lamented the limited view of human activities that is reflected in measures of functional health, such as ADLs, which they regarded as largely about basic physiological functions and not about positive health. Some 12 years later Becker et al (2010) concluded that a pathogenic framework still dominated in health services, with progress continuing to be measured by reference to negative outcomes, such as fewer consultations with a doctor. With a particular focus on the US, Becker et al called for a renewed emphasis on salutogenesis within healthcare systems and a change of emphasis from treating illness to promoting good health.

Nettleton (2006) presented a strong critique of New Public Health and health promotion. First, she distinguished the rhetoric from the reality of public health and argued that in both New Public Health and health promotion a focus on individual life-styles, risks and behaviours remains the dominant framework for practice. This, she argued, represents a major gap between the radical rhetoric of principles and the more conservative reality of practice (2006: 241). Second, targeting both the educational and medical approaches, Nettleton questioned the underlying presumption of health promotion that, once obstacles are removed, people will be able to make rational healthy choices. Moreover, she points out that this presumption takes for granted that rationality is as defined within the biomedical paradigm. Third, Nettleton argued that health promotion targets particular groups for attention, and in so doing reinforces sexist, racist and homophobic tendencies, which tend to privilege particular conservative moral codes. This point is particularly relevant where health promotion is conducted as a professional, officially sanctioned activity and where public health action is taken which curbs individual freedom. However, Nettleton went further, to argue that even the bottom–up community development approach to health promotion runs the risk of appropriating the agendas of groups that have challenged professional definitions of need so that professionals end up in control.

Petersen and Lupton (1996) acknowledged that while supporters of the New Public Health regard it as a means of tackling gross socioeconomic inequalities, its practices might not be in line with their vision. Not only are the core principles of community engagement and equity likely to be eclipsed by the competitive, individualistic ideals of neoliberalism, but these also divert attention from the bigger issues of increasing inequalities in wealth and power at a societal level. Like other commentators, Peterson and Lupton pointed to the potential of health promotion and New Public Health to act as a form of social regulation through the scrutiny of individual behaviour. They argued that the New Public Health was essentially a *moral* enterprise that contributed towards the development of ideas about self-regulation, the control of human bodies and the 'proper way' to live. For Peterson and Lupton, then, the New Public Health was an important means of self-regulation and self-governance. What is more, they argued that the adoption of a wide definition of health put in place conditions for self-regulation to become yet stronger, with a range of obligations placed on individual citizens. For Peterson and Lupton, then, the underlying philosophies and practices of the New Public Health were open to far greater critical scrutiny than they received.

There are therefore several critiques of upstream approaches in public health and health promotion, all of which are highly relevant to this discussion of health and care in later life. They can be summarised as follows:

1. Upstream approaches that emphasise the socioeconomic determinants of health have had very limited influence in health policy and practice, which is dominated by a scientific, biomedical approach.
2. It is impossible for the ideals of salutogenesis to be realised in practice within the current context of healthcare, which is dominated by a neoliberal agenda.
3. There is a discrepancy between calls for intersectoral action to promote health and the persistent emphasis on individual behaviour in policy and practice.
4. Practices of the New Public Health divert attention from socioeconomic determinants, being a moral enterprise designed to encourage self-governance in health.

To this list might be added the point raised by Labonté and Schrecker (2009) and discussed in the previous chapter about the weakness of the WHO in maintaining its stance on the socioeconomic determinants of health; the eclipse of the WHO by the World Bank as the pre-eminent global body speaking out on health; and the associated involvement of the global commercial sector in health services. Despite these critiques, the ideals of upstream approaches to illness-prevention retain widespread appeal in policies on ageing, particularly those aimed at promoting the compression of morbidity.

Ageing, disease prevention and health promotion

This section will consider how developments in public health and health promotion have influenced thinking on strategies to promote older people's health, taking into account the critiques outlined above. In her book *Promoting Health in Old Age*, Bernard (2000) identified three strands of health promotion: *health protection*, which encompasses traditional public health measures such as banning smoking in public places; *health prevention*, which is concerned with actions to prevent or reduce ill-health and conserve health; and *health education*, which emphasises information and advice about healthcare and access to it. To these, Bernard added a fourth, *health preservation* strand, which is concerned with achieving optimal levels of functioning. Bernard (2000) argued for attention to be focused less on health systems and what they can do for older people and more on how older people act to achieve optimal levels of functioning, how they keep themselves healthy and how their actions can be promoted and facilitated. She argued also that it is necessary to combat the stereotypes of old age as being about disease, illness and death, which have been exacerbated by ageist and discriminatory attitudes among health professionals and others. Bernard's emphasis on understanding health from the perspective of older people was an important contribution to the debates about ageing and health promotion and remains a vital reminder of older people's continuing agency. Her focus on 'combating the stereotypes of old age' raised a question that continues to be relevant, concerning whether an emphasis on older people's capacities to continue an active and healthy life and to engage in self-care runs the risk of making it more difficult for them to ask for help when they need it.

A global perspective on health throws into sharp relief the value of traditional public health measures, the high levels of mortality and morbidity in low-income countries being attributable to a large extent to the lack of the prerequisites for health set out in the Ottawa Charter. Indeed, Vera-Sanso (2006) pointed out that in parts of India conditions of work are sufficiently arduous for some groups to create the onset of functional old age long before people reach chronological old age. The particularly oppressive conditions under which scheduled caste people in India work and live have led to a range of illnesses and malnutrition, as well as enforced exit from paid employment at the ages of 40 to 50 years. Environmental factors, such as the lack of sanitation and safe drinking water are frequently cited in relation to their impact on premature deaths, particularly deaths in infancy and childhood, but their direct and indirect effects on health in old age are also significant. The direct benefits of public health measures, such as the provision of affordable housing, accessible healthcare services, sanitation and transport are of great importance to older people's health. The indirect effects are evident in the epidemiological evidence of the links between health in old age and exposure to health risks at earlier stages of the lifecourse.

Age intersects with social and economic factors to produce unequal effects on health, and there are environmental concerns of particular relevance to older people. Birn et al (2009), for example, pointed out that in poorer households older people, along with women and children, are among the most vulnerable to indoor air pollution, as a result of the use of biomass fuels for cooking and inadequate ventilation. Agrawal and Arokiasamy (2010) referred to the poor water and sanitation facilities available to older people in rural areas of Maharashtra and Uttar Pradesh in India, which together with the risk of smoke inhalation from cooking stoves create major environmental health risks. Older people, particularly those that are poor, are also among the most vulnerable to environmental disasters (HelpAge International 2005). Environmental concerns are not restricted to low- and middle-income countries. Older people in relatively affluent countries also experience the direct effects of unhealthy environments, as can be seen in the prevalence of hospital-acquired infections in the UK. Age also appears to be implicated in the susceptibility of individuals to forms of food poisoning, such as listeriosis (Keller et al 2007). Deaths from hypothermia and hyperthermia in old age can also be understood as a public health concern. During the 2003 heat-wave in France 15,000 older people died and many of these deaths could have been avoided with more effective public health measures (Ogg 2005). For example, the care homes where many died were ill equipped to deal with extremes of temperature.

In 1996 Peterson and Lupton pointed to a lack of firm evidence on causal pathways between upstream conditions and health outcomes and contended that such firm evidence is needed to ensure that preventive action will be effective. Since then, researchers in a range of disciplines, particularly epidemiology, have tackled the issue of causation. The Health Evidence Network of the European Region of the WHO, for example, reviewed the evidence on risk factors for disability in old age and called for further research from a lifecourse perspective, including on the impact of resources acquired throughout life on abilities to cope with health and function in old age (WHO 2003b). As discussed in Chapter Three, developing a lifecourse approach that explains the pathways between childhood and adult chronic disease has been a growing interest within epidemiology (Kuh and Davey Smith 2004). The impetus for this research lies in the view within epidemiology that medical care has limited value in promoting health. The view is summed up in this quote from Daniels et al (2000):

> By the time a sixty-year-old heart attack victim arrives at the emergency room, bodily insults have accumulated over a lifetime. For such a person, medical care is, figuratively speaking 'the ambulance waiting at the bottom of a cliff'. (p 4)

The need to understand what causes differences and inequalities in health within countries where the majority of people have access to the basic requirements for health has generated more research within high-income countries on the links between socioeconomic determinants and individual health. However, Gu et al (2011) have made the pertinent point that little such research has been conducted in developing countries, where individuals often lack the personal economic resources to invest in health at earlier stages of the lifecourse. There is an increasing realisation of the need for such research. For example, the International Network on Public Health and Aging (Wahlin et al 2008) aims to tackle this gap in knowledge through scientific research and to assist in the development of culturally appropriate interventions to promote healthy ageing. This sharing of knowledge has the potential to enable newly ageing countries to examine critically the experiences of those that are 'already aged', taking into account differences in geo-political contexts. Importantly, the benefits are not perceived to flow one way, since new knowledge of benefit to the already aged countries is likely to be generated through comparative research, including a better understanding of the underlying mechanisms of risk factors for disease. An important point about policy attention to upstream factors in preventing illness (particularly non-communicable diseases) is that the focus is on reducing *future* levels of illness, and there is a danger that the needs of people with chronic disease in the present time will be overlooked, particularly in the context of resource constraints.

When the focus is on the perceived burden of disease associated with ageing societies it is not surprising that policy and research activities favour the identification of risk factors or 'predictors' as a prelude to preventive action at the individual level. Research into genetic predisposition and susceptibility to diseases associated with ageing, such as Alzheimer's disease, is a clear example of this. However, it is the interaction of factors that is increasingly regarded as important (McKee and Samuelsson 2000, Allet and Crimmins 2010). Ayis et al (2006), for example, identified a range of psycho-social factors associated with the onset of 'catastrophic decline' in mobility in older people, and argue that a purely disease-centred approach will provide only a partial picture of the determinants. In this study, the interrelationship of the physiological, psychological, social and environmental dimensions of mobility is a key finding, lending weight to the view that the value of uni-dimensional medical interventions is very limited. From their review of health promotion interventions to prevent isolation and loneliness in older people, Cattan et al (2005) also concluded that traditional trials alone were ineffective and that these should be supplemented by qualitative, observational and multilevel evaluations.

When prevention is understood at a population level the range of factors associated with health is far greater and the causal chains are more complex. An example of this is given by Jawad et al (2009), who examined the effect of life stressors on mental health in old age among older people in Lebanon, who had lived through years of civil war. They argued that it was impossible to generalise from their findings because of the significance of cultural, social and historical contexts particular to Lebanon.

Understanding the operation of upstream factors as determinants of health therefore requires a much wider set of research methodologies than those used in clinical and epidemiological research and a greater synthesis of evidence from a range of sources that connects socioeconomic factors to health and healthcare.

Indeed, as Labonté and Schrecker (2009) argued, it is questionable whether setting a water-tight 'burden of proof' is necessary or desirable in relation to many public health measures. It is especially questionable when the consequences of doing nothing are taken into account. The research agenda is therefore replete with controversy about where attention should be focused and what methodologies are desirable and effective.

From research to action

An important issue in preventive health is whether actions should aim to promote health and well-being across the board (horizontal) or should be targeted to particular conditions (vertical). The eradication of smallpox is a clear example of the latter, as is the current campaign to eradicate malaria (Bill and Melinda Gates Foundation 2009). The debate about the relative value of vertical and horizontal action is long standing (Rifkin and Walt 1986) and is echoed in Bernard's 'health preservation' concept, which emphasised the importance of bottom-up strategies to promote health, led by older people (Bernard 2000). Such horizontal actions are regarded within public health as having broad-based benefits for health which include not only improvements in physical and mental health but also better social health through community cohesion.

By contrast, vertical or selective actions focused on particular diseases are usually led 'top-down' by professionals or policy makers. The WHO's 2008–13 Action Plan for the prevention and control of non-communicable diseases (WHO 2008c) exemplifies the vertical approach. It focused on four conditions: cardio-vascular diseases, diabetes, cancers and chronic respiratory diseases. It acknowledged the importance of environmental, economic and social determinants in the growth in the prevalence of these conditions. It cited policy measures, such as banning smoking and reducing salt levels in food production, as beneficial strategies that have been tried and tested. However, it placed greater emphasis on individual behavioural determinants and the modifiable risk factors that are common to the four conditions: tobacco use, physical inactivity, unhealthy diets and the harmful use of alcohol.

The need for action on the socioeconomic determinants of health in later life is widely accepted in theory, yet in practice policy makers still tend to direct their attention to strategies to change individual behaviour. Another example is the UN's World Economic and Social Survey for 2007, which focused on health and long-term care systems for ageing societies. It considered the evidence on the relationship between, on the one hand, the prevalence of non-communicable disease in later life and, on the other hand, living conditions, nutritional status in childhood and levels of education. However, despite acknowledging the strength of this evidence, it concluded that individual behaviour such as smoking cessation, exercise and diet was 'more policy relevant': 'Much of the preventable component of the non-communicable disease burden is linked to a number of risk factors that can be modified through individual behaviour' (UN 2007: 122) . As discussed in

Chapter Two, evidence from Latin America and the Caribbean concerning the rise in prevalence of diabetes demonstrates clearly that political and economic contexts make a difference to individual behaviour and the choices people make. The impact of the liberalisation of trade on the diets of poorer people in low- and middle-income countries has led inexorably to an increase in the availability and promotion of foods that are high in calories and low in nutrients (Palloni and McEniry 2007).

Yach et al (2006) concluded that the role of the WHO and public health agencies is often to urge individuals 'to stop smoking; eat less fat, sugar and salt; do more physical activity; and eat more fruits, vegetables, nuts and grains', even though it is well known that that individual action without government and multisectoral support does not achieve sustained change (2006: 299). However, their own perspective on multisectoral support is somewhat limited. They argued that, in the context of chronic illness, prevention strategies would need to extend beyond exhortations on healthy living, to incorporate also 'individual self-care, self-monitoring and links to supportive community resources'. Hence, the individual is still the main focus, with communities taking a supporting role.

Some prevention strategies adopt a broader, horizontal view of health (as opposed to being focused only on disease prevention), but are specific in their focus on particular actions and interventions. The promotion of exercise in later life is an example, where individual behaviour remains the primary focus but the benefits of behavioural change are evidently far reaching. There is extensive evidence over many years of the benefits of exercise for health in later life (WHO 2003b). The Better Ageing Project (Fox et al 2007), for example, examined the benefits of exercise for physical and mental health and well-being in old age. This project is located within the scientific medical paradigm, taking as its starting-point the need to improve older people's locomotor function through exercise in order to prevent a range of disorders, including depression and Alzheimer's disease. The Never Too Late study (Fuller et al 2010) examined the benefits of exercise for older people living with chronic illness. This took an ecological view of exercise that highlighted the importance of context and of ensuring that opportunities for physical activity are consistent with the interests and life-styles of groups.

Active ageing: the moral message of health promotion in later life

The moral agenda of the New Public Health described above extends to old age and, in the context of concerns about older people's use of health services, acquires greater urgency. A health promotion booklet, *Demystifying the Myths of Ageing*, produced by the European Region of the WHO (Ritsatakis 2008) conveys a strong moral message, describing as a myth that 'people should expect to deteriorate mentally and physically' as they age. Instead, it claims that the exercise of mind over matter is vital to maintaining health and preventing the diseases of ageing: 'Nothing holds more power over the body than the beliefs of the mind' (p 3). Older people are consequently encouraged to take part in physical activity, to avoid smoking and excessive drinking and to follow a healthy diet in order to tackle the health problems frequently associated with old age. The 'use it or lose it' message is powerful but should be critically analysed in the context of older people's decisions about whether or not to seek help with health problems. As discussed in Chapter Three, when older people begin to develop health problems the danger is that they will be seen as having failed. The sociological perspective on this developed by Higgs et al (2009) and discussed in Chapter Three traces the growth of third-age identities in modern consumerist societies in which health is understood as a 'fundamental expectation and required goal of individual lifecourses' (p 690). The role of health promotion has, they argued, overwhelmed our understanding of later life because it is through health that an older person can still be seen as active agentic individual disassociated from sick and dependent fourth-agers. From this perspective, decisions about whether or not to consult a doctor over perceived health problems assume a moral dimension.

The concept of 'health literacy' has taken hold in health promotion campaigns (and, as discussed in the next chapter, is linked with the concept of self-care in the context of long-term illness). For Katz (2006), functional health literacy 'is held aloft as a self-skill that permits the ageing individual entry into the privileges and professionally approved realm of quality-of-life autonomy and choice-making' (p 133). The shift of perception about ageing from the chronological to the functional, discussed in Chapter Three, is highly significant and its alignment with neoliberal policies on independence and successful ageing is an essential part of the overarching policy aim of containing the cost of support for older people in the context of population ageing.

The moral message, in which older people as individuals are charged with responsibility for maintaining their health through adopting an appropriate life-style and through self-vigilance, finds its way into policies on social care. An example of this is an OECD working paper on policies for healthy ageing: 'In general, the elderly do not exercise enough', this paper argued, before acknowledging that 'the degree of exercise is very hard to measure as formal measures do not necessarily take into account exercise of a casual nature – i.e. shopping or housework' (Oxley 2009: 16). According to this policy paper, the aim should be to promote moderate exercise in pleasant and congenial surroundings. However, it goes further, to suggest policy incentives for informal exercise: 'In some cases, home help for the elderly may effectively eliminate the only exercise that they do undertake' (p 17). Prevention strategies are evidently, therefore, not only about ideas of normal and abnormal ageing but also about placing conditions on the allocation of public services, as a means of obliging older people to take part in the expected level of physical activity.

Like Petersen and Lupton (1996), Higgs et al argued that health promotion entails surveillance through practices of screening and monitoring by experts, where older people's state of health is judged by reference to standards of normal functioning. Screening provides a basis for decisions about whether interventions are to be targeted at those with the greatest risk of developing disease and disability, or applied universally. When the cost of intervention is an overriding concern, such decisions assume greater urgency. The promotion of 'Age-Friendly Primary Healthcare' (WHO 2004b) identifies the screening function of primary healthcare centres as an important means of pursuing preventive strategies with older people, and the moral message comes across clearly in this extract:

> The onset of disability must be delayed or prevented for as long as possible if the success story of increased longevity is to be a time for independence, rather than dependence, activity rather than inactivity, and participation rather than marginalization from family and community life. (p vi)

Normal functioning as activity rather than inactivity is the overriding message: even the reference to family and community life is about 'participation' from a position of independence, rather than about mutual bonds of affection and support.

Not surprisingly, older people express a wide variety of views about what they regard as 'ageing well' (Keating 2005, Bowling 2009). Torres and Hammarström (2009), for example, found that among their interviewees in Sweden many had a problem formulating ideas about what ageing well entailed. Some saw it as 'not ageing at all', since ageing was associated with deterioration. The term 'active ageing' is often used interchangeably with terms such as 'successful ageing' or 'positive ageing'. It embraces a range of perspectives and practices on health and well-being, all of which are to a greater or lesser extent salutogenic in nature. Danyuthasilpe et al (2009) identified how 'following family practices' and 'being interdependent' were regarded as key to healthy ageing in their research in northern Thailand, which entailed the integration of physical, social and spiritual elements. Following family practices included attention to eating and exercise as well as religious practices. Being interdependent included giving and receiving support to and from others in one's family and community. Bowling (2005) argued that the concept of 'quality of life' is compatible with older people's own definitions of 'successful ageing'. In her research in the UK this included social activities, interests and goals, and was in contrast with other models of successful ageing focused on individual achievement.

The roots of the WHO's active ageing agenda can be traced back to the 1995 programme on Ageing and Health (WHO 1998), which was entirely focused on physical activity as the way to age in good health. The WHO's *Active Ageing: A Public Policy Framework*, which was launched at the 2002 Madrid Assembly on Ageing, offered a more comprehensive approach. This Framework defined active ageing as:

> the process of optimizing opportunities for health, participation and security in order to enhance quality of life as people age. (WHO 2002b)

Health, participation and security are referred to as the three pillars of active ageing. The word 'active' thus refers not only to individual physical activity but also to active *contributions* to family, community life and national life. The key goals of the WHO's active ageing policies are to extend healthy life expectancy and quality of life and to maintain autonomy and independence as people age (Kalache and Keller 1999). The Framework adopted a lifecourse approach that stressed the need to prevent non-communicable diseases in later life through action at earlier stages of the lifecourse, based on the understanding that the gap between life expectancy and healthy life expectancy can be influenced to the benefit of older people. The WHO's active ageing agenda has been taken up by governments in most parts of the world and has generated a wide range of activities, the breadth of its conceptualisation of active ageing being capable of adoption in almost any ageing-related policy. As Stenner et al (2011) pointed out, active ageing is presented both as an observable process that is influenced by a range of determinants and as an explicitly political strategy intended to change understandings of what ageing is.

For Walker, active ageing is 'the leading global policy strategy in response to population ageing' (2009: 75). Walker focused in particular on the European context, where he identified that a narrow, employment-focused model had been adopted in preference to the more comprehensive approach of the WHO. Vidovićová (2005) similarly argued that the European model of active ageing has drawn closer to the US concept of 'productive ageing', rather than holding to the WHO's broader vision. Walker identified seven principles for a strategy for active ageing in its broader meaning:

1. Activity should consist of all meaningful pursuits that contribute to the well-being of the individual, their family, community and society at large, not only concerned with paid employment or production.
2. Activity should be a preventive concept – applicable throughout the lifecourse.
3. Active ageing should encompass all older people, including those who are frail and dependent.
4. Active ageing should maintain intergenerational solidarity and fairness.
5. Active ageing should encompass rights and obligations, so that rights to education and training and so on should be accompanied by obligations to participate in these.
6. A strategy for active ageing should be participative and empowering, including both top-down policy action and bottom-up civic action.
7. Active ageing should respect national and cultural diversity.

Walker thus regards active ageing as a broad and inclusive strategy which is relevant to the whole lifecourse, not just old age, and which takes account of the physiological effects of ageing as well as cultural differences. However, the fifth of these principles, concerning the relationships between rights and obligations, echoes the discussion above concerning the moral message of health promotion.

In this vein, Chapman (2005), for example, made the point that much has been written about how older people *should* age, rather than how they *do* age. However, placing obligations on older people to be active in later life takes the moral message a stage further. This approach is open to question, generally in terms of the moral pressure it places on older people, but particularly so in relation to older people who are socioeconomically disadvantaged and more likely to experience poor health and disability. Questions remain over active ageing, concerning who has control over the agenda and how progress on active ageing policies is identified and measured.

Vidovićová (2005) argued that a 'funnel effect' is taking place, in which all the noble ideas concerning active ageing are being translated into narrow and restricted forms within policies. It is the narrow focus on activities within the labour market that Vidovićová criticised most, together with the lack of awareness on the part of policy makers of variations in health status between older people, so that an undifferentiated view of what constitutes activity is developing. In the context of the Czech Republic she pointed to long-standing cultural norms concerning retirement, which is largely still seen as a 'deserved rest'. Vidovićová's observations raise questions about the relevance and value of a pan-European approach to active ageing.

Deeming (2009) examined the roots of the 'active ageing' concept, seeing it as a reaction to 'disengagement theory' (Cumming and Henry 1961). Disengagement theory held that successful adaptation to old age would be achieved by *withdrawal* from roles and relationships built up over the lifecourse. With its emphasis on prolonging active life for as long as possible through paid work and community activities, active ageing is the antithesis of disengagement. Deeming conducted a case study in East London, which focused on the activities that older people engaged in voluntarily, including residents' groups, church groups, evening classes, sport and exercise and social clubs, and found evidence of a positive impact on participants' quality of life. There were evident direct benefits to health from these various activities, but also indirect benefits, seen in the cementing of friendships and the enrichment of people's social lives. For some, these friendships took the place of families living some distance away. As Deeming pointed out, many of the activities that were so beneficial have very insecure resources and there remains an important role for the state in supporting voluntary efforts. Like Vidovićová, Deeming also raised questions about the extent to which active ageing agendas are sensitive to cultural contexts. He noted that older people from ethnic minorities in the area of his study did not benefit in the same way from activities and concluded that active ageing agendas tend to take a blanket view of what would be beneficial, irrespective of culture.

When examined from the perspective of global inequalities, yet more critiques of active ageing emerge. Research by Cameron et al (2010) on the productivity of over-60s in Bangladesh identified how older people there remain active for as long as they are able, for reasons of survival rather than health promotion. They pointed out that while research in more developed countries highlights the benefits for health and well-being of active living and delayed retirement, in countries such as Bangladesh the picture is very different. In Bangladesh demands on older people to earn money and to take care of family and household necessitate levels of activity that are injurious rather than beneficial to health. In this research, it was evident that older people's roles in domestic and community life represented an important contribution to the general good, but this contribution came at personal cost in terms of their health.

Research conducted by Mudege and Ezeh (2009) also highlights the lack of relevance of Western models of active ageing. Their focus on ageing and health in Nairobi highlighted the extensive caring activities of older people whose grandchildren have become orphaned by the HIV/AIDS pandemic. Like Mackintosh and Tibandebage (2006), Mudege and Ezeh argued that, at a time when these women's own health is declining through a range of illnesses and chronic pain, the obligation to care was an additional stress. The idea that active ageing policies are needed to ensure that older people have a meaningful role in life bears little relation to the circumstances of the people in Nairobi, where Mudege and Ezeh conducted their research. The women in this research were more in need of policies to provide relief from being over-extended in their roles. There are compelling reasons, therefore, to adopt a critical stance on the concept of active ageing as it has developed and to consider both its applicability in different contexts and its potential as a basis for promoting older people's health where resources are uncertain.

Socioeconomic determinants and social capital

Analyses of the relationship between socioeconomic factors, on the one hand, and individual health, on the other, have raised questions about whether socioeconomic inequalities are susceptible to moderation through social capital. Bourdieu (1986) describes social capital as:

> the aggregate of the actual or potential resources which are linked to possession of a durable network of more or less institutionalized relationships of mutual acquaintance or recognition – or in other words to membership of a group. (p 248)

Social capital can be seen as a means by which individuals can gain access to benefits, as well as a benefit in and of itself. At a superficial level it might appear obvious that the accumulation of social capital throughout the lifecourse would lead to better physical and mental health in later life, but the evidence on how this occurs still needs to be clearly established. Studies of social networks have focused on their *structures* – the strength and nature of the ties between members – and on the *meaning of the relationships* within the network, especially levels of trust between members.

Despite the prevalence of policy discourses on the dependency of older people, it is increasingly recognised that older people are not simply the passive recipients of the benefits of social networks, sitting back on their laurels after a life-time of contribution. There is a proliferation of evidence that even at the oldest ages people continue to contribute to social networks at both individual and community levels. Boneham and Sixsmith (2006), for example, identified the important role played by older women in the north of England in creating and maintaining social capital and playing a key role in the health of their local communities. Similarly, Fernández-Ballesteros (2002) identified strong family ties in Spain, where older people make a significant contribution to local communities through their care of children. The older people in the Spanish study derived a great deal of satisfaction from their participation in community networks. The context of grandparents' care for HIV/AIDS orphans is also relevant in this respect. Like Mudege and Ezeh (2009) discussed above, Chazan (2008) identified significant stresses on women looking after their grandchildren orphaned by HIV/AIDS in South Africa. Chazan highlighted financial and emotional stresses faced by women as a result of the responsibility of supporting an increasing number of people in their family networks on a diminishing income. She concluded that grandmothers were playing an important role in cushioning the wider societal impact of the HIV epidemic but were receiving little support or income security for themselves. Mudege and Ezeh identified how the social networks that women had built up over the years provided them with a much-needed source of help, enabling them to cope. These two studies exemplify both practical and emotional dimensions of support from social networks.

A distinction should be drawn between Bourdieu's conceptualisation of social capital, which is focused on the individual level, and the community-level conceptualisation attributed to Putnam (2000). Nyqvist et al (2006) argued that individual-level social capital is of greater relevance to the oldest age groups. Their study of social capital and health in people aged 85 and over in Finland highlighted the positive effects on physical and mental health of social networks. They concluded that networks are an especially important resource with regard to preventing depression in later life. However, as they commented, because older people are more likely to be bereaved than other age groups, they are also the most vulnerable to the loss of social networks. Furthermore, because people's social networks diminish as they age, they become more reliant on more formal networks of support that are accessed through health and social care services or community groups. The cultures of care that prevail in formal services will thus have a significant bearing on the health of older people using them, not only in a direct sense through the provision of services but also through the disposition and behaviour of care workers. These observations demonstrate the importance of caring *about* in the context of caring *for*, and of the need for practices of care to acknowledge and respond to social and emotional needs in order to maximise social capital.

The relationship between formal and informal networks is important to consider for another reason. What older people need from their personal social networks will be affected directly by what they get from societal resources. At the same time, what people are able to obtain from societal sources will be affected by the bridging capacity of personal networks that mediate between the individual and society.

Summary

This chapter has explored a range of 'upstream' factors concerned with the prevention of illness and the promotion of health. The broad socioeconomic determinants of health were identified at the outset as a fundamental aspect of public health knowledge and practices, but it was argued also that the focus on multisectoral upstream action has been displaced by a narrower focus on individual behaviour as the key determinant of health. This narrowing of focus is reflected in debates concerning health in later life, which follow the pattern established within health promotion more generally and which bear the hallmarks of its moral agenda. The conclusions that can be drawn from this discussion resemble those of the previous chapter. The focus on self-regulation seen in the active ageing agenda and in behavioural strategies to promote activity in later life present a strong moral message to older people about their personal responsibility for health. This message has found its way into welfare policy agendas, and what is presented as a policy for older people is in fact more properly understood as applicable more specifically to those older people who rely on public services. The active ageing agenda has been taken up as a global strategy and is perceived as universally relevant, but it obscures the conditions of ageing experienced by vast numbers of older people whose conditions of life point to the need for urgent multisectoral action upstream. This would include the provision of an income to enable them to stop work for the benefit of their health, rather than continue in work, to the detriment of their health. The importance of a salutogenic environment is also evident in relation to older people's social capital. Formal support services become increasingly important to older people as their individual circumstances change with increased age and because they are more likely to be bereaved of their partners, friends and families. The need for both formal and informal sources of support for health is underlined in the context of the grandmothers in Africa who provide care for their orphaned grandchildren. This last point is central to the ethics of care perspective, reflecting what Kittay referred to as 'nested dependencies'. A truly salutogenic environment would replenish social capital. It would enable relationships of care to flourish, and generate support for those whose social networks had diminished with ageing.

SIX

Medicine, ageing and healthcare

Introduction

At the secondary level of health promotion, the focus is on restoring health and alleviating symptoms. In this chapter the focus is on healthcare systems, which are understood as incorporating a wide range of treatment and support in response to illness. A number of ethical issues are raised in this discussion, including a revisiting of the discussion about the medicalisation of old age, which is discussed in relation to particular disorders associated with later life, as well as anti-ageing medicine. Population ageing has been regarded as a 'driver of health system change' because of the epidemiologic transition and because of concerns about the potential rises in the costs of healthcare. The response of health systems to the epidemiological transition is therefore also explored. This includes a discussion of the ways in which the management of chronic illness has shifted relations between health professionals and older people as patients.

Health services and health

The relative importance of health services to health is a matter of debate, and particularly contentious in relation to medical practice. The popular 'McKeown thesis' (McKeown 1976) was that improvements in health in the UK between the mid-19th and mid-20th centuries should be attributed to wider social and environmental change, rather than to health services per se. During the second half of the 20th century, however, developments in medical treatment for diseases such as coronary heart disease and breast cancer have had a significant impact on life expectancy and on quality of life in old age. The McKeown thesis therefore needs to be understood in its historical context, and the time is right for a re-evaluation of the contribution of medical practices to health (Davey-Smith et al 2000).

In the context of health in later life, the value of medical practices can be demonstrated by reference to the 60-year-old heart attack victim in the emergency room who was introduced in the previous chapter. Daniels et al (2000) argued that this man's need for treatment could have been circumvented had not a 'lifetime accumulation of insults' been inflicted on his body, and placed him in a position of dependency on the health services. Pursuing the metaphor, the health services were there to pick up the pieces that ensued from the lifetime's accumulation of insults, and over the past few decades they have done this with significant success. For example, the widespread use of statins by older people across the Western world has had a major impact on cardio-vascular disease, one of the major causes of mortality. In addition, the value of secondary prevention is not unrelated to primary prevention. Primary prevention can bolster people's capacity to cope with illnesses when they occur in later life, through building up health capital throughout the lifecourse. At the same time, contact with medical practitioners because of illness can generate commitment to a healthier life-style. Gu et al (2009) argued that, as in Western societies, access to healthcare in China demonstrably makes a difference to older people's chances of survival, but that this difference is reduced where people's 'health capital' is low – pointing once again to the importance of lifecourse factors and primary prevention. According to Adeyi et al (2007), health outcomes for people with cardio-vascular disease in all parts of the world could be improved through clinical interventions, including access to drugs such as statins. They argued that there is ample evidence in particular that strong primary care services play a part in reducing deaths from preventable chronic diseases, since they can provide continuity of contact with a range of professionals and staff, which helps people to manage their diseases. On the other hand, like most commentators, Adeyi et al made the point that such secondary prevention interventions should be part of a wider approach to improving health outcomes, not a replacement for primary prevention strategies, such as tobacco control.

Evidence from America and Europe demonstrates that although there is an increase in the numbers of people with chronic illnesses, therapeutic advances have led to a decline in the numbers who report having a disability (Pomerleau et al 2008). Medicine has an important role to play in the space between disease and functional impairment, and appropriate medicines can maintain functional health, and thus people's ability to work. As argued by Davey-Smith et al (2000), the relationship between socioeconomic status and health cuts both ways. Inequities in the availability of treatments contribute to poorer health, and thus to socioeconomic differentials and a widening mortality gap. It follows also that the restoration of functional health can play an important role in older people's family and social life and help to maintain a better quality of life. There are therefore moral and political reasons to consider how healthcare can be developed so as to play a part in the reduction of socioeconomic inequalities.

Adeyi et al (2007) argued that pressure on healthcare systems in low- and middle-income countries could be relieved in the long run by judicious spending on healthcare. In fact they concluded that, on balance, in those countries healthy ageing is more likely to be the *result of more* medical care rather than the *cause of less* medical care. The adverse consequences of a poorly developed healthcare system were described by Leonard (2005), arising from her research on the management of illness by poor households in Chad. Here, some families resorted to the market as their only available form of healthcare and purchased medications according to what they could afford. Others who did have access to healthcare practitioners received medication only for their most pressing health problems. The consequences of these practices were seen in poor health outcomes. Leonard referred to evidence of the 'indigenisation' of healthcare, a term that describes the way in which the privatisation of healthcare practice minimises the distinction between health workers in the 'official sector' and 'folk practitioners' as both groups tailor their treatments according to customers' ability to pay rather than to their healthcare needs.

It is notable that in discussions of policy priorities for healthcare development in low- and middle-income countries little reference is made to older people's health needs specifically. As Lloyd-Sherlock (2010) pointed out, policies on reducing inequalities in health focus overwhelmingly on TB, malaria and HIV/AIDS and rarely raise the particular concerns of older people. Policies on promoting equity in access to healthcare show a similar picture (Oliveira-Cruz et al, Gu et al 2009). Within the policy process there is a disjuncture between the strongly expressed concerns about the effects of population ageing on healthcare systems and the policy priorities for those systems. Instead, in most parts of the world, older people are subjected to age-related inequalities, age discrimination and ageism in healthcare.

Population ageing and healthcare systems

Healthcare systems are variable and are frequently categorised according to the method by which they are financed (for example, through taxation or insurance schemes); the access that people have to services (whether universal or selective); the organisation of services (the combination of generalist and specialist services); how healthcare is paid for (service-user payment at the point of delivery or through insurance schemes); and what is covered by the payment (comprehensive or selective). As discussed in Chapter Four, a system of health services and care provision includes not only formal services provided through the state but also those provided by the market, NGOs and – above all – families. As Abu-Sharkh and Gough (2010) pointed out, a welfare *system* needs to incorporate all the elements that make a difference to outcomes. Focusing only on what is organised within the formal structures misses the point about the interconnectedness of different spheres of activity. The formal organisation of healthcare within welfare states in modern societies over the course of the 20th century has influenced the development of healthcare systems in many parts of the world. At the current time healthcare systems throughout the world are responding in different ways to the pressures of globalisation and economic upheaval, as well as to demographic and epidemiologic trends.

According to a report published by the European Commission in 2009, demographic change is a 'positive opportunity' for the development of healthcare (European Foresight Monitoring Network 2009). This optimistic view was related to the perception that the needs and demands of older age groups would generate new goods and services that would boost economic growth and international trade. The positive opportunities listed in this report provide insight into the way modern science is seen by policy makers as providing a solution to the problem of cost containment in healthcare. The opportunities referred to include a range of new technologies (genomics, biotechnologies, nanotechnologies and robotics); regenerative medicines; and tissue engineering, all of which could play a part in reducing the costs associated with 'age-related diseases'. Assistive technologies (telemedicine, telemonitoring, telediagnosis) were also harnessed to the strategy of reducing costs by enabling people to remain in their own homes and reducing the level of in-patient care needed. Developments in information and communications technology are also valued for their potential in research into neurodegenerative diseases and in the organisation and management of healthcare. This would be of benefit in contexts where there is a lack of healthcare professionals or where new configurations of services are needed to link professionals between different healthcare settings. At the far reaches of medical technology are human enhancement technologies (HETs), which are used not only for treating diseases but also 'for improving the capabilities of healthy individuals' (European Foresight Monitoring Network 2009: 21). With HETs, the report commented, the traditional borders between prevention, treatment and improvement break down and significant ethical issues emerge, including equity questions for public health. The benefits of new scientific and technological developments in healthcare are, according to the report, very significant.

While the report envisaged that reductions in cost would flow from the implementation of these new technologies, it also recognised that there are costs associated with research and development, at least in the short term. A more muted view was presented in the 2007 UN World Economic and Social Survey of the cost and value of new medical technologies. This survey identified technological progress as a major *driver* of health expenditure. It referred to evidence that the majority of medical procedures, technical equipment and pharmaceuticals in use today were developed in the past 50 years and that these advances played a part in driving up both life expectancy *and* the costs of healthcare. The UN report acknowledged that, over time, medical advances can help to contain costs. It also argued in favour of adjustments to healthcare systems in line with changing needs in ageing populations. However, its conclusions were far less enthusiastic than those presented in the European Commission's report. Policy priorities depend to a large extent on choices about the funding of scientific and technical research and development, where investments are made, and how they are financed, distributed and paid for. In the context of major economic crisis, scientific research and development might well be confined to projects where a profitable return on investment is most likely, rather than where quality of life in old age can be enhanced.

The 2010 World Health Report focused on universal coverage of healthcare through health systems financing (WHO 2010). Of course, whether or not a healthcare system in any society can afford to provide universal coverage is as much a political as an economic matter. At the time of writing, a fierce debate is taking place in the US about how its healthcare system should be financed and what rights of access to healthcare should be guaranteed. These debates raise issues that are seen to go to the heart of that country's culture, and the aims of its founding fathers are invoked to support opposing views. At their most basic, these issues are whether the risks of expenditure on meeting health needs should be borne by the individual or should be pooled through a social insurance scheme.

Two aspects of healthcare system financing need to be considered: first, whether the system is financed sufficiently to ensure that people have access to an adequate range of services, and second, the financial effect that using the service will have on the person using it. Thus a well-resourced healthcare system might be available to all as long as they can afford to pay, or, at the other end of the spectrum, a healthcare system that is poorly resourced might be freely available to all, irrespective of ability to pay. Both aspects have implications for ageing, since the risk of illness, and thus the need for services, increases with age, while income in later life is likely to have decreased.

Households with children or elderly members are more likely than others to experience 'catastrophic' health expenditures associated with out-of-pocket payments for healthcare. The WHO 2010 report pointed to four main strategies that could overcome these problems, promote universal coverage and encourage people to use healthcare:

1. Increased efficiency in revenue collection – ensuring that taxes are collected and stamping out tax avoidance.
2. Reprioritisation of government budgets towards health.
3. Innovative financing – a strategy that is relevant to high-, middle- and low-income countries. Examples of innovation include a levy on foreign exchange transactions. This would be highly appropriate in a country such as India, which has a substantial foreign exchange market. Other examples are raising taxes on tobacco, alcohol and harmful food products, which would have the double effect of reducing demand as well as raising money for the healthcare system.
4. The fourth strategy entails global solidarity, as it points to the help needed by the vast majority of low-income countries to achieve the spending levels needed to ensure an adequate healthcare system. This would require high-income countries to honour their pledges made on aid.

A list such as this indicates clearly the extent to which healthcare is a political issue. As discussed in Chapter Two, the comparisons drawn between countries of relatively equal wealth demonstrated that political decisions about the funding of healthcare and the extent of its coverage across the population make a difference to health outcomes. However, the neoliberal, low-tax and low public-spending policies that dominate at a global level run counter to the WHO's proposal concerning the reprioritisation of budgets towards health. The question of development assistance is also politically contentious. As welfare budgets in high-income countries have been subjected to stringent cuts in response to the current economic crisis, overseas aid is also at serious risk.

The sphere of secondary prevention has more commercial potential than either primary or tertiary prevention, and globalisation has a direct effect on the markets in healthcare. As already discussed, the development of drugs and other technologies is seen, at least within the high-income countries of the European Union, as a priority for healthcare systems in the context of population ageing. The global trade in pharmaceuticals, healthcare and medical knowledge has raised a raft of ethical questions about the cost of and access to drug therapies and about how controls over the market can be exerted by national governments. The 2010 World Health Report listed 'inappropriate prescriber incentives and unethical promotion practices' as, *inter alia*, common reasons for inefficiencies in healthcare systems (WHO 2010: 63). There is growing evidence of the need for better regulation, and the need for action is widely accepted, but progress towards achieving this is patchy. In the absence of adequate progress, the power of the pharmaceutical companies has increased, but is it still open to challenge. In 2007, for example, the then health minister of Indonesia announced that Indonesia would not share samples of H5N1 (bird 'flu) for use in the development of a vaccine unless it could be guaranteed that Indonesian people would benefit (Sukarsono and Wulandari 2007). The concern of the Indonesian government was about the outflow of information from Indonesia that would be of benefit only to transnational pharmaceutical corporations. In this case, the Indonesians held an unusually powerful position, but this episode served as a reminder that the power of transnational corporations can be challenged. A different kind of challenge is described by Mackintosh et al (2011), who explored the role of NGOs in the market for medicines in low- and middle-income countries, particularly for HIV/AIDS, TB and malaria medicines. They concluded that social enterprises are improving access for poorer people and, importantly, that they introduce an unexpected competitive element into the market, which commercial manufacturers respond to. NGOs thus can have an influence on the culture of the markets for medicine in particular contexts.

Health work migration

The migration of healthcare workers – also fuelled by demographic trends – has been a highly contentious issue (see Chapter Seven also for a discussion of migration and care workers). Migration patterns are complex, as countries react to a range of push and pull factors. For example, the accession of several former Eastern Bloc countries to the EU was followed by the movement of skilled healthcare workers to better-paid jobs in Western European countries. More contentious is the movement of professionals from low-income to high-income countries, which was the subject of a voluntary code in the 2008 World Health Assembly. Points of contention often concern the transfer of skills from countries of origin where they are most needed to countries of destination. The exploitation of workers in destination countries is also condemned. Loewenson (2008) pointed out that the countries of origin can benefit from health-worker migration because it can provide greater economic security for the workers and their remittances are an important source of income in the home countries. Despite these advantages, Loewenson argued, there are considerable costs to the healthcare systems in the migrants' countries of origin. His key point is that the protection of freedom of movement as a fundamental human right should not be used to undermine the equally fundamental rights of communities to access health services in the countries of origin or conditions of labour in the destination countries.

The movement of health workers around the world is influenced both by international labour market forces and migration policies and by the relationship between these, producing a varied picture. Variations in patterns of migration in the UK, the US, France and Germany were analysed by Pond and McPake (2006), with particular attention to the balance between market forces and policy effects. They noted that policy effects could be striking, and that the movement of workers could not be attributed to market forces alone. For example, increased expenditure on healthcare in the UK in the late 1990s led to an increase in demand for healthcare workers. In the US, demand dipped, and then grew in line with changes in policies and practices in healthcare over the 1990s. The relaxation or tightening of work permits and visas also has a direct effect on the movement of healthcare workers (Kanchanachitra et al 2011). Pond and McPake concluded that increased pay for nurses in the destination countries, as well as opportunities for higher numbers of people to take up training and education, would go some way to solving labour shortages. This in turn would help to overcome the drainage of skilled workers from low-income countries.

Age and equity in access to healthcare

Age is implicated in access to healthcare in a number of ways. These include a range of factors on the supply side, including the type of services available and whether attention to older people's health needs is included in these; and on the demand side, including whether older people know about what is available and can obtain the help they need. Primary care is widely regarded as being more accessible than other forms of healthcare. The 2009 World Health Report (WHO 2009) described the advantages of comprehensive primary care services over specialist interventions for priority needs in terms of their accessibility and acceptability for local populations. This is particularly so where local communities have ownership and control over the services, where the usage of services increases. The WHO's claim is supported by a review of a range of primary care initiatives in low- and middle-income countries by Kruk et al (2010), who identified improved access as one of their strengths.

Lloyd-Sherlock (2010) argued that there is considerable scope for mainstreaming older people's needs into primary healthcare. Not only does it improve access, but primary care can also bridge the gap between hospital care and care at home, particularly in the context of incurable diseases and the need for palliative care. Primary care in high-income countries is also regarded as being an appropriate first port of call and as a gateway to specialist healthcare, as well as being associated with health promotion. In policy terms, GPs – often described as 'family' doctors – are characterised as the health practitioners who 'know' their patients, conferring a warm glow around this particular patient–doctor relationship. In the UK at the current time, this description permeates plans to reshape fundamentally the National Health Service, giving GPs a role as the major driving force within a marketised approach to healthcare. Evidently, the ideals of primary healthcare can be appropriated in many ways in health policy.

In some countries, particularly in remote rural areas, in order to improve the accessibility of healthcare a range of traditional medicines have been incorporated into healthcare systems. By their nature, traditional medicines are well established and have a long-standing role and function in rural areas, making them generally accessible. There are, however, other advantages. Dummer and Cook (2008), for example, argued in favour of the incorporation of traditional medicines into plans for healthcare systems in China and India not only so as to improve accessibility but also in order to maintain local traditions. On the other hand, traditional medicines vary in terms of efficacy and safety. In 2003 in the South East Asian region of the WHO an inter-country working group was established to improve knowledge sharing and quality control in traditional medicines. It was envisaged by this group that traditional medicines would be incorporated as 'an adjunct to' allopathic medicine. In Thailand, for example, traditional medicine is practised in hospitals and in the community, and is supervised by the Medical Registry Division within state health system. This approach to incorporation is not without its critics and there are apparent tensions and contradictions in policies on traditional medicines, which are reflected in this WHO report. The many and varied forms of traditional medicines are regarded as one of their strengths – as recognised by the WHO – but the strategy to impose a standard assessment of quality and efficacy runs counter to this view. Hence, the inter-country working group agreed that medications should be tested for safety and quality, but that modern scientific methods of assessment (randomised control trials) would not be appropriate. Instead the working group recommended that tests should be according to the methods appropriate to traditional medicine. Similarly, it was agreed that there should be a standardised policy framework on the use of traditional medicines, but also that interregional variations should be considered in establishing this. Finding ways of establishing and enforcing internationally agreed quality standards in the context of local traditional practices is evidently a struggle for the WHO.

For policy makers, ensuring access to healthcare is a more complex challenge than arranging a supply of affordable services. As discussed in Chapter Three, there are many factors that will determine whether or not an individual will consult or seek help from a healthcare system. Of the list of 10 factors presented by Blaxter, only one relates to the supply side – the 'availability of treatment resources and the costs of taking action' (2004: 71). It is noteworthy that the other nine, demand-side factors, such as perceptions of illness symptoms, the seriousness and tolerability of these and how they affect everyday life and responsibilities, are inextricably linked with social and cultural norms and practices. It is therefore crucial to take into consideration cultural variations in people's perceptions of their *entitlement* to services, the significance of becoming a patient and whether health systems encourage or deter people's use of healthcare. For example, Agrawal and Arokiasamy (2010) found that in parts of India higher levels of education were consistent with higher usage of services. So too was the family structure surrounding the older person related to service usage – families with more daughters were more likely to seek help than those with more sons.

Evidence on the relationship between gender, health and illness highlights the point about cultural variations. Long-standing evidence shows how women are, in general, at greater risk of illness. Their need for healthcare is greater than that of men. As far as healthcare *usage* is concerned, the international picture is mixed. In high-income countries there is a mass of evidence indicating that women are greater users of healthcare than are men, although there are divergent opinions as to why this should be. In low-income countries, on the other hand, the picture is different and, as discussed in Chapter Two, there is evidence that despite their higher levels of illness, women use services less than men (Buvinić et al 2006). According to Yount et al (2004), the means by which gender affects the use of healthcare in later life are not yet fully understood in the West, while in the contexts of developing countries there is a dearth of relevant data on which to draw any firm conclusions. Yount et al's own study of gender and the use of healthcare in Tunisia and Egypt (conducted in 1990) showed how economic resources interacted with age, gender and illness in complex ways and how lifecourse differences and inequalities tended to persist into later life. They concluded that research in all contexts is needed that focuses on 'the effects of perceived *and* observed illness, the quality of informal support and the availability and quality of services' (Yount et al 2004: 2493).

Trust in the healthcare system is also a crucially important factor. In deciding whether their symptoms are serious enough to warrant a visit to the doctor, people will take into account previous experiences, how they were treated and whether they trust the doctor. Questions of trust involve perceptions of professional competence, behaviour and attitude, as well as the cultures that prevail at the institutional level, and the macro-context has a strong bearing on organisational cultures. The adequacy and management of resources for healthcare influence encounters between people and healthcare professionals and, consequently, expectations and levels of trust. Hui (2010) described how, in China, following the marketisation of healthcare and the devolution of powers from the central state, hospitals were given carte blanche to raise funds through treatments and therapeutic procedures. The linking of hospital finances to treatment decisions led to widespread public scandals as evidence was produced to show that hospitalised patients had been prescribed unnecessary and expensive treatments. As a result, fears that a stay in hospital would drain them of their life savings deterred people from seeking help with health problems. The numbers of people using hospitals dropped, and there was a damaging loss of trust.

Similar concerns have been raised in other contexts where out-of-pocket payments for healthcare are the norm. The 2009 World Health Report noted that around 47% of Latin America's population is excluded from health services, for reasons including a lack of protection from financial exploitation and the fear of this – irrespective of whether such fears are well founded. The policy of charging out-of-pocket payments can be regarded more positively. In the US a strategy of cost sharing has been introduced, through which out-of-pocket payments are raised to relieve pressure on Medicaid budgets and to discourage inappropriate prescribing. As older people comprise 13% of the population of the US but account for 30% of prescription drug expenditure, this policy is particularly relevant to them and could offer a degree of protection for them from iatrogenic disease. However, evidence suggests that although there has been an impact on overall prescription costs, the reduction is not confined to inappropriate prescribing. As a consequence, older people are at risk of complications in their health conditions (Costa-Font and Toyama 2011).

The injection of funds into global health initiatives (primarily focused on HIV/AIDS, TB and malaria) has, according to the WHO, done little to improve the governance or financing of healthcare, as it tends to provide free access to services for particular conditions but without effecting changes to the existing systems. Of course, all age groups are affected by the problems arising from out-of-pocket payments, and socioeconomic rather than age-related inequalities are a more direct concern than age per se. However, where family resources are limited, decisions about how to prioritise spending will be necessary. Such decisions will be influenced by older people's social status and their roles within families. Influencing factors will include whether they have their own income and whether they are able to contribute to family life (Mudege and Ezeh 2009, Cameron et al 2010). In Ghana, Aboderin (2006) identified how, in the context of limited resources, the needs of conjugal families took precedence over the needs of older parents.

Age discrimination and ageism in healthcare are further important considerations in this discussion of accessibility and affordability. Both of these act as barriers to older people's uptake of services, and although they are different phenomena, there is a strong relationship between them. For example, Lloyd-Sherlock (2010) identified pervasive negative attitudes towards older people in developing countries, which were expressed openly by health professionals. He pointed out how these attitudes are framed by the underlying assumptions within research and policy about the burdensomeness of older people and the problems associated with the ageing of populations. In high-income countries, even where resources are available, there are age-related inequalities in obtaining access. There is ample evidence of age discrimination in health programmes, such as screening, and in drug trials. In the UK the use of QALYs (Quality Adjusted Life Years) to determine the cost-effectiveness of treatments contains an inbuilt assumption that, with fewer years left to live, a treatment is less cost-effective on an older than a younger person.

There is also ample evidence that the health conditions affecting older people are marginalised within healthcare systems around the world and that medical practitioners dismiss symptoms of disease in older people on the spurious grounds that these are merely the manifestations of old age. Older people are thus denied access to treatment that could be life saving or, at least, could help to restore their functional abilities. Twigg (2006) gave the example of incontinence, which, she argued, is a low priority within healthcare, despite its having far-reaching consequences for the health and well-being of those who suffer from it.

The pressure to minimise the cost of care is placed on health professionals, and influences their practice. In the UK and in other Western countries this is seen in hospital discharge schemes, in which it is expected that people will be moved out of hospital beds as quickly as possible to maximise the efficient use of beds. However, for older people, the question of discharge is often complicated by the possibility that they will be unable in either the short or long term to care for themselves. In addition, the health problems that brought them to hospital in the first place might well have life-changing consequences. For example, a fall, a stroke or a heart attack might well herald a sudden and significant change of life-style, meaning that discharge from hospital is fraught with difficulties. The pejorative term 'bed-blockers' has been coined to describe those who are seen to linger too long in hospital while arrangements are made for their discharge. Another example from the UK of ageism and age discrimination is presented in a confidential inquiry into the deaths of older people undergoing surgery. This found numerous problems with pre- and post-operative care among people aged over 65, including ageist attitudes and a lack of attention to the complex health needs of older people (Wilkinson et al 2010).

There is considerable consistency around the world in the kinds of concerns raised by older people in relation to their treatment within healthcare services (WHO 2004b, Lloyd-Sherlock 2010). Apart from discriminatory factors such as the inaccessibility of the buildings or the cost of care, the ageist attitudes of staff are also cited as presenting a major barrier to older people using services. Examples of concerns raised with the WHO include being shunted around in overly bureaucratic institutions; being spoken to in rude and disrespectful language; having basic needs, such as the need to use the lavatory, ignored; being treated roughly when being given hands-on treatment; not having healthcare interventions explained; and not being listened to or having concerns understood (WHO 2004b). Hence the WHO's call for age-friendliness in healthcare, amid growing recognition that there is a relationship between institutional cultures and the adequacy and governance of resources.

Ageist attitudes are perhaps more comprehensible in the context of hard-pressed, resource-poor institutions. However, the problem goes deeper than this. As Higgs and Rees-Jones (2009) argued, simply to look for solutions in institutional reform does not fully engage with the deeper questions that concern attitudes to growing old and the material consequences for older people that flow from age discrimination and ageism. Exhortations to people working in institutions to change their behaviour and attitudes towards older people are unlikely to succeed because such behaviour and attitudes are a manifestation of broader cultural attitudes and, in the view of Higgs and Rees-Jones, an expression of resistance on the part of health professionals to old age.

How should arguments about the need for equity in healthcare be understood in the context of the debate about the medicalisation of old age? In gerontology, age-related inequalities in access to healthcare, the low priority given to health conditions associated with ageing, and discrimination against older people are deplored but, as discussed in Chapter Three, the practice of biomedicine is also deplored for its tendency to medicalise and pathologise the ageing process (Estes et al 2003). There is therefore a tension in the relationship between gerontology and biomedicine. However, it should also be acknowledged that concerns about medicalisation have changed over time. According to Mykytyn (2008), the notion of 'ageing as a disease' is now less prevalent than it used to be. On the other hand, there is a widely shared understanding within biomedicine of what constitute the 'diseases of ageing'. Mykytyn argues that the definition of older people's conditions as diseases is rarely challenged. From this perspective, it is the power of medicine to define what is or is not a disease state that is the problem.

Concerns about medical decisions reflect and are reflected by policy and organisational priorities. With reference to the UK context, for example, Ebrahim (2002) argued that the medicalisation of old age should be encouraged in order to combat the de-medicalisation of services for older people and the relabelling of their health conditions as 'social'. In the UK context this relabelling has a significant financial impact on older people because, while healthcare is free at the point of delivery, social care is means-tested. As a consequence, people with conditions such as dementia are seriously disadvantaged financially because they must meet the high cost of care in nursing homes, instead of receiving services through the health service. A different view on the division between health and social care is taken by Means (2007), who argued that policies that emphasise health over and above other dimensions of life risk imposing too narrow an interpretation of needs, so marginalising the things that matter to older people and that are relevant to their health, such as housing. In reality, it does not follow that the labelling of older people's needs either as health or as social care needs will necessarily produce any kind of service at all, especially in the context of cost containment. Again, it depends on where the power lies to categorise needs and determine eligibility for services and what older people's entitlements are. However, in highlighting that decisions on how to distribute resources for healthcare are not necessarily the responsibility of a doctor, Ebrahim raises an important point. Doctors are not always responsible for the consequences that flow from decisions about older people's eligibility for services or their obligation to pay for them. Indeed, it is also argued that policies to minimise the cost of healthcare create organisational structures that interfere with professional medical judgements.

A further twist to the question of age-related equity comes with the question of the *appropriateness* of health interventions in what is the final stage of life. It is widely accepted that towards the end of life palliative rather than curative care might be the better option, in order to avoid the possibility of sustaining life without any quality. The danger is that, in the context of ageism and age discrimination in healthcare, decisions not to offer curative treatment might be interpreted as a form of passive euthanasia. Trust is particularly important in the context of treatment at the end of life (Lloyd et al 2011).

Age discrimination in healthcare is manifest in many ways. Perhaps most surprisingly it is apparent in the WHO's own campaign for Age-friendly Primary Healthcare. One rationale for this campaign is the growing numbers of older people, which are seen to place unsustainable pressures on over-stretched health services. The WHO links this concern with its active ageing agenda, so placing responsibility on older people for adhering to a healthy life-style and minimising their need for services, in order that these can be freed up for use by younger age groups.

> An older population in good health releases resources which can be used for other needs, such as child and maternal health. While healthy ageing is important for developed countries so that health care spending can be controlled, it is vital for developing nations where health care resources are sorely lacking. (WHO 2004b: 6)

The moral agenda of active and healthy ageing is thus inextricably linked with questions of entitlement to healthcare. This is not to underestimate the scale of the challenge to healthcare systems worldwide, or to overlook the difficulties of managing the double burden of disease in low-income countries. However, the WHO's approach places conditions on age-friendliness and runs the risk of reinforcing the already widely held view that older people's entitlement to services is lower than that of other groups, so undermining its own position on age-friendliness.

Anti-ageing medicine

In the context of equity in access to healthcare, the ethical questions raised by the phenomenon of anti-ageing medicine are of fundamental importance. In the discussion in Chapter Four concerning health capabilities, the question was raised whether resource priorities for healthcare should favour children and younger people who are at risk of premature death over older people who have already had a full life span. In anti-ageing medicine the moral and ethical issues raised by this question are magnified. Anti-ageing medicine challenges the idea that the human life span is limited to what is currently known. The priority for anti-ageing medicine in affluent countries is to find ways of extending already lengthy life spans and to use resources to this end. This is not the only ethical question: there is a deeper question, which concerns the *value and meaning* of the additional years of life gained and whether, in seeking to defy the 'natural' allocation of years, anti-ageing medicine is devaluing life itself. Anti-ageing medicine is not a single, homogeneous practice. Vincent (2003, 2006b) presented a spectrum of activities. At one extreme are practices that he refers to as 'abolition'. Abolition seeks to change the fundamentals of biological ageing so as to remove the boundary between old age and death. It is this version of anti-ageing medicine that gives rise to accusations that scientists are 'playing God' as they seek immortality.

At the other end of the spectrum, Vincent identifies 'symptom alleviation'. This version of anti-ageing activities consists of attempts to hide, postpone or relieve the effects of biological ageing. Symptom alleviation straddles the boundary between primary and secondary prevention. Activities include, respectively, 'cosmetic', such as anti-wrinkle cream; 'prophylactic', such as diet and exercise; and 'compensatory', such as Viagra. These activities can also be defined as achieving 'optimal health', defined by Mykytyn (2002) as 'the-best-a-body-can-and-has-ever-been'. This definition points to the supreme desirability of a younger, fitter body. With its echoes of fitness and vigour, Mykytyn's 'optimal health' concept could be interpreted as a salutogenic approach to life, although it is more firmly fixed within the framework of individual responsibility for health, without any reference to environmental factors.

The idea of anti-ageing medicine as achieving optimal health is also consistent with what Vincent refers to as 'life-expectancy extension', because the focus is on the risk of disease faced by older people and the need to eliminate this so as to extend healthy life expectancy. The European Foresight Monitoring Group Report (2009) referred to above, for example, cites regenerative medicine (tissue engineering to regenerate damaged tissue *in vivo* or externally for transplant) as offering the prospect of repairing damage caused by ageing, by degenerative diseases (such as strokes, Parkinson's disease and cardio-vascular disease) and by the treatments for diseases. Developments in artificial organs, neuro-implants and cyborgs are also part of the anti-ageing medicine repertoire (Bradshaw and ter Meulen 2010).

Healthcare needs in later life

This section of the chapter is focused more specifically on patterns of illness in later life and the responses of healthcare systems to these. It is not intended to be a comprehensive discussion of the diseases associated with growing older, but to look at particular health conditions that highlight the points discussed above.

As discussed previously, the epidemiological transition has generated a considerable amount of discussion among policy makers about how healthcare systems should respond to changing patterns of disease. It is worth restating the point that infectious diseases remain a problem for older people throughout the world. In developing countries this is experienced as a 'double burden' of disease, which presents particular stresses on healthcare systems that are ill equipped to deal with them – hence the policy emphasis on primary prevention. Older people are at risk of infections in high-income countries also, and appear to be particularly vulnerable to some pathogens, such as new strains of influenza, listeria (food poisoning) and hospital-acquired infections, such as *clostridium difficile*. However, it is the need to reorient services to manage growing levels of chronic and non-communicable diseases that emerges as a major challenge to policy makers. This challenge is particularly great in the context of contemporary global economic pressures and the drastic reduction in spending on health and welfare programmes. There is a challenge also to biomedical practitioners, whose training and background has been largely focused on treatments with a view to cure rather than the management of non-communicable diseases. A further challenge to practitioners and service providers also comes from the co-morbidities that are characteristic of illness in later life. The need for better standards in healthcare for chronic diseases throughout the world is not disputed. Nolte and McKee (2008) pointed out the failure of even relatively well-resourced healthcare systems to achieve globally agreed standards, so that conditions are left untreated until serious complications arise.

Some medical interventions have demonstrable benefits to older people. A clear example is the treatment of cataracts – a relatively common age-related visual impairment (Margrain and Boulton 2005). Treatment for cataracts is low cost and highly cost-effective, but is very unevenly spread in global terms. In high-income countries cataract treatment is widely available and relatively routine, but this is not so in low-income countries, where there are consequently high levels of avoidable blindness. The WHO and the International Agency for the Prevention of Blindness (2007) estimate that almost 18 million people worldwide are blind as a result of cataract. In high-income countries this represents only about 5% of cases of blindness, as compared to around 50% in low-income countries. The consequences of blindness are many and varied, including loss of opportunities to work and increased levels of dependency on others. Factors other than cost influence the availability of treatment. 'Low cost' does not equal 'widely available', because health systems may have other priorities that take precedence in the allocation of resources. In some settings, even where treatments are freely available, older people do not always make use of them. The reasons for this are difficult to pin down, but Lloyd-Sherlock (2010) points to the presence of socio-cultural and educational factors that inhibit older people from seeking help for cataracts. In some contexts, loss of sight is considered to be a normal part of the ageing process.

Dementia

Dementia provides a good example of the above discussion concerning ideas about normal and pathological ageing (Innes 2009). Bond and Corner (2004) pointed to the identification of Alzheimer's disease as a distinct disease entity in the 1970s as marking a shift in the way that cognitive decline in old age was understood. They argued that the pathologisation of conditions such as Alzheimer's disease imposed a degree of order to the condition, and gave a more precise and specific terminology from which medical practitioners could work and challenged unacceptably vague and general concepts, such as 'senile decay'. The biomedical model of dementia has subsequently remained in a dominant position, despite the critiques discussed in Chapter Three. However, Innes (2009) pointed out that, although the biomedical model has its place, because dementia entails decline over time, it has not brought unalloyed benefits. Alzheimer's disease is still a condition that stigmatises, and scientific understanding has not overcome social and cultural prejudices. It has also been argued by a number of commentators that, since the development of a biomedical understanding of dementia, attention has turned to the search for a cure, rather than to the care of people who live with condition.

International variations in prevalence indicate that the *identification* of dementia as a medical condition is not straightforward. In fact, data on which an accurate estimate of prevalence could be made are lacking, and this gap in knowledge has implications for policy making. From their Delphi consensus study, Ferri et al (2005) estimated that 24 million people in the world have dementia and that the number will double every 20 years, assuming no change in mortality or any medical developments. Prince et al (2008) estimated 24.2 million, with an additional 4.6 million new cases annually. China and neighbouring Western Pacific countries have the highest numbers of people with dementia (6 million), followed by Europe with 4.9 million and North America with 3.4 million. Prince et al projected that the growth in numbers would fall into three broad groupings of countries that reflect the current age profile of the countries, current numbers of people with dementia and their projected increases:

1. Developed countries, which start from a relatively high base and which will experience a moderate proportionate increase (around 100% between 2001 and 2040).
2. Latin America and Africa, which start from a low base and will experience a rapid increase in numbers (between 235% and 393%).
3. India, China and other South Asian and Western Pacific countries, which start from a high base and experience rapid growth (between 314% and 336%).

Reasons why there are lower rates of dementia in parts of the developing world are unclear, but they could include lower survival rates of people with dementia rather than lower incidence rates. Alternatively, there might be differences in perception of mild cognitive disorder as dementia per se. Prevalence studies provide an incomplete and partial form of knowledge and there remains a need for a better understanding of what it means in different contexts to live with dementia, or how the condition impacts on the lives of families (Prince et al 2008).

Innes identified a growing convergence of dementia care policies in the European Union around three main themes: first is the politico-economic theme, which is focused on concerns about growing prevalence and the perceived cost; second is the humanitarian theme, focused on the development of person–centred care and self-care; and third is the rights–based theme, focused on advance directives and decision making and related ethical matters. There are complex political factors to be taken into account in analysing the development of policies and services for dementia care. In their international study, Knapp et al (2007) identified a range of factors related to these three themes. They include a shortage of skilled staff and poor conditions of employment, poor-quality care homes and a low level of development of systems for 'ageing in place' rather than care home provision. On the other hand, they also noted that in a number of countries dementia is increasingly seen as a policy priority, which has generated activity on policy initiatives. The perceived cost to societies of increasing numbers of people with dementia focuses the minds of policy makers, but, as Innes (2009) noted, this cost is difficult to estimate because there is such variation between geographical and cultural contexts. Dementia is estimated to be one of the non-communicable conditions with which people can live longest (on average 11.2 years, as compared with 2.4 for cancer (Innes 2009)). This alone generates concern about cost. Diagnosis is a particular concern and is directly linked to cost concerns, since early diagnosis can be cost-effective, enabling people to plan ahead and pre-empt problems. However, there are barriers to diagnosis, including reluctance on the part of physicians to give the condition official recognition, particularly as there is a lack of effective medication for it. The issue of medication is contentious and there is no coherent basis for agreement on which drugs should be financed or how they should be paid for.

The contribution of family care needs to be taken into account, and there is generally poor understanding of the cost to families of providing care to a family member with dementia. In high-income countries such as the UK, institutional care is being displaced in favour of ageing-in-place schemes. In these circumstances costs to the public purse vary, depending on the level of support that is given to families and how home-based care services are combined with family care. In low-income countries responsibility falls on families to a greater extent because of the lack of alternatives. In some countries families are put under emotional pressure through cultural assumptions about care homes being for 'the destitute'. In others, legally enforceable penalties are imposed if families fail to provide the practical and financial support (Prince et al 2008).

Depression

In the case of depression, as with dementia, there are ethical questions surrounding the recognition and diagnosis of the condition as a disease. There are also questions about the prevalence of depression in later life, but depression has not received the same attention as dementia among policy makers (Manthorpe and Iliffe 2005). Within the confines of this discussion it is not possible to explore in depth the causes of depression, but it is important to note its association with other health problems. There are differing opinions as to the relationship between chronic illness, disability and depression. From the US, a study by Schnittker (2005) of people aged over 50 examined the effects of age on the relationship between chronic illness and depressive symptoms. This suggested that the onset of chronic illness and disability in middle age was associated with more serious depressive symptoms. This led Schnittker to conclude that there are points of convergence between the idea of 'age as decline' and 'age and transcendence'. Thus, while chronic illness can cause depression in old age, the symptoms might be less severe and are therefore not so easily diagnosed. It is possible that older people have higher expectations than younger people that they will be ill, and the illness therefore has a less depressing effect. It is also possible that older people are better able than younger people to cope with chronic illness or have more effective ways of compensating for its effects and are therefore less severely depressed as a consequence. Manthorpe and Iliffe (2005) provided another insight into the relationship between depression and other age-related health factors. They pointed out that while most disabled older people are not depressed, disability and depression can each have a causal effect on the other. A related point from the Netherlands was made by van Gool et al (2005), who found that being depressed had the effect of accelerating the process of disablement in middle age and later life.

It is thought that depression is widely under-diagnosed. From the UK, Murray et al (2006) estimate that between one-quarter and one-third of older people attending GP surgeries are depressed and that this figure might represent the tip of an iceberg because older people are reluctant to acknowledge psycho-social problems and unlikely to report them to their GPs. The view that early interventions are beneficial to older people who are depressed is widespread. However, primary care practitioners are in a difficult position. Since older people experience life events known to have depressing effects (bereavement and social isolation, for example) doctors might be concerned about medicalising these problems. On the other hand, evidence suggests that medical interventions are of value in treating depression. While there is no cure there is considerable potential for alleviating or reducing its symptoms. Medical interventions are also used in combination with other kinds of support. Analysis of data from the SHARE study (the Study of Ageing and Retirement in Europe) by Abu-Rayya (2011), for example, suggested that more social participation has a positive impact on people who are depressed. In 2001 the World Health Report recommended that a priority for mental health was to incorporate it into primary healthcare settings in low- and middle-income countries. Medical interventions can be counter-productive if they are not appropriate. Manthorpe and Iliffe (2005) noted that inappropriate treatments such as pain relief or treatment for anxiety are sometimes offered to older people. Patel et al (2006) argued that problems associated with medical interventions for depression in North America and Europe pointed to the need for a more multifaceted strategy in low- and middle-income countries, with less reliance on medication.

Secondary prevention in chronic and non-communicable diseases (NCDs)

Among health policy specialists there is a fair degree of consensus about the way in which healthcare systems should respond to chronic diseases. Primary care is seen as providing an essential link with health promotion as well as being a gateway to specialist care. Adeyi et al (2007) identified a need for *sustained contact* and *continuity of care* between different parts of the healthcare system, while Yach et al (2006) identified a need for *comprehensiveness*. An OECD Health Working Paper (Oxley 2009) referred to the need to achieve *better coordination*, as does the WHO's Innovative Care for Chronic Conditions (ICCC) framework (WHO 2002d). In summary, there is a general perception that, given the nature of chronic and non-communicable diseases, there is a need for coordination across a broad spectrum of services and for continuity over time.

Nolte and McKee (2008) identified a number of ways in which healthcare is changing as a result of the epidemiological transition: increasing opportunities for early intervention and of combining prevention and treatment; a trend towards treatment outside of hospital settings, including in people's own homes; a shift in the balance of power in relationships between patients and doctors; a greater reliance on evidence in place of intuition as a basis for medical interventions; a more proactive approach to seeking need, rather than simply responding to it; and greater use of information technology to offer bespoke forms of healthcare. Nolte and McKee argued that the challenge to the workforce will be to respond to all of these changes in the way that healthcare services are currently run. The idea that health services would actively seek out rather than respond to need is hard to square with the overarching concern to keep a tight rein on health expenditure, but this idea needs to be understood in the context of the discussion in the previous chapter, which noted how primary care services were seeking to carve out a niche in the field of health promotion.

The changing nature of relationships between doctors and patients is a common theme in health policies, and in the context of chronic disease is strongest. Adeyi et al (2007) referred to the need for improved 'health literacy' among patients, which in chronic disease is an essential prerequisite of effective 'self-management'. The change in relationship cuts both ways: patients are responsible for becoming more health literate and self-managing, but doctors are also expected to play their part in enabling this. Yach et al (2006) and Nolte and McKee (2008) see it as the responsibility of healthcare systems to be *patient centred* – to recognise the patient as a person, ensure they are fully informed about treatment options, share power and responsibility and develop their ability to participate in their care. Clearly, the message of individual responsibility extends beyond the sphere of primary prevention, through healthy and active ageing. Experiential and lay knowledge gained through the experience of chronic illness poses a challenge to the hierarchical boundaries that have traditionally existed between professionals and patients. It places patients in a position of responsibility for monitoring their symptoms and the effects of medication. The Department of Health in England (DH 2011) refers to the value of the internet and of telecare and telehealth technology, which, together with telephone coaching, will enable people to 'self-care' for as long as possible.

Health literacy or expertise is relatively easy to imagine in settings where people can obtain access to information about medical conditions and treatment options. Those who are able to access web-based information become better informed as individuals and are also able to link up with others in the same situation. The internet can thus provide a platform for groups of people who share the same conditions, and from this empowered position, health-literate 'consumer patients' emerge to make more demands of health services. However, the self-managing, expert patient is an idealised individual, and the realities of living with long-term illness can be very far from such an ideal. The challenges to people managing their chronic conditions are many and varied and increase with multiple morbidities (Meinow et al 2006). As Nolte and McKee (2008) pointed out, individuals may experience an aggravation of one condition as a result of treatment for another and iatrogenic disease is more likely in the context of chronic conditions. Medication management becomes extremely complex in the context of polypharmacy and where prescription drugs interact with non-prescribed alternative medicines or over-the-counter remedies. The use of medication is increasingly understood as impinging on individuals' identity, sense of self and moral outlook (Ballantyne et al 2011). Looked at from the perspective of the older person, the experience of living with long-term illness has a significance that is rarely acknowledged in policy debates, as is discussed further in the next chapter.

Summary

There is strong evidence to support the view that secondary prevention is particularly important in the context of later life and the health problems that are associated with old age. The organisation of healthcare and the provision of services have been strongly influenced by both demographic trends and economic globalisation. This influence is seen in inequalities and inequities in access to healthcare. The commercial activities related to healthcare indicate that, of the three levels of prevention considered in this text, the secondary level has the greatest commercial potential and the power of pharmaceutical companies has not been effectively controlled through regulatory regimes. Access to healthcare is highly complex, and both demand and supply factors affect people's ability to obtain treatment. Socioeconomic factors exacerbate existing inequalities in health through the barriers to healthcare faced by many older people, especially the poor. Ageism and age discrimination in health are evident deterrents to older people obtaining healthcare. However, concerns over age discrimination are not always easy to reconcile with concerns over medicalisation, and ethical questions are particularly acute in the contexts of medical practices relating to life extension and of end-of-life care. Questions of trust in health systems in general and in healthcare professionals in particular are of great significance in older people's use of healthcare.

Demographic and epidemiological trends have generated an impetus for system change in healthcare, in which the containment of costs is the overarching concern. But system change is also needed because long-established models of acute care are no longer sufficient. Approaches to treatment and care for non-communicable diseases have developed in the context of the overarching need for cost-containment as well as globalisation. The spread of ideas about self-care, supported by the use of new technologies, is entirely in keeping with individualised forms of welfare and the shift of responsibility for health onto the individual. The policies discussed in this chapter place a heavy responsibility on older individuals to care for themselves, not only to reduce their own levels of illness but also to release scarce healthcare resources for other, younger groups. Integrated models of care in the context of chronic disease management transcend the boundaries between primary, secondary and tertiary prevention. Primary prevention seeks to promote the compression of morbidity and make long-term illness as short as possible. Primary prevention can also improve underlying health so that chronic diseases are less disabling in their effects. Secondary prevention is responsible for treating symptoms and minimising the effects of illness, so restoring people to functional health. At the tertiary level, disease management (including self-management) can be empowering to older people as well as keep the cost of care to a minimum. From a policy and management perspective it looks like a rational plan to get a grip on the expensive and unpredictable business of care for people with long-term illness. These themes will be discussed further in the next chapter.

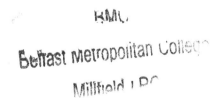

BML,

Belfast Metropolitan College

Millfield LRC

SEVEN

Care for health in later life

Introduction

The focus of this chapter is on the tertiary level of health promotion – action to promote health in the context of long-term or incurable illness. It is in these circumstances that the link between care and health takes a qualitative turn, and that the importance of care for health is at its most stark. As discussed in Chapter Three, the circumstances in which an increasing number of older people live during the last stage of life before death involve long-term illness and increased dependency on others, and because these illnesses are associated with the end of life they take on greater significance. In high-income countries, at no other time in history has death been so closely associated with old age, and demographic trends show that this association is strengthening in most other parts of the world. The concentration of mortality in old age has profound implications for the way that the care of older people with long-term health problems is perceived. Because of demographic trends and because the much-hoped-for compression of morbidity has not yet occurred, the need for care is increasing rather than decreasing (OECD 2005) and socioeconomic inequalities are reflected in differing levels of long-term illness. Poorer people are likely to suffer from more severe long-term health conditions in old age and to have their health problems occur earlier.

This chapter discusses older people's need for care and analyses policy responses to this. It considers the provision of unpaid care by families and friends as well as paid care by care workers, and critically examines the relationship between these two spheres of care. The intention is not to attempt a comprehensive account of care policies but to highlight key debates in order to pursue the analysis of how the overarching policy aims of cost containment and promotion of active ageing are played out in the context of dependence in old age.

Dependence on others: the need for care

A recurring theme within this text has been that an over-simplistic portrayal of global demographic trends has generated a particular view of rising dependency levels as a global economic problem. Dependence is portrayed as a function of chronological age, and also as capable of being modified through healthy life-styles and active ageing. The promotion of independence is an essential element of the active ageing agenda. However, the concepts of dependence and independence are both open to widely varying interpretations. As Plath (2009) points out, cultural variations are evident, and these are reflected in national policies. Independence can be used as a shorthand term to mean living in one's own home and not in an institution, or being functionally well and able to perform activities of daily living without assistance. At the same time, an older person might be considered independent if the care they receive is from family members, rather than from a paid carer, and particularly so if the care they receive is not paid for by the state. Just as the availability of healthcare influences views of illness, so too the availability of long-term care influences views of dependency. Policy shapes the mix of informal and formal care and therefore plays an important part in shaping perceptions of older people's dependency. In most parts of the world the only form of care available is from the family and in some the obligation to care for older relatives is enshrined in law, but in virtually all settings the benefits of family care over institutional care are emphasised. This applies also where the role and functions of family carers have become more akin to those of paid carers. In the UK, for example, recent policies have introduced training for carers in practices previously associated with formal healthcare, such as stoma care and wound care. In many European countries 'cash for care' policies – discussed below – are promoted on the basis that enabling older people to remain in charge of their own care arrangements helps to maintain their independence and dignity. As discussed in the previous chapter, new approaches to self-care in the context of chronic disease, including the use of new technologies, have been presented in a very optimistic and positive way. Encouraging individuals to take responsibility for their own care, these policies portray a message of empowerment rather than of decline.

However, the positive spin placed on self-care does not engage with the effects of long-term illness in old age. Reference was made in the previous chapter to policies in the Department of Health for England which spoke of the desirability of promoting self-care 'for as long as possible'. The question this provokes is: 'What happens in the next stage, when self-care comes to an end?' The insights from Twigg (2006) and Gilleard and Higgs (2010) are highly relevant to this discussion, particularly the view that optimistic accounts of the third age are only possible by projecting into the fourth age all that is negative about ageing as the battle for mastery over the body is lost. Attempts to extend these optimistic accounts further into the fourth age for as long as possible overlook the circumstances of dependence on others in the last stage of life. The impact of serious illness on an individual's life affects not only their activities and everyday living arrangements but also their relationships, identity and sense of self. Higgs and Rees-Jones (2009) argued that older people resist attempts to place them in the category of 'fourth age' because this entails a reduction in agency, a loss of autonomy and control over decisions. Jolanki (2009) similarly argued that in Western cultures the meaning of agency has become inextricably linked with health, so that it becomes difficult to imagine agency in old age in other ways. The loss of agency comes with being categorised as 'old' – a categorisation that generally occurs when bodily health declines and which has the effect of barring older people from engaging in the activities associated with consumer citizens. Older people's resistance to being so categorised is boosted by the active ageing agenda. With the assistance of medical interventions they might extend their resistance further, but eventually a degree of dependence is inevitable and it is in these circumstances that the inextricable links between health and care are seen most clearly.

At this point it is worth exploring the evidence that has emerged concerning older people's experiences of long-term health problems and what these signify. As discussed in previous chapters, ageing brings increased risk of life-threatening conditions such as cardio-vascular disease, diabetes, chronic obstructive pulmonary disorder, cancer and dementia. Ageing also increases the risk of visual and hearing impairment, as well as mobility problems from conditions such as osteoarthritis. In old age co-morbidities are common, as are complications in symptoms. The long-term nature of such health problems exacerbates their impact, and medication can generate complications as well as provide relief.

In the context of economic concerns about containing the cost of care, the impact of illness on physical function has received most attention. Although policies are open to criticism for their too narrow focus on physical function, it is important not to overlook the importance to older people of functional health. From their analysis of findings from the English Longitudinal Study of Ageing, Blane et al (2008) concluded that quality of life in old age is most affected by those aspects of health that have an impact on functional limitation. They called for more attention to be paid by policy makers to problems such as falls, urinary incontinence and osteoarthritic pain, all of which are prevalent in old age and cause avoidable reduction in quality of life. The loss of functional health is important therefore not only because it generates costs in assistance with activities of everyday living but also because it reduces quality of life more generally. The problem with the focus of policies is largely to do with the narrow focus on what constitutes an activity of daily living and the individualistic focus that ignores relationships and quality of life.

In Chapter Three the perception of health as absence of illness was discussed and contrasted with the medicalised view of health as the absence of disease. It was pointed out that older people can often describe their health status as good, even though they have identifiable diseases and disabilities. This is a crucial point that draws attention to what functional impairment signifies. For example, research in the UK by Sanders et al (2002) focused on the impact of osteoarthritis on older people. The participants in this research described how becoming limited in their functioning had an impact on their sense of self, their sense of security and their relationships. Their physical limitations, the pain they experienced and the psychological effects of these had caused some of them to withdraw from their usual activities and roles. Sanders et al noted how arthritis as a condition is often seen as synonymous with old age. This was reflected in the responses of their participants, who regarded arthritis as something to be expected, given their age. At the same time, the interviewees were also worried about the significance of their arthritis in terms of how their disability would be perceived in the context of social activities and whether they would be regarded as a burden on society.

These research findings reflect the observations of Higgs and Rees-Jones (2009) that illness in later life can be seen as both normal and abnormal: normal because it is usual and to be expected, but abnormal in the sense that it is pathological and has far-reaching effects on relationships and way of life.

The language of policies contributes significantly to the cultural meanings attached to long-term illness in old age. In English-speaking Western cultures terms such as 'frail' and 'vulnerable' are commonly used. In the context of welfare services the term 'vulnerable' is used to describe certain categories of people: this categorisation contributes to their objectification and ignores the threat to which they are vulnerable. Being described as one of 'the vulnerable' carries stigma and humiliation and this is easily compounded in the context of welfare. In the UK, in an example of conceptual slippage, the term has come to be applied specifically to people who have already been abused, ill-treated or neglected. The use of the term 'frail' is almost entirely limited to old age. In medical contexts a frail person is identified by reference to the presence of particular factors (Rockwood, 2005). In the US, if an older person has three or more of muscle weakness, slow walking speed, exhaustion, low physical activity levels, or unintentional weight loss they are considered to be frail and at greater risk of disability, hospitalisation and death. The significance of a medical diagnosis of frailty is that from this diagnosis flow decisions about the need for care and how this is best arranged. The consequent decisions about how to live, where to live and whom to turn to for help exemplify how dependency through poor health can lead to a loss of agency, as the voice of the older person categorised as frail is easily overlooked. In this sense, it is the practices of care that make an individual vulnerable to loss of agency. This is a precarious period of life that highlights the complex nature of care.

The inevitability of illness in old age can enable older people to make better sense of what is happening, despite the distress caused, as identified by Schnittker (2005) and others. The expectation of illness and the experience of seeing one's contemporaries in a similar position can act as a buffer against the shattering impact of disease. An important factor in this is the suddenness of the onset of disease and whether symptoms develop gradually, as in the case of osteoarthritis, or occur suddenly, as with a stroke. However, a wide range of other factors influence how older people interpret their symptoms and how they then act on their interpretation. The findings from Sanders et al (discussed above) highlight the influence of social and cultural factors. In the context of cultures that regard dependency as abhorrent, it is not surprising that a dependent identity is avoided. When coupled with old age, the problems of dependency are further complicated by the realisation of the relative nearness of death, the prospect of going downhill and being seen to be going downhill. The risk of being considered as socially dead before biological death is particularly acute. In these circumstances care is particularly complex, as it involves helping people to negotiate their way through a process of acceptance of the inevitable loss of an accustomed way of life, on the one hand, and maintenance of a sense of selfhood on the other. Gooberman-Hill and Ebrahim (2006) observed how older people's relationships with family members altered and fluctuated subtly and significantly in line with changes in health and mobility. From this point of view, care *relationships* are not only about the provision of practical support (caring for) but also about the maintenance of a sense of self and the reshaping of identities. The importance of relationships to older people's self-perception is also highlighted by Hammarstrom and Torres (2010) in their research on understandings of dependency and independence among older people receiving home help services. The older people in this study distinguished between 'being', 'feeling' and 'acting' dependent. Thus, being dependent as a consequence of receiving home help services did not necessarily lead to a feeling of dependence or a change in older people's capability for agency. One important influencing factor was the nature of the relationship with the home help, how reliable and adequate the support was and whether they had adult children or other social networks that could be counted on to provide additional support if necessary. A pertinent point made by Downs (1997) is that the idea of 'personhood' in dementia care was regarded as a way of overcoming the problems of objectification, but in reality personhood was in fact the responsibility of the cognitively intact carer. The idea of personhood falls short of perceiving the cognitively impaired person as having agency.

Dependence at the end of life

Understanding older people's experiences of health and illness, independence and dependence in the fourth age cannot be separated from their experiences of dying and death. In Chapter Three reference was made to Twigg's view (Twigg 2006) that in secular societies the fourth age is emptied of meaning because it is the period of life adjacent to death, which has also lost meaning. Jolanki (2009) questioned whether, at the stage of being bedridden in an institution, it would be legitimate to refer to an individual as having agency at all, since the only remaining question was whether or not to accept one's own fate. When agency is associated with resisting or at least 'pushing back' decline, what meaning is left? Here it would be fruitful to consider the insights that have emerged from studies of death and dying, to identify how dependence and agency are understood through the dying trajectory. In end-of-life studies the concept of a 'good death' takes into account that a dying trajectory has both length and 'shape'. The shape relates in part to the physical changes that occur (relapses, periods of remission and so on), and also to the interpersonal and psychological dimensions. Johnson (2009), for example, refers to the biographical pain that is experienced by some through the process of dying, where family tensions and conflicts are unresolved. Walter (2009) pointed to three key factors that influence ideas about a 'good death': the extent of secularisation, the extent of individualism and how long the typical death takes. From this perspective, long-term illness in old age is significant because it is an increasingly prevalent form of dying trajectory. Certainly, in cultures that place a high value on independence and autonomy the dependency associated with long-term illness can be regarded as worse than death. Contemporary demographic trends strengthen the links between old age and death (Lloyd 2010). Old age is widely regarded as the 'right time' to die, but in spite of this there is a serious risk that perceptions of burdensomeness will increase through the period of dying when the long-term conditions common in old age lead to a protracted dying trajectory. Even in societies with cultural norms about treating older people with reverence, there are expectations that older people should not linger too long (van der Geest 2004, Kreager and Schröder-Butterfill 2007). The length of a dying trajectory is thus inextricably linked with its shape, as an individual with a 'too lengthy' dying trajectory becomes vulnerable to neglect or ill-treatment. There is a strange contradiction between the widespread neglect of dependent older people and the policy aims that encourage people to live to old age. Scarcity of resources is a major factor in most settings, and in low-income countries helps to explain (although not justify) the neglect of older people; but in high-income countries the perception of older people as burdensome seems inexplicable. The description of the fourth age as a 'social imaginary' (Gilleard and Higgs 2010) goes some way to providing an explanation. In cultures where the last stage of life is an imaginary, where the darkest of human fears resides, the dying are hard to associate with, and their care is separated both organisationally and professionally.

On the other hand Seale and van der Geest (2004) identified a number of near-universal ideals concerning 'a good death', including that old age is the best time to die, after having lived a long and productive life. Other ideals are a death at home without violence or pain, where the dying person is at peace with his environment and having a degree of control over events. The ability to exercise control over events is usually highly circumscribed and confined to the micro-context of individual care, but is also influenced by the policy framework. The practice of drawing up Advance Directives or 'living wills' has been incorporated into a number of legal and policy systems. These can be understood as a particular way of extending the civil rights of individuals to the point of death, enabling them to exercise choice and control even after they lose mental capacity. Several commentators have made the point that Advance Directives suit the highly individualistic values of secular cultures. Importantly, Seale and van der Geest also commented on the significance of differences *within* cultures concerning what makes a death good or bad. They pointed to economic and professional status and political interests as important factors. An example of this is research in the US by Johnson et al (2009), who identified how African Americans were very reluctant to make Advance Directives. They argued that this reluctance should be understood by reference to inequalities in power and a lack of trust of health professionals among African Americans. A similar argument can be made in relation to physician–assisted deaths. While these have become part of the overall provision of healthcare in the Netherlands, there is resistance among older people's organisations in the UK, on the grounds that older people are in a relatively powerless position and the risk is too great that they could be persuaded against their will to agree to a physician–assisted death (Seymour et al 2004, Lloyd 2010).

The observation by Seale and van der Geest about the importance of the dying person's being at peace with their environment also draws attention to the importance of family and social networks. Not wanting to linger too long or to take up precious family resources also feature in older people's accounts of their feelings at the end of life (van der Geest 2004). Older people's concern for family harmony and for the well-being of family members after their death has been identified repeatedly in research. Being with others who understand their needs provides reassurance, protection and help with existential anxieties (Bito et al 2007, Kwok et al 2007, Seymour et al 2004). As Johnson (2009) argued, being at peace with others is crucial for spiritual health. These concerns influence older people's decisions about where and how to be cared for, whether or not to accept treatment or food. These findings echo Jolanski's point above, that the decision whether or not to accept one's fate characterises agency at this stage of life. However, the evidence from end-of-life studies demonstrates that these decisions are highly nuanced and complex and, as Jolanki recognises, that the social, cultural and relational dimensions need to be better understood in terms of how we understand older people's agency in conditions of dependence (Lloyd 2004).

The provision of formal care at the end of life

Ideas about a 'good death' have developed primarily within palliative care for cancer patients in Western cultures. Shanmugasundaram et al (2006) questioned the adoption of Western models of palliative care in India and argued that other forms of care, including those that draw on traditional healing practices, would be more appropriate. WHO policies on palliative care are almost entirely confined to cancer and HIV/AIDS, while its action plan on non-communicable diseases makes no reference to palliative care at all (WHO 2008c). Instead, it emphasises that non-communicable diseases (including cardio-vascular diseases, diabetes, cancers and chronic respiratory diseases) are largely preventable. Moreover, the priority for action is to reduce deaths from non-communicable diseases in people aged below 70 years. We can conclude from this strategy, first, that palliative care is not seen as appropriate in the context of these diseases, and second, that deaths in the over-70s are not a priority for attention.

Over the years it has become evident that age discrimination operates in palliative care and that older people are less likely to be referred to palliative care services. At the same time, there is increasing recognition that palliative care as currently practised is not necessarily suitable for the circumstances in which the majority of older people die and that the impact of age on the dying process needs to be better understood (Gott et al 2008). As discussed, apart from the complications that arise from co-morbidities, there are particular existential aspects of living and dying in the fourth age.

In response to the growing evidence of poor standards of services for older people at the end of life in the UK, Davies and Higginson (2004) called for palliative care to be reconceptualised to embrace the care of older people through their long and complex dying trajectories. A problem commonly cited is that it is often difficult to know whether an older person is living with disease or dying from it. Bern-Klug (2004) referred to this as the 'ambiguous dying syndrome'. Defining someone as terminally ill and informing them of this is often regarded as an essential element of the palliative care approach. Arguably, however, if older people's needs are being responded to throughout the period of illness, with its changes and fluctuations, the distinction between living with and dying from becomes unimportant. It is also the case that palliative care was envisaged as applicable in the context of enduring and non-curable disease, not only in relation to the period immediately prior to the end of life.

Conceptualisations of care in policies

This part of the chapter turns attention to policies on care, which is conceptualised in many different ways, influenced by a range of lobby groups and policy agendas. Williams (2010) identified three major conceptualisations in European welfare states: first, care as the object of *claims making*, which includes interventions to support carers and people in need of care; second, care as a *set of relationships* between givers and receivers in both formal and informal settings; and third, care as a *moral orientation* that includes values such as love, commitment, empathy and interdependence (p 2). One of the central themes of this text is that policies have emphasised the importance of the first of these and have paid scant attention to the other two. For decades, the preoccupation of policy makers has been with defining and restricting eligibility for claims making and establishing criteria for inclusion in or exclusion from services. The lack of attention to other conceptualisations of care does not mean that policy preoccupations with claims making do not have an impact on care relationships or on the moral dimensions of care. On the contrary, restrictions on access to care services have a direct impact on conditions of family care and on moral and ethical perceptions of care.

Williams argued that the dominant frame for European care policies has been 'investment in human capital' (2010: 11), which refers to the way in which – partly as a result of population ageing – policies on care have been incorporated into labour-market and associated work-centred welfare policies. As a consequence, those who are not seen to have productive capacities – including 'frail' older people – are reduced to the status of objects of care. She also argued that there have been some positive effects, such as greater recognition of the needs of carers in employment. However, the overall framing of care policies as investment has had the effect of reinforcing the unequal, gendered division in working and care responsibilities. At the same time, the increase in women's paid employment has also played a part in the generation of global care chains, with greater dependency in Europe on migrant care workers. As discussed below, these workers typically have severely curtailed rights. In 2009, in the UN Commission on the Status of Women a debate was held with the intention of producing a 'roadmap for care policy', mostly but not exclusively in the context of HIV/AIDS (Bedford 2010).

This debate was important in terms of framing the international debate on care, setting out key themes that would then be picked up by UN member states to be acted upon. Bedford commented that the sporadic references to disability within this debate framed disabled people 'as a care burden, alongside the sick and the elderly' (2010: 18) and that there was no acknowledgement of the voices or needs of disabled people in debates about care.

As pointed out in Chapter Three, some disabled people have called for the idea of care to be scrapped, on the grounds that it is demeaning and disempowering (see, for example, Beresford 2008). The 'custodial' potential of care undoubtedly has led to ill-treatment and institutionalisation, and it is easy to see how acknowledgement of this becomes a step towards adopting the view that care in itself is undesirable. The influence of this view is seen in policies that promote independence and non-institutionalised services. At the same time, unpaid carers have argued that the contribution of their care work to the well-being of society is grossly undervalued and that the physical, mental and emotional labour that it involves is unrecognised. However, struggles for recognition by both groups can lead to the entrenchment of divisions between them, so that shared interests between them and diversity within them are unacknowledged. It is worth repeating the point that older and disabled people are also care providers, as has been acknowledged widely in the context HIV/AIDS in sub-Saharan Africa. At the same time, the disabled people's lobby against care does not distinguish between experiences of disability of different age groups, so that the particular needs of older people disabled by long-term illness are not given due attention.

Family obligations and unpaid care

As discussed previously, unpaid care constitutes the vast majority of care provided to older people throughout the world. In some countries, including Brazil, China and India, reliance on families is built into legal and policy structures (Gragnolati et al 2011). In high-income countries with more or less developed welfare systems there is also heavy reliance on families (Gooberman-Hill and Ebrahim 2006). Saltman et al (2006) estimated that in Europe the percentage of people relying on care from families alone was as high as 80% in some countries, including Spain and Austria. Even strongly developed publicly funded state welfare systems such as Sweden's are increasingly dependent on unpaid carers. The numbers of people who are providing unpaid care are rising across Europe. In the UK it is estimated that 6.4 million people provide unpaid care, around 10% more than indicated in the Census figures for 2001. Around a third of them provide care for more than 20 hours a week. In North America also, there is heavy reliance on unpaid care in families. In the US it is estimated that one in four households is providing help for someone aged 50 or over with care needs, while in Canada about 80% of care for older people is provided by family and friends (OECD 2005). Against this backdrop of an overall emphasis on unpaid care, there are also important differences between countries to take into account. Glaser et al (2004) identified differences between European countries in levels of support for older people and identified a number of influencing factors, the most important of which were attitudinal and cultural. Hence, in more individualistic cultures a heavier emphasis was placed on the voluntary nature of care, while in more familistic cultures the sense of obligation was stronger. Other factors included were socioeconomic (such as levels of pension) and demographic (such as numbers of older women living alone). As Glaser et al pointed out, these various factors have a bearing on each other, and differences in the policy environment are reflected in cultural attitudes. These attitudes did not run only in the direction of children's support for ageing parents but also in levels of support given by older people to their children.

Policy debates are replete with discussions about what constitutes 'a carer' or 'informal care'. In Europe, Mestheneos and Triantafillou (2005) defined family care as 'care and or financial support provided by a family member for a person 65-years of age or over needing at least four hours of personal care or support a week, at home or in a residential care institution'. A partial explanation for the preoccupation with definitions is that they represent *recognition* and can act as a gateway to welfare state support. Recognition by policy makers has been a major thrust of policy activity by organisations representing carers because of its association with eligibility for resources. There is widespread agreement among policy makers everywhere that support for family carers is a high priority – which is of little surprise, since in most contexts it is woefully inadequate. Where support is provided, it has mostly taken the form of cash benefits, tax-relief schemes, 'respite' care in the form of breaks from the caring role and recognition of carers' needs by employers. In 2007 support for carers was identified as a top priority by the European Ministers of Employment and Social Affairs (Glendinning and Moran, 2009), although a report by the Eurofamcare Consortium (2006) argued that these policy moves have been driven by economic and pragmatic concerns, rather than by humanistic concerns about the conditions of caring. The realisation that Europe is approaching a 'tipping-point' in the balance between the need for and the provision of care has concentrated the minds of policy makers (Buckner and Yeandle 2011).

Encouraging women to participate in the labour market is an important element of the wider agenda to contain the cost of welfare. Replacing the 'family breadwinner model', common to many welfare states, with the 'adult-worker model' aims to reduce dependency on state benefits for all who are able to work. In many European countries women's entitlement to state benefits has been curtailed. At the same time, the adult-worker model has also necessitated action to make employment more amenable to women's caring responsibilities. Encouraging women to participate in the labour market is also a key policy aim in countries with rapidly expanding economies, such as Brazil, where the need for alternative forms of long-term care beyond family care is regarded as pressing (Gragnolati et al 2011).

The need to support family carers is sometimes linked to concerns over the potential for abuse of older people. For example, the OECD working paper on policies for health in ageing (Oxley 2009) noted that injuries among older people are sometimes caused by violence in both family and institutional settings: 'Such problems reflect the fact that living with the elderly can be a daunting task as individuals become more dependent on others' (2009: 22). Such statements are very revealing about the abhorrence of dependency that permeates Western cultures. The importance of support for carers is undeniable: the concept of 'nested dependencies' discussed above stresses this (Kittay 1999). But what is striking about this comment is that the dependency of elderly people is framed as the cause of the violence. Also striking is how living with elderly people is characterised as a 'task'. This framing of the problem of violence places the carer at the centre of policy attention, while the older person is marginalised, and objectified as a problem to be coped with.

The abuse of older people in care homes is a long-standing concern which, as argued in the introduction to this book, has been the subject of numerous policies and strategies. Actions to regulate care homes, establish quality of care standards, improve the training of care workers and the governance of homes have been developed over the years and yet, despite examples of improvements, abusive treatment appears to be an intractable problem. Entry into a care home can increase the risk of institutionalisation and objectification, particularly in a context where the overriding interest is in containing costs. The model of efficiency that underpins care practices sets the context for the enforcement of institutional regimes and for conflicts of interest between care workers and residents, and increases the risk of abuse.

However, understanding the abuse of older people necessitates a broader understanding of the nature of vulnerability and the cultural significance of vulnerability and of the privatised nature of care work. Evidence from the US demonstrates that when more professionally qualified nurses are employed in care homes the quality of care improves. One of the reasons for this is that professional registration engages workers with an alternative set of accountabilities, placing them in a stronger position in relation to the care home regime (Harrington 2001). Professional accountability can enable employees to resist participating in poor standards of service and can offer protection. Harrington's point about the differing accountabilities of nurses is important, as it illustrates a wider concern about who is responsible for practices of care. However, it does not provide a complete answer to the question of how older people's dependency makes them so vulnerable to abuse, since the evidence suggests strongly that the majority of abuse occurs in people's own homes.

From the perspective of the feminist ethics of care, competent care is not possible without a sharing of responsibility and the provision of support for older people and carers. A relevant and important observation by Kreager and Schröder-Butterfill (2007) illustrates this point. In rural Indonesia, where strong cultural traditions of family responsibility still prevail and where care for elders is a mark of a family's reputation and solidarity, the problems of infantilisation and exclusion of older people are still evident. The likelihood of problems occurring is greatest where an older person's decline is long term, where the demand for bodily care increases and where responsibility for care becomes more concentrated on one or two carers. In these circumstances, the quality of care diminishes in very similar ways to those that have been observed in the UK and elsewhere. The evidence from a range of settings suggests that when care is conducted privately and out of sight and when responsibility for care is concentrated on sole or few carers – either within the family or in care homes – accountability is minimised. Shared responsibility not only relieves the pressure on carers but also exposes the practices of care to the view of others, and thus can increase accountability.

An important aspect of this discussion concerns the way that care within families and within formal services is perceived in dichotomous ways. As discussed in Chapter Three, this characterises care in the family as being natural and imbued with emotion, and care in services as objective and rational. Over the years, this dichotomy has been the subject of critique by feminists in particular, yet it remains a strong feature of policies which often lament the loss of family care that has come about through modernisation. The view that economic development has jeopardised traditions of filial obligation is entrenched in policies. Aboderin (2006), for example, commented on how assumptions that traditions of filial obligation in Africa and Asia were being eroded were built into the Vienna Plan and became firmly established in debates on modernisation and development. However, Aboderin also pointed to an alternative perspective that has developed in Africa. This emphasises the centrality of the family as the provider of care and support to older people, not merely as a means of limiting public spending but also as a way of reinforcing cultural values and building a system of care that reflects African traditions, rather than copying a Western model. She argued that to realise this vision of care requires policies that support families, and strengthens family responsibility. Hence, instead of care being understood in dichotomous ways, the need is for policies that understand better the ways in which different forms of care interact.

This point is echoed in studies in Asia, where cultural traditions of family care have influenced relationships between formal and informal care. Izuhara (2010) and others have argued convincingly that traditions of filial piety are flexible, and capable of adapting to changing economic circumstances. However, government policies play a powerful role in forcing the direction of change. In China, Chou (2010) identified the impact of economic development and internal migration on traditions of filial piety (see also Giles et al 2010). The Chinese government has invested substantially in the development of care homes – seen by some commentators now as the 'cornerstone of China's development of eldercare' (p 586) – and this has inevitably had an impact on the balance of care as between families and institutions. The input of the for-profit and not-for-profit sectors is a key issue and the growth of a wealthier class of people in China is seen as providing opportunities for profitable enterprise in institutional care provision. Ochiai (2009) argued that in Japan policies on the marketisation of care as well as the activation of communities are essential because the level of dependency on relatives is unsustainable. A culture of avoidance of institutional care is strong in many contexts, not only in countries with a strong tradition of filial piety. Institutionalisation signifies the subjection of individual identity and vulnerability to overbearing controls and an abuse of power. This perspective underpins the emphasis on home-based care, but it is important to point out that institutionalisation is not necessarily associated with a place, but with practices of care. In the context of inadequate resources, home-based care can be equally institutionalised because older people are obliged to follow schedules imposed by care agencies.

The labelling of care practices as 'cultural' can mask structural factors that pertain in situations where, because of poverty, families have little choice other than to provide care (Flores et al 2009). Aboderin (2006) makes the pertinent point that the chance of developing policies with the right balance of family and state responsibility, with support for rather than exploitation of traditions of family responsibility, hinges to a great extent on how norms of filial obligation operate at the micro-level. From her research in Ghana, she highlighted in particular the need to understand better the interactions between cultural norms on filial obligation, on the one hand, and personal relationships and structural factors, on the other. Crucially, Aboderin pointed out that there are limits to filial obligation and that within families there are 'hierarchies of priorities'. In Ghana, in the context of severe constraints on resources, support to aged parents was reduced in order to meet the needs of conjugal families.

Policy developments in long-term care

Long-term care is the description given to a range of services and interventions that support people with long-term conditions with activities of daily living. An OECD report (OECD 2005) studied trends in long-term care in 19 countries of the OECD, looking at the support given over an extended period of time with activities of daily living, which covered help with bathing, dressing, eating, getting in and out of a bed or chair, moving around and using the lavatory. The services were often provided in conjunction with rehabilitation and other medical services. As discussed previously, views on what constitutes an activity of daily living are very narrow, and where resources diminish so too does the range of activities. The OECD study bears out the view of Ryff and Singer (1998) that ideas about positive health rarely make their way on to policy makers' agendas. Despite these limitations, it is constructive to examine the information on long-term care in such range of countries because the similarities and differences between them highlight the extent to which and the ways in which global trends shape national experiences, and vice-versa.

The trends in long-term care in OECD countries are towards individual, 'personalised packages' of care, towards self-care in the older person's own home supported by assistive technology for as long as possible. A move to a nursing home or residential care home after that is common, but the length of time older people spend in care homes before their deaths has become shorter (Lloyd 2010). The terms 'spectrum of care' or 'continuum of care' are often used in policy circles to describe the kinds of care required by older people as their circumstances change in line with declining health. At one end of the spectrum are low-level forms of support in the older person's own home, such as home-help services, including assistance with heavier household tasks. At the other end are nursing homes, providing comprehensive care for all needs. Along the continuum between these are more personal and nursing care services for people with more serious health problems, as well as supported housing schemes. Decisions about whether a person should continue to be supported at home or in a care home will be based on financial considerations, as well consideration of the older person's health.

Waerness (2001) commented on the separation between the public management of care services and the 'real world' discourses on care for older people. When policy makers speak of social care for older people their focus is not on the daily activities of helping them to wash and dress or to prepare and eat their meals, but on the economic challenge generated by their dependency and ways of managing this. Demand has grown for more sophisticated measures to predict need and demand for care through predictions of chronic disease in later life. However, while an improved understanding of likely levels of disease can assist in predicting need, it is insufficient as a basis for predicting demand for care services. Predictions of both need and demand must also factor in the accessibility of treatments to modify symptoms and the availability of unpaid family carers (Batljan and Lagergren 2005).

Within health and welfare services the focus is on care as a commodity, with procurement, funding and management being the chief priorities. Part of the managerial agenda has been the categorisation of needs in ways that make them capable of being measured. Hence the focus on functional health, rather than on quality of life and on specifying which activities should be included in provision of services, as well as in what circumstances. This distinction between ADLs and IADLs is relevant to the question of who might be expected to provide care (Glaser et al 2004). Older people are more likely to obtain support from family, friends and neighbours with *instrumental* activities, such as shopping and delivering food, than with ADLs, such as eating or bathing. It is organising help with ADLs within the limits of available resources that is most taxing for service providers. As a consequence, time and money values are attached to activities, which are broken down into units, and the provision of care becomes a matter of calculating the unit costs. This approach makes procurement easier, but it generates numerous problems. On a practical level, it does not distinguish between people in terms of the time it takes them to have a bath or to get dressed, nor does it allow for differences in individual requirements between one day and another. As Williams pointed out, it reduces older people to objects of care, where care is seen wholly in terms of a set of tasks. Of course, when the pressure is on to keep the cost of care down, the time available to provide a service becomes more and more limited, and this pressure is exerted on (mainly female) front-line workers (Dyer et al 2008).

An important observation made by Land and Himmelweit (2010: 17) sums up the impact of this reductionist approach to care:

> Care is a quintessentially 'soft' product whose essential characteristics are not easily measured. It is possible to monitor the attainment of certain physical tasks, such as, whether a client has been bathed or taken their medicine. Market-driven provision, in its drive for efficiency, will tend to meet these measurable outputs and economise on the less tangible aspects of good care. But these are of the very essence of good care, which in nearly all cases needs to include the development of a warm relationship between care provider and recipient.

The provision of care, even in its reduced form, varies between countries. The OECD report referred to above noted that across the 19 countries studied there was a trend towards more universal public provision of long-term care. The term 'universal' does not necessarily mean freely available at the point of use. There are differences between countries in how they approach the task of meeting and containing the cost and there appears to be a trade-off between maintaining more public funding, on the one hand, and offering a higher quality of services, on the other. Some countries (such as Sweden) have targeted services on people who are sicker and more disabled, while others (such as the Netherlands) have introduced service-user payments. In Austria, Germany, Japan and Luxembourg long-term care has been brought into the social insurance schemes. In general there are low levels of spending on long-term care: even in countries with comprehensive coverage it amounts to only 10–20% of total healthcare expenditure. Low spending has been made possible through high levels of charging and through the provision of informal family care. In several countries 30% or more of total spending is covered by private payments for care.

The OECD report also identifies a growing trend towards consumer empowerment, which is underpinned in some countries (Australia and the US, for example) by advocacy schemes and in others by residents' councils and complaints procedures, which have had some success in improving the standard of services. The influence of consumer perspectives on long-term care also underpins the development of cash-for-care schemes in several OECD countries. These schemes are regarded as maximising choice for service users and overcoming the problem of institutionalisation associated with monolithic state-run services. They take the form of allocation of personal budgets to service-users over which they have more or less control. The cash in a personal budget is most often used to employ a care assistant (or several assistants) directly, although in some countries cash payments are made directly to carers. Personal budgets can also be used to purchase goods that will support independent living, such as adaptations to the home or mobility aids. An interesting aspect of this particular trend is the way in which policies on cash for care have also tapped into the perspectives of older people who wish to remain at home rather than enter an institution, and of carers who have demanded recognition of their role and reward for their labour. Cash for care has come to represent a convergence of aims between the consumerist (providing more choice), the liberationist (providing greater control over conditions of care) and the neoliberal (minimising the cost of care).

In reality there is less convergence than at first appears and there are several unresolved problems with cash–for–care schemes, including the low level of payments, the conditions of care work and restrictions on choice (Lloyd 2010). Some countries allow for cash to be paid to family or other informal carers, while others restrict payment to non–co–resident carers. In the UK the rate of pay for the employment of a care assistant is higher than the rate of allowances given to carers, the reasoning behind this being that the carer's allowance is intended to be a compensation for not being able to work, rather than a wage for working. In some countries (including Australia and Ireland), the carer's allowance is means-tested. Not all countries in the OECD have opted for cash payments. Japan bucks the trend, preferring instead to expand in-kind benefits through its long-term care insurance scheme. Other countries lack a welfare infrastructure to enable them to implement cash–for–care schemes. In countries such as Mexico, Spain and Poland there is a heavy reliance on unpaid care, and the OECD report warns that this is becoming unsustainable.

Cash–for–care schemes are very popular with some groups of service users, but evidence suggests that, when given a choice between a personal budget and services, older people are among those least likely to choose personal budgets. Rummery (2009) analysed schemes in six countries in order to explore their gendered nature. As she pointed out, they can exacerbate existing socioeconomic inequalities, the wages and conditions of work for the mainly female carers are generally poor and there is a risk of exploitation because the emotional labour involved in the work can lead to expectations that carers will provide more than they are paid to. On the other hand, there are potential gains. Facilitating the employment of personal assistants can enhance women's citizenship status either by conferring an 'employed' status on the carer who was previously an unpaid carer or by freeing up unpaid carers to join the labour market. They can improve the conditions of caring, enhancing carers' well-being and enabling them to make a choice about whether or not to engage in care work. Rummery (2009) concluded that these marketised approaches to care can offer gains in citizenship if the state maintains a strong influence over the governance of schemes and enable carers and service users to exercise choice and control. However, they can generate a problem if the regulation of cash–for–care schemes is experienced as an overbearing intrusion into people's private lives, as was identified in the UK, the Netherlands and France. In contrast, in countries where there is less regulation (such as Austria and Italy) there is greater potential for workers to be exploited. The question of regulation and monitoring is also of crucial importance in relation to the potential for abuse of older people, which, as discussed, is greatest in the context of private care arrangements.

The accountability of long-term care providers is a contentious point. As services have become increasingly concentrated in non-state settings the state has greater responsibility for inspection and regulation. The classic neoliberal demand for a 'light touch' regulation of for-profit provider organisations has been challenged by scandals over practices. It has also become evident that the need for regulation extends beyond the practices of care, to the financing of care. This was illustrated graphically in the UK with the collapse of the largest for-profit care home provider, Southern Cross, in July 2011, as pointed out in Chapter Four.

There has not been a great deal of attention to long-term care in low- and middle-income countries (Gragnolati et al, 2011). Lloyd-Sherlock (2010) sees the explanation for this in a lack of appreciation of the speed of population ageing, particularly the growth of very old populations, and the continuing policy emphasis on younger populations. There is in fact a rapid increase in demand for long-term care in many developing countries but, as Lloyd-Sherlock pointed out, in the context of limited resources and regulatory regimes, the need for a better understanding is essential. His study of residential care in Argentina underlined this need, as it identified that many homes are unregulated and run on an informal basis but that anecdotal evidence on substandard care practices and cases of abuse is increasingly prominent. Importantly, many of the older people in the care homes he researched had been admitted for reasons other than health needs, including poverty and housing problems, while, perversely, people with dementia were excluded. He argued that there is a serious need to develop specialised forms of support and care for this group, which is increasing in number as populations age.

In their report for the WHO, Brodsky et al (2003) predicted an increase in demand for long-term care in developing countries as a consequence of two interrelated processes: a growth in the factors that increase the prevalence of long-term disability and a change in the capacity of informal support to address these needs. Thus, while there are differences in the way that both of these processes play out in national contexts, there is a great deal of similarity between developing and OECD countries in terms of demand for long-term care. There is also some convergence of ideas about how to meet demand. The spread of ideas about care, models of care practice and management beyond OECD countries to low- and middle-income countries is described by Mahon and Robinson as 'travelling social policy discourses', in which the WHO and the OECD play a crucially important role (2011: 10). However, as discussed above, there is no straightforward policy transfer from developed welfare states to low- and middle-income countries, and path dependency factors also need to be taken into account. Local histories and traditions concerning family obligations as well as local socioeconomic conditions play an important part in shaping policy agendas. Brodsky et al (2003) pointed to high HIV/AIDS rates in sub-Saharan Africa, as well as armed conflicts and significantly increased accident rates, both of which have increased the numbers of disabled people.

Brodsky et al (2003) identified policy directions for long-term care in 10 case-study countries: China, Costa Rica, Indonesia, Lebanon, Lithuania, Mexico, the Republic of Korea, Sri Lanka, Thailand and Ukraine. The trends they identified were that more formal care services are being developed (home care, personal care and home health), with different approaches to the funding of services, the age of eligibility for help and the range of services offered. In most cases eligibility is based on income levels. Brodsky et al argued that a pattern of services is developing which at first involves 'home health' services, with an emphasis on training family carers, and subsequently personal care and home-making services. In general, long-term care services are heavily health oriented, with healthcare systems playing the major role in providing support to family carers. At the same time Brodsky et al identified a heavy reliance on community-based volunteers organised through NGOs. They also identified variations between the case-study countries in the emphasis given to institutional care, with more extensive provision in Lithuania and Ukraine, less in China, Lebanon, the Republic of Korea and Sri Lanka, and hardly any at all in the remaining countries. The balance between formal and informal care is to a large extent dependent on wider changes in economic policies and labour market conditions, as discussed above in relation to China (Chou 2010). In Brazil, high levels of unemployment have contributed to high levels of co-residence between elderly parents and adult children – 42.2% of households containing 'frail elderly' people also contain adult children aged 21 or over. Intergenerational dependency is evidently a two-way process in these circumstances (Gragnolati et al 2011).

Global chains of care

There is growing recognition that the increased numbers of migrant care workers have changed the landscape of care. Yeates (2005) argued that it is no longer justifiable to analyse regimes of care without reference to the global political economy, while Mahon and Robinson (2011) emphasised the importance of recognising not only differences between national regimes of care but also the increasingly permeable boundaries around them. The concept of 'global chains of care' describes the flow of workers, mostly women, from low- to high-income countries to work in a range of settings. The push and pull factors behind women's decision to migrate to work in care homes in the formal care services of high-income countries are many and varied. Current demographic trends and changes in the labour market affecting women's position as carers increase the demand for care. Redfoot and Houser (2008) examined the international migration of nurses to the US and also pointed to the trend towards more home-based rather than institutional care and quicker hospital discharges as contributing factors in increasing the demand, as well as the particularly low status of care work and high levels of vacancies in nursing. The long-standing disadvantaged position of women in the labour market has thus been internationalised and racialised, as colonial histories influence the patterns of care-worker migration.

Redfoot and Houser (2008) also highlighted how the education levels and professional credentials of care workers are processed in destination countries. Establishing workers' credentials is necessary to ensure an appropriate level of competence, but the procedures that have been established have also been used as a means of managing the numbers of workers and their deployment in different parts of the care system. For example, in the US the procedures for screening and examination of migrant nurses have resulted in a high failure rate (a process of 'decredentialing'), which often means that nurses qualified overseas end up working in care homes in lower-paid, lower-status jobs than they had expected when they were recruited in their home countries. Similar patterns are evident elsewhere.

The issue of recognition of overseas education and professional credentials is contentious, but what is striking is that the expectations of migrant nurses is so far removed from the reality they face when they arrive in the destination country. This directs attention to the circumstances in which they are recruited. The demand for nurses in the already aged countries of North America and Europe has provided new business opportunities for recruitment agencies operating out of low- and middle-income countries, but these agencies have come in for criticism on the grounds that they misrepresent to would-be migrants the opportunities that are available. Redfoot and Houser also point out that many of these agencies are unregulated, or weakly regulated. The impact of migration on migrant nurses' home countries has produced international guidelines and bilateral pacts to limit the numbers employed in public health services in high-income countries, but many migrants end up working in private, for-profit care homes which are exempt from such guidelines.

For many migrants, entry into the workplace in destination countries is, as Lund (2006) observed, a 'step into vulnerability' (p 222). Not only do they face poor conditions of work and low status, but they also leave behind their families and other networks of support, and sometimes their entitlements to citizen rights in their home countries, including their rights to healthcare and pensions. The work that they do in home-based social care also exposes the falseness of the dichotomy between paid and unpaid work, as their roles often entail unpaid overtime, which is unrecognised but is regarded as an essential part of the caring role, modelled on the ideal of family care.

Summary

The need for care in circumstances of dependency and loss of capacity for self-care raises major questions about human vulnerability and interdependence. It is perhaps in this context that the inadequacy of policy agendas appears most starkly. Policies that attempt to capture the concerns raised by bodily breakdown in later life and to frame them in ways that conform to a managerial agenda are counter-productive. The counter-trend to the institutionalisation of older people, exemplified by cash-for-care schemes, offers some potential for better forms of care, but even here older people are still at risk of institutionalisation if resources are inadequate, and worse still, of abuse as a result of the private nature of care within the home. Conversely, an increase in demand for care within care homes is evident in a number countries where economies are expanding, but the cost of these can restrict access to the minority with resources (as in China) or expose older people to neglectful and abusive regimes (as in Argentina). In the context of resource constraints, the emphasis worldwide is on policies to reduce demand through shortening the period of dependency and to promote better health. Yet the dependency of older people in the fourth age is inextricably linked to the end of life and there are inevitable limits to this strategy. The insights from research on end-of-life and palliative care highlight the need for a better understanding of dependency over the long term. Understanding long-term illness as a prolonged dying trajectory shifts the focus from primary and secondary forms of prevention to the promotion of health in its broadest sense, including the health of those who care for and care about the older person.

EIGHT

Conclusion

The discussion in this text has spanned a range of issues of relevance to understanding health and care in ageing societies. At the outset, attention was drawn to the overarching policy principles that shape policies and practices in health and care: first, the focus on the gap between life expectancy and healthy life expectancy so as to maintain health and independence, and second, the need for a tight rein on public spending on health and social care services so that the cost of older people's eventual dependency on services is contained. The discussion has covered a wide range of policies and practices in which these two principles can be seen to operate and which shape experiences of ageing, health and care. This concluding chapter identifies the key issues that have arisen and discusses the value of an ethics-of-care approach as an explanatory framework.

Demographic trends and patterns undoubtedly affect the ways in which ageing, health and care are perceived, but the impact of political and economic interests on these perceptions is powerful. In spite of the evidence of a double burden of morbidity in low- and middle-income countries, differences in the speed at which populations are ageing and the lack of welfare infrastructures in those countries, it is the experience of ageing in high-income countries that has dominated the picture. The idea of the compression of morbidity, despite its uncertainty, occupies an important place in the policy process and, coupled with an individualistic focus on the determinants of health, has reinforced a health policy message that is highly moralistic in tone.

The influence of this policy message is evident in policies on health in later life, which repeatedly present health in ageing as something within the control of individual older people. The 'mind over matter' message of the WHO's health advice to older people stands in stark contrast to the evidence that the WHO has produced on the socioeconomic determinants of health. The intention is not to suggest that individual behavioural factors are unimportant, but to point to the need to understand better how they interact with socioeconomic factors throughout the lifecourse. Evidence on the role of supportive social relationships as a prerequisite for health throughout the lifecourse is a crucially important message from this exploration of health and is of direct relevance to policy. It draws attention to the fundamental necessity of care and provokes a critical response to policies on care that focus almost exclusively on the individual rather than the social.

Policies reflect and reinforce cultural values, and the moral imperative for action on inequalities in health is strong. Yet actions to tackle inequalities in health have been ineffective, despite decades of debate and policy making. When the policy process is analysed, the way in which it is influenced by powerful interests goes some way to explaining why this should be so. The global reach of neoliberal policies has exacerbated inequalities and, despite a belated realisation of the effects on health and welfare in low- and middle-income countries, the effects of policies begun in the 1980s are still being felt. These effects are significant for experiences of ageing, including older people's health and their access to health and social care services. Differentials in power between actors in the policy process have resulted in a framing of older people's needs in particular ways and in establishing policy priorities that privilege economic interests over public health and well-being. Analysis of the policy process demonstrates how difficult it is for relatively powerless groups to pursue the moral case for action on inequalities in health and on the provision of healthcare as a human right. The themes of prevention, treatment and care that have been explored all have strong implications for ageing. A key point is that health and care should be understood as a complex and many-faceted phenomenon. Health in old age is more than the absence of disease and more than the outcome of individual capacity for self-care.

The concept of salutogenesis provides a useful framework for exploring health at the individual and social levels and the value of health-promoting social and physical environments. The 'upstream' actions explored in Chapter Five demonstrated how the focus on the social and on the importance of multisectoral approaches to policies has been overshadowed by the narrow, individualistic focus. The concepts of social capital and of 'bonding and bridging' social networks were explored. These concepts also have value for understanding old age because of the increased likelihood of loss of and changes in social relationships in later life. In this chapter another important theme of relevance to the whole discussion was raised, which concerns the relationship between formal and informal sources of support. Both are necessary for the prevention of illness, and this was demonstrated powerfully in the evidence from grandmothers in Africa who provide care for their orphaned grandchildren. It was argued that a salutogenic environment would replenish social capital, enable relationships of care to flourish and generate support where social networks have diminished with ageing.

The relationship between ageing and medicine is also complex. Critiques of medicalisation are important because the pathologisation of ageing plays an important role in the policy process and the characterisation of older people as a drain on resources. However, these critiques should not disregard the importance of medicine to older people. The secondary level of health promotion becomes more important at later stages of the lifecourse as the risk of disease increases. Inequalities in access to healthcare and inequities in the provision of services also have strong implications for older people, which were discussed in Chapter Six, where barriers to healthcare were explored, including ageism and age discrimination in health. It was also argued that the secondary level of health promotion was more strongly influenced by economic globalisation than the other two levels because of its commercial potential and because of weakened systems and regimes of regulation and control.

System change in healthcare is necessary in order to keep pace with demographic and epidemiological trends and the need to shift from an over-reliance on traditional acute models. But system change has taken place in the context of an overarching concern about cost, which has affected approaches to treatment for non-communicable diseases. The spread of ideas about self-care supported by the use of new technologies is consistent with individualised perceptions of health, and shifts responsibility for care to the individual. A further implication for older people is that this responsibility is sometimes expressed as a duty to the young.

At the tertiary level, policies on self-care take on a greater economic importance, since it is at this stage that care becomes a 'long-term' necessity. Self-care is regarded as both empowering to older people and good for minimising the cost of care. However, it is in the context of long-term illness and dependence that the importance of a broad and inclusive conceptualisation of health is most needed. The evidence, however, is that policies are moving in the opposite direction. Individualistic conceptualisations of preventive health are reflected in the prevalent view that the long-term conditions experienced by older people could be prevented by healthier life-styles. In fact, the UN's World Economic and Social Survey for 2007 disregarded evidence on the link between living conditions and non-communicable diseases and chose to focus on life-style factors as being 'more policy relevant'.

At the last stage of the lifecourse the loss of capacity for self-care exposes most clearly the importance of understanding our embodied nature and the essentially vulnerable and interdependent nature of human life. It was argued in Chapter Seven that it is in this context – at the tertiary level – that the policy process appears most counter-productive to older people's health because of the framing of older people's needs to conform to a managerial agenda. It was argued that policies to de-institutionalise care, seen in a number of established welfare states, have been only partially successful because of inadequate resources and the pre-eminence of concerns about the cost of care. It was also argued that in privatised forms of care the risk of abuse was heightened but had not been given due attention. The counter-trend in countries with expanding economies, towards more institutional care, was also discussed, where the picture of family care and obligation is changing. At the tertiary level the limitations of individualist health-promotion strategies are shown clearly because of the dependency of older people at the end of life. It was argued that long-term care could be informed by the experiences of palliative care. Understanding long-term illness as a prolonged dying trajectory shows how the promotion of health in its broadest sense is possible.

The ethics of care as a framework for analysis

Throughout this text, a range of ethical and moral questions have been raised. These include questions concerning relationships of trust between older people and professionals, which emerge in the context of medical practices in life extension and in end-of-life care, as well as in the context of regulation of care and out-of-pocket payments for healthcare. Socioeconomic inequalities also raise deep moral and ethical questions, and these were discussed in relation to age-related resource allocation for healthcare. It was pointed out that in these debates questions of older people's rights to healthcare cannot be separated from socioeconomic inequalities, since it is older people's access to *public* resources that is in question.

At the outset, it was argued that the ethics of care provides a valuable framework for analysis, explaining the relationship between the three levels of health promotion and critiquing the role of policies. Tronto's model for an ethic of care (Tronto 1993), discussed in Chapter Three, can be easily understood as a way of understanding how care as the combination of attentiveness, responsibility, competence and responsiveness can inform – and indeed provide an organising framework for – caring relationships at the micro-level. However, it is important to reiterate that the ethics of care does not only apply to the micro-contexts of caring relationships or where individuals are clearly in acute need of help because of illness and impairment. The essential need for care and to care applies across the lifecourse, between generations and at the broader social level. The concept of nested dependencies (Kittay 1999) is a useful explanation of interdependence that does not balk at acknowledging the realities of dependence or seek to deny the need for care. Instead it demonstrates that the need for care is not confined to particular categories of vulnerable or frail people but is inherent within the human condition and therefore applies to the givers as well as the receivers. The potential for conflicts of interest between givers and receivers is also acknowledged. An ethic of care requires that attention is paid to ways of resolving these.

Because the ethics-of-care approach is not confined to actual practices of care in a narrow sense, its relevance extends to all three areas of health promotion discussed in this book. It is entirely compatible with salutogenic approaches to health. As pointed out by Sevenhuijsen (1998), care is primarily about quality of life and how this is interpreted and experienced. The salutogenic conceptualisation of health is of direct relevance to a lifecourse approach to health, with its strong emphasis on upstream measures. It is also of direct relevance to health in old age through its holistic perspective on health, which provides an optimistic account of how the many dimensions of health can be promoted, physical health being just one. While it is undoubtedly true that eating well, taking exercise and not smoking will increase an individual's chances of living in good health to an old age and through old age, the broader view of health promotion, which focuses on the importance of socioeconomic determinants of health, has been eclipsed whereas an ethic of care would place socioeconomic determinants at the heart of policy-making.

Dominant neoliberal agendas have also effectively stifled opposition to the individualistic view of health. The WHO has come under fire from Katz (2009) and others for its capitulation to neoliberalism and its compromise on the social determinants of health. An example of compromise is the comment in the WHO's age-friendly primary care strategy (WHO 2004b) that the need for good health in old age is more pressing within low-income countries, where resources for healthcare are 'sorely lacking'. The argument that healthier old people would mean that resources would be freed up for use by younger people characterises older people's healthcare needs as conflicting with those of younger people. This is a diversion from the concerns about the sore lack of resources that the WHO might reasonably have been expected to prioritise, given its history. However, the WHO's position reflects a more general tendency, heightened in the context of neoliberalism, to characterise a need for care as a threat to societal well-being. It appears that any health-promotion strategy can be turned to the benefit of neoliberalism, including placing responsibility for inadequately resourced health and care services on the shoulders of sick older people. Because of their increased risk of illness, older people are at a particular disadvantage from the framing of health as the outcome of individual effort. Those who fail in the effort become a burden on the rest. From this point, the policy of placing constraints on eligibility for health and care services is a logical step. From the perspective of the ethics of care, the discourse of burdensomeness is a way of marginalising older people and also of disassociating the young, fit and able-bodied from their own vulnerability and their own future old age.

As argued, the need to see health as complex and multifaceted is crucially important, but functional conceptualisations of health in later life are dominant and are consistent with individualistic approaches to care. As Blaxter (2004) argued, health is defined by the governments who exercise surveillance over it and by the commercial interests who turn it into a commodity. Definitions are evident in the managerialist model of health and social care service provision, in which care for older people is reduced to a set of measurable tasks that can be achieved for minimum cost. In the context of neoliberal frameworks, the service provider becomes first and foremost the guardian of public resources. In these circumstances older people are easily objectified. In terms of Tronto's model, narrow functional conceptualisations of health represent an all-round failure to care through a lack of attentiveness to broader health needs; a lack of responsibility on the part of those who control resources to act to meet need; a lack of competence in carrying out the tasks of care; and a lack of responsiveness to the perspectives of older people on the receiving end of the service. A clear example of this is in the OECD working paper on *Policies for Healthy Ageing* (Oxley 2009), discussed in Chapter Three, in which the suggestion was made that the provision of a home-help service might be bad for the health of older people because it would effectively eliminate the only exercise they take. At the same time, there is also a lack of attentiveness to the needs of carers and their conditions of work, as argued by Kittay et al (2005), Land and Himmelweit (2010) and Mahon and Robinson (2011).

Consumerism in care services can be regarded as responsive, but only partially so. The development of ideas about personalisation in health and care services has been attractive to service providers as a way of demonstrating that they are attentive to the particular needs and requirements of individuals. However, the ideals of personalisation are not always implemented in practice, and in the context of resource constraints are jeopardised. If the ideals of personalisation are reduced to an agenda of promoting cash-for-care schemes in a bid to reduce the cost of welfare, older people in declining health are highly likely to miss out on a responsive service. This is particularly the case where cash-for-care schemes place restrictions on payments to family carers. In Tronto's terms, to be competent the amount of cash provided should be adequate, and for responsiveness, schemes should allow for a range of caring relationships to be supported, not only those that fit institutional criteria. For some, a consumerist approach means that services are more responsive and better organised around personal need, but for those who are unable to engage with the consumerist agendas of choice-making it is meaningless and hollow. Again, global socioeconomic inequalities are inextricably linked with the micro-context of care. Older people in high-income countries might be able to exercise their choice to have personalised services in their own homes, but their choice is made possible by the migration of low-paid workers from low- and middle-income countries to carry out the work. The capacity of the ethics of care to draw the links between the micro- and macro-levels of care is of particular importance in revealing the global nature of caring work.

The capabilities approach remains influential in global policy circles and has offered an important alternative to narrow, economistic perspectives on social development. It provides a critique of neoliberalism that has been taken up by many in public health and social development. Yet, the capabilities paradigm has also generated ethical debates about priorities for resource allocation, which have positioned age as a prominent factor. These questions are placed into sharp relief in the context of resources for anti-ageing medicine and life-extending medical practices (Daniels 2008, Ruger 2010). In this discussion, a crucial point of departure from the capabilities paradigm is its *individualistic* nature (Held 2006, Lewis and Giullari 2006, Dean 2009). The capabilities paradigm relies for care on sympathy for those who are at times dependent on others. In so doing it presupposes that dependency is a deviation from the norm, rather than being a basic human characteristic. It is in this respect there is a wide divergence between the ethics-of-care and the capabilities paradigms.

The ethics of care and gerontology

A number of themes in this text are of particular relevance to gerontology. Demographic trends do not generate policies, but in terms of the understanding of care as 'claims-making' they cannot be ignored, because of the powerful discourse of older people's burdensomeness in the policy process. The insight of feminist ethicists into the false division between the moral and political agendas is relevant to this point. Tronto (1993) identified how the false division has led to a position in which the moral agenda of rights (such as the right to health and care) is overshadowed by the political agenda of resources. The falseness of this division is that in reality the agenda of rights is inextricably linked with the political agenda of resources. Keeping the policy process focused on the right to healthcare is a difficult matter, expressed wearily by Banerji (2008) as the WHO's 'decennial ritual of remembering Alma Ata'. Over and over again, the argument is repeated about the importance of intersectoral action to promote health and to tackle inequalities, but the dominance of political and economic agendas prevents such action. Older people are particularly disadvantaged by this because of their increased need for health and social care.

This leads to the second point of importance for gerontology, which is that the struggle to obtain equity in health and social care has been shaped by the positive ageing agenda. It should be emphasised that, in arguing in favour of an ethics of care, the intention is not to belittle efforts to counteract negative images of ageing but to point out the problems associated with it. These are, first, that because neoliberal agendas are dominant, ideas about positive ageing have been appropriated as an acceptable rationale for cutting services. Positive ageing has been an important strategy to counteract negative portrayals of ageing in welfarist or medicalised accounts, which emphasise decline and death. Ironically, this effort is being made at the very time when decline and death are more closely linked with old age than ever before. As discussed, the active ageing agenda has been incorporated into the neoliberal agenda of personal responsibility and of the model of citizenship based on paid work. Walker (2009) observed that, in the European context at least, the active ageing agenda has become reduced to a narrow employment model. Second, positive accounts of ageing have promoted an idealised version of the autonomy of a self-reliant individual who does not need care.

From the perspective of the ethics of care, the problem lies in the narrow view of autonomy which is regarded as 'normal'. It is scarcely surprising that groups that are marginalised and 'othered' because they are seen as having lost their autonomy wish to disassociate from the perception that they are abnormal. But it is the characterisation of the normal that is the primary problem, and the particular way that autonomy is understood within Western cultures. The discussion in this book has included different ways of understanding independence and dependence. It has emphasised the necessity of social relationships for health and well-being, which demonstrates the feminist ethicists' view of autonomy as a characteristic that emerges from relationships. These are not abstract ideals. The discussion of evidence from non-Western cultures – including that presented by Aboderin (2006) – demonstrates that self-reliance is not a prerequisite for well-being and that it is older people's relationships that are of paramount importance.

The idea of relational autonomy also highlights the potential for conflicts of interest, which might be characterised as an intergenerational conflict, but in any case draws attention to the importance of attention to nested dependencies. Research has demonstrated repeatedly the value of the sharing of care tasks, and of support for carers. The evidence of older people's role as providers of care is crucially important but, as argued, there has been a spectacular failure to recognise this. At the same time, external pressures make care by younger family members for older people harder. This is particularly so in the context of high unemployment and job insecurity. The need to work long hours and meet employers' demands for flexible working runs counter to the need to provide care. The pressure on families is also fierce because of the lack of alternative forms of care. Family carers are in a double bind, under greater pressure to care but in worsened circumstances. The subjugation of care practices to the dictates of the market impinges directly on the circumstances in which care is provided. But there is also an indirect effect, which is the way in which expectations of help and support are shaped, how older people perceive their needs and how they decide whether to seek help, what they should do and who they should turn to.

The othering of older people also increases the likelihood of neglect and abuse. The dichotomous thinking between private and public forms of care referred to above has deflected attention from the potential for abuse within older people's families, despite evidence that the abuse of older people is most likely to take place within their own homes. The question of how private arrangements for care should be exposed to the scrutiny of others is fraught with difficulty, but the concept of nested dependencies does offer a way of thinking about the sharing of care that at least reduces the isolation that is often experienced in caring relationships. The challenge to the public/private dichotomy of care is a major contribution from feminist ethicists. This is of particular relevance to ageing, since the invisibility of practices of care and the culture of privacy surrounding both institutional and family care place dependent older people in a vulnerable position and impoverish public understanding of what care involves or how it could be practised differently.

One of the critiques of the ethics of care is that it presents an over-generalised view of care and that, while the need for care and to care can be recognised at the micro-level, at the societal level an ethic of justice should take precedence over an ethic of care. The counter-argument to this is that the practices of care are inextricably linked with political and economic agendas. The ethics of care starts from an understanding of what is happening in practice, rather than regarding justice as an abstract principle. Of fundamental importance is the view that the contemporary ideal of autonomy has overlooked the essentially social nature of human life and that autonomy is achieved through relationships. This is a particularly important point for gerontologists to consider because of the profound impact of ageing on relationships.

The feminist ethics of care provides a sound basis for analysing health and care in the context of ageing societies because of its explanatory power in relation to the dependency of human beings and their essentially social nature and interdependency, and in relation to the moral and political agendas that shape these. In the context of ageing societies, policy processes on health and care are exceptionally active, and within them a raft of political, economic and ethical questions are raised which reverberate around the world, affecting even those societies that do not regard ageing as a political priority.

The overarching policy principles that were the starting-point for this discussion have been demonstrably counter-productive to older people's health and well-being. As Robinson (2010) argued, the time is ripe for an alternative political vision, and the ethics of care provides a framework for rethinking the nature of social relationships. The ethics of care is of central importance to gerontology. It challenges long-established ideas about autonomy, independence and dependence. It provides a way of understanding how global and local contexts of care are inextricably linked and how global political agendas shape individual experiences of ageing. It therefore commands attention not only for its explanatory value but also because it offers an alternative way of conceptualising health and care. It provides a lens through which the study of ageing can be enriched, through its explanation of the links between care and health in later life.

References

Abe, A.K. (2010) *The changing shape of the care diamond: The case of child and elderly care in Japan*, UNRISD Gender and Development Programme Paper no 9, Geneva: UNRISD.

Abu-Rayya, H.M. (2011) 'Depression and social involvement among elders', *The Internet Journal of Health*, vol 5, no 1, pp 1–10.

Abu-Sharkh, M. and Gough, I. (2010) 'Global welfare regimes: a cluster analysis', *Global Social Policy*, vol 10, no 1, pp 27–58, DOI: 10.1177/1468018109355035.

Aboderin, I. (2006) *Intergenerational support and old age in Africa*, New Brunswick: Transaction Publishers.

Aboderin, I., Kalache, A., Ben-Shlomo, Y., Lynch, J.W., Yajnik, C.S., Kuh, D. et al (2002) *Life course perspectives on coronary heart disease, stroke and diabetes: Key issues and implications for policy and research*, Geneva: WHO.

Adeyi, O., Smith, O. and Robles, S. (2007) *Public Policy and the challenge of chronic noncommunicable diseases*, Washington, DC: The World Bank.

Agrawal, G. and Arokiasamy, P. (2010) 'Morbidity prevalence and health care utilization among older adults in India', *Journal of Applied Gerontology*, vol 29, no 2, pp 155–79.

Agyei-Mensah, S. and de-Graft Aikins, A. (2010) 'Epidemiological transition and the double burden of disease in Accra, Ghana', *Journal of Urban Health*, vol 87, no 5, pp 879–97.

Allet, D. and Crimmins, E. (2010) 'Epidemiology of ageing', in D. Dannefer and C. Phillipson (eds) *The Sage handbook of social gerontology*, London: Sage, pp 75–95.

Anand, S. (2004) 'The concern for equity in health', in S. Anand, F. Peter and A. Sen (eds) *Public health, ethics and equity*, Oxford: Oxford University Press, pp 15–20.

Anand, S. and Hanson, K. (2006) 'Disability-adjusted life years: a critical review', in S. Anand, F. Peter and A. Sen (eds) *Public health, ethics and equity*, Oxford: Oxford University Press, pp 183–200.

Anderson, T. (2006) 'Policy coherence and conflict of interest: the OECD guidelines on health and poverty', *Critical Public Health*, vol 16, no 3, pp 245–57.

Antonovsky, A. (1979) *Health, stress and coping*, San Francisco: Jossey-Bass.

Antonovsky, A. (1996) 'The salutogenic model as a theory to guide health promotion'. *Health Promotion International,* vol 11, no 1, pp 11-18.

Apt, N.A. (1996) *Coping with old age in a changing Africa*, Aldershot: Avebury.

Ashton, J. and Seymour, H. (1988) *The new public health*, Milton Keynes: Open University Press.

Ayis, S., Gooberman-Hill, R., Bowling, A. and Ebrahim, S. (2006) 'Predicting catastrophic decline in mobility among older people', *Age and Ageing*, vol 35, pp 382–7.

Baars, J. (2006) 'Beyond neomodernism, antimodernism and postmodernism: basic categories for contemporary critical gerontology', in J. Baars, D. Dannefer, C. Phillipson and A. Walker (eds) *Aging globalization and inequality: The new critical gerontology*, New York: Baywood, pp 17-42.

Ballantyne, P.J., Mirza, R.M., Austin, Z., Boon, H.S. and Fisher, J.E. (2011) 'Becoming old as a "pharmaceutical person": negotiation of health and medicines among ethnoculturally diverse older adults', *Canadian Journal on Aging/La Revue Canadienne du Vieillissement*, vol 30, no 2, pp 169–84, DOI:10.1017/S0714980811000110.

Banerji, D. (2008) 'The World Health Organization's decennial ritual of "remembering" the Alma Ata Declaration', *Global Social Policy*, vol 8, no 2, pp 149–52.

Bardage, C., Pluijm, S.M.F., Pedersen, N.L., Dorly, A.E., Deeg, J.H., Jylha, M., Noale, M., Blumstein, T. and Otero, A. (2005) 'Self-rated health among older adults: a cross-national comparison', *European Journal of Ageing*, vol 2, pp 149–58.

Barrientos, A. (2010) 'Protecting capability, eradicating extreme poverty: Chile solidario and the future of social protection', *Journal of Human Development and Capabilities*, vol 11, no 4, pp 579–97.

Batljan, I. and Lagergren, M. (2005) 'Future demand for formal long-term care in Sweden', *European Journal of Ageing*, vol 2, no 3, pp 216–24.

Beaglehole, R. and Bonita, R. (2009) 'Strengthening public health for the new era', in R. Beaglehole and R. Bonita (eds) *Global public health: A new era*, Oxford: Oxford University Press, pp 283-298.

Becker, C.M., Glascoff, M.A. and Felts, W.M. (2010) 'Salutogenesis 30 years later: where do we go from here?', *International Electronic Journal of Health Education*, vol 13, pp 25–32.

Bedford, K. (2010) *Harmonizing global care policy? Care and the Commission on the Status of Women*, UNRISD Gender and Development Programme Paper no 7, Geneva: UNRISD.

Bengston, V.L., Elder, G.H. and Putney, N.M. (2005) 'The lifecourse perspective on ageing: linked lives, timing and history', in M. Johnson (ed) *The Cambridge handbook of ageing*, Cambridge: Cambridge University Press, pp 493–501.

Beresford, P. (2008) *What future for care?*, York: Joseph Rowntree Foundation.

Bern-Klug, M. (2004) 'The ambiguous dying syndrome', *Health and Social Work*, vol 29, no 1, pp 55–65.

Bernard, M. (2000) *Promoting health in old age*, Buckingham: Open University.

Bill and Melinda Gates Foundation (2009) *Malaria: Strategy overview*, http://www.gatesfoundation.org/global-health/Documents/malaria-strategy.pdf.

Billings, J. and Hashem, F. (2009) 'Literature review: salutogenesis and the promotion of positive mental health in older people', presented at the European Union Thematic conference Mental Health and Well-being in Older People – Making it Happen, Madrid, 19–20 April, Brussels: European Communities.

Birn, A.-E., Pillay, Y. and Holtz, T.H. (2009) *Textbook of international health: Global health in a dynamic world*, Oxford: Oxford University Press.

Biswas, P., Kabir, Z.N., Nilsson, J. and Zaman, S. (2006) 'Dynamics of health care seeking behaviour of elderly people in rural Bangladesh', *International Journal of Ageing and Later Life*, vol 1, no 1, pp 69–89.

Bito, S., Matsamura, S., Kagawa Singer, M., Meredit, L.S., Fukuhara, S. and Wenger, N.S. (2007) 'Acculturation and end-of-life decision making: comparison of Japanese and Japanese-American focus groups', *Bioethics*, vol 21, no 5, pp 251–62.

Blane, D. (2006) 'The lifecourse, the social gradient and health', in M. Marmot and R.G. Wilkinson (eds) *Social determinants of health*, Oxford: Oxford University Press, pp 54–77.

Blane, D., Netuveli, G. and Montgomery, S.M. (2008) 'Quality of life, health and physiological status and change at older ages', *Social Science & Medicine*, vol 66, pp 1579–87.

Blaxter, M. (1983) 'The causes of disease: women talking', *Social Science and Medicine*, vol 1, no 2, pp 9–17.

Blaxter, M. (2004) *Health*, Cambridge: Polity.

Bond, J. and Cabrero G.R. (2007) 'Health and dependency in later life', in J. Bond, S. Peace, F. Dittmann-Kohli and G. Westerhof (eds) *Ageing in society: European perspectives on gerontology*, 3rd edn, London: Sage, pp 113-41.

Bond, J. and Corner, L. (2004) *Quality of life and older people*, Buckingham: Open University Press.

Boneham, M.A. and Sixsmith, J.A. (2006) 'The voices of older women in a disadvantaged community: issues of health and social capital', *Social Science & Medicine*, vol 62, pp 269–79.

Bourdieu, P. (1986) 'The forms of capital', in J. Richardson (ed) *Handbook of theory and research for the sociology of education*, New York: Greenwood, pp 241–58.

Bowden, P. (1997) *Caring: Gender-sensitive ethics*, London: Routledge.

Bowling, A. (2005) *Ageing well: Quality of life in old age*, Maidenhead: Open University Press/ McGraw Hill.

Bowling, A. (2009) 'Perceptions of active ageing in Britain: divergences between minority ethnic and whole population samples', *Age and Ageing*, vol 38, pp 703–10.

Bozorgmehr, K. (2010) 'Rethinking the "global", in global health: a dialectic approach', *Globalization and Health*, vol 6, no 1, pp 6–19.

Bradshaw, H.G. and ter Meulen R. (2010) 'A transhumanist faultline around disability: morphological freedom and the obligation to enhance', *Journal of Medicine and Philosophy*, vol 35, no 6, pp 670-684.

Brodsky, J., Habib, J. and Hirschfield, M. (eds) (2003) *Long-term care in developing countries: Ten case studies*, Geneva: WHO and JDC-Brookdale Institute.

Buckner, L. and Yeandle, S. (2011) *Valuing Carers 2011: Calculating the value of carers' support*, London: Carers UK.

Buvinić, M., Médici, A., Fernández, E. and Torres, A.C. (2006) 'Gender differentials in health', in D.T. Jamison, J.G. Breman, A.R. Measham, G. Alleyne, M. Claeson, D.B. Evans, P. Jha, A. Mills and P. Musgrove (eds) *Disease control priorities in developing countries*, 2nd edn, Washington, DC: The World Bank and Oxford University Press, pp 195–210.

Cameron, L.J.H., Kabir, Z.N., Khanam, M.A., Wahlin, A. and Streatfield, P.K. (2010) 'Earning their keep: the productivity of older women and men in rural Bangladesh', *Journal of Cross-Cultural Gerontology*, vol 25, pp 87–103.

Carpenter, M. (2009) 'The capabilities approach and critical social policy: lessons from the majority world?', *Critical Social Policy*, vol 29, pp 357–73.

Caselli, G., Meslé, F. and Vallin, J. (2002) *Epidemiologic transition theory exceptions*, http://www.demogr.mpg.de/Papers/workshops/020619_paper40.pdf.

Cattan, M., White, M., Bond, J. and Learmouth, A. (2005) 'Preventing social isolation and loneliness among older people: a systematic review of health promotion interventions', *Ageing & Society*, vol 25, no 1, pp 41–67.

Chapman, S.A. (2005) 'Theorizing about aging well: constructing a narrative', *Canadian Journal on Aging*, vol 24, no 1, pp 9–18.

Charusheela, S. (2009) 'Social analysis and the capabilities approach: a limit to Martha Nussbaum's universalist ethics', *Cambridge Journal of Economics*, vol 33, pp 1135–1152.

Chazan, M. (2008) 'Seven "deadly" assumptions: unravelling the implications of HIV/AIDS among grandmothers in South Africa and beyond', *Ageing and Society*, vol 28, pp 935–58, DOI:10.1017/S0144686X08007265.

Chou, R.J.A. (2010) 'Willingness to live in eldercare institutions among older adults in urban and rural China: a nationwide study', *Ageing & Society*, vol 30, pp 583–608.

Colebatch, H.K. (2005) 'Policy analysis, policy practice and political science', *Australian Journal of Public Administration*, vol 64, no 3, pp 14–23.

Coleman, P. (2011) *Belief and ageing: Spiritual pathways in later life*, Bristol: The Policy Press.

CSDH (Commission on Social Determinants of Health) (2008) *Closing the gap in a generation: Health equity through action on the social determinants of health. Final report of the Commission on Social Determinants of Health*, Geneva: WHO.

Costa-Font, J. and Toyama, M.G. (2011) 'Does cost-sharing really reduce inappropriate prescriptions among the elderly?', *Health Policy*, vol 101, pp 195–208, DOI:10.1016/j.healthpol.2010.09.001.

Craig, R. and Mindell, J. (eds) (2005) *Health survey for England: Volume 2, Chronic diseases: The health of older people*, London: NatCen.

Crimmins, E.M. (2004) 'Trends in the health of the elderly', *Annual Review of Public Health*, vol, 25, pp 79–98.

Cumming, E. and Henry, W.E. (1961) *Growing old: The process of disengagement*, New York: Basic Books.

Daniels, N. (2008) *Just health: Meeting health needs fairly*, Cambridge: Cambridge University Press.

Daniels, N., Kennedy, B. and Kawachi, I. (2000) *Is inequality bad for our health?* Boston, MA: Beacon Press.

Dannefer, D. (2003) 'Cumulative advantage/disadvantage and the lifecourse: cross-fertilizing age and social science theory', *Journals of Gerontology*, vol 58B, no 96, pp S327–37.

Dannefer, D. and Settersten, R.A. (2010) 'The study of the life course: implications for social gerontology', in D. Dannefer and C. Phillipson (eds) *The Sage handbook of social gerontology*, London and Thousand Oaks: Sage, pp 3–19.

Danyuthasilpe, C., Amnatsatsue, K., Tanasugarn, C. and Kerdmongkol, P. (2009) 'Ways of healthy aging: a case study of elderly people in a northern Thai village', *Health Promotion International*, vol 24, no 4, pp 394–403.

Davey-Smith, G., Frankel, S. and Ebrahim, S. (2000) 'Rationing for health equity: is it necessary?', in G. Davey-Smith (ed) *Health inequalities: Lifecourse approaches*, Bristol: The Policy Press, pp 513-522. Davies, S. and Higginson, I. (2004) *Palliative care: The solid facts*, Copenhagen: WHO.

Day, P., Pearce, J. and Dorling, D. (2008) 'Twelve worlds: a geo-demographic comparison of global inequalities in mortality', *Journal of Epidemiology and Community Health*, vol 62, pp 1002–10.

Deacon, B. (2007) *Global social policy and governance*, London: Sage.

Dean, H. (2009) 'Critiquing capabilities: the distractions of a beguiling concept', *Critical Social Policy*, vol 29, no 2, pp 261–78.

Deeming, C. (2009) '"Active ageing" in practice: a case study in East London, UK', *Policy & Politics*, vol 37, pp 93–111, DOI 10.1332/030557309X397946.

DH (Department of Health) (2011) *Improving the lives of people with long-term conditions*, 14 March, http//:www.healthandcare.dh.gov.uk/improving-the-lives.

Dixon, T., Shaw, M., Frankel, S. and Ebrahim S. (2004) 'Hospital admissions, age and death: a retrospective cohort study', *British Medical Journal*, vol 328, p 1288.

Downs, M. (1997) 'The emergence of the person in dementia research', *Ageing and Society*, vol 17, pp 597–607.

Dummer, T.J.B. and Cook, I.G. (2008) 'Health in China and India: a cross-country comparison in a context of rapid globalisation', *Social Science & Medicine*, vol 67, pp 590–605.

Dyer, S., McDowell, L. and Batnizky, A. (2008) 'Emotional labour/body work: the caring labours of migrants in the UK's National Health Service', *Geoforum*, vol 39, pp 2030–8.

Earle, l. (2007) 'Promoting public health: exploring the issues', in S. Earle, C.E. Lloyd, M. Siddell and S. Spurr (eds) *Theory and research in promoting public health*, London: Open University/Sage, pp 1-36.

Ebrahim, S. (2002) 'The medicalisation of old age: should be encouraged', *British Medical Journal*, vol 324, pp 861–3.

Engelman, M. and Johnson, S. (2007) 'Population aging and international development: addressing competing claims of distributive justice', *Developing World Bioethics*, vol 7, no 1, pp 8–18.

Eriksson, M. and Lindström, B. (2005) 'Validity of Antonovsky's sense of coherence scale: a systematic review', *Journal of Epidemiology and Community Health*, vol 59, no 6, pp 460–6.

Estes, C., Biggs, S. and Phillipson, C. (2003) *Social theory, social policy and ageing: A critical introduction*, Maidenhead: Open University/McGraw Hill.

Eurofamcare Consortium (2006) *Services for supporting family carers of older dependent people in Europe: Characteristics, coverage and usage: the Trans-European Survey Report*, Eurofamcare Consortium, http://www.uke.uni-hamburg.de/eurofamcare/.

European Foresight Monitoring Network (2009) *Healthy ageing and the future of public healthcare systems*, EUR 24044, Brussels: European Commission.

Fernández-Ballesteros, R. (2002) 'Social support and quality of life among older people in Spain', *Journal of Social Issues*, vol 58, no 4, pp 645–59.

Ferri, C.P., Prince, M., Brayne, C., Brodaty, H., Fratiglioni, L., Ganguli, M., Hall, K., Hasegawa, K., Hendrie, H., Huang, Y., Jorm, A., Mathers, C., Menezes, P.R., Rimmer, E. and Scazufca, M. (2005) 'Global prevalence of dementia: a Delphi consensus study', *Lancet*, vol 366, pp 2112–17.

Fisher, B., and Tronto, J.C. (1990). 'Toward a feminist theory of caring', in E. Abel and M. Nelson (eds) *Circles of care: Work and identity in women's lives*, Albany: State University of New York Press, pp 35-62.

Fletcher, A.E. (2007) 'Major eye diseases of later life: cataract and age-related macular degeneration', in A.D. Dangour, E.M.D. Grundy and A.E. Fletcher (eds) *Ageing well: Nutrition, health and social interventions*, Boca Raton, FL: CRC Press, pp 25–34.

Flores, Y.G., Hinton, L., Barker, J.C., Franz, C.E. and Velasquez, A. (2009) 'Beyond familism: a case study of the ethics of care of a Latina caregiver of an elderly parent with dementia', *Health Care for Women International*, vol 30, no 12, pp 1055–72.

Fox, K.R., Stathi, A., McKenna, J. and Davis, M.G. (2007) 'Physical activity and mental well-being in older people participating in the Better Ageing Project', *European Journal of Applied Physiology*, vol 100, no 5, pp 591–602.

Frenk, J., Bobadilla, J.L., Sepulveda, J. and Cervantes, M.L. (1989) 'Health transition in middle-income countries: new challenges for health care', *Health Policy Plan*, vol 4, no 1, pp 29–39.

Fries, J.F. (1980) 'Aging, natural death and the compression of morbidity', *New England Journal of Medicine*, vol 303, pp 130–5.

Fuller, B.G., Williams, J.A.S. and Byles, J.E. (2010) 'Active living – the perception of older people with chronic conditions', *Chronic Illness*, vol 6, pp 294–305.

Giles, J., Wang, D. and Zhao, C. (2010) 'Can China's rural elderly count on support from adult children? Implications of rural-to-urban migration', *Population Ageing*, vol 3, pp 183–204.

Gilleard, C. and Higgs, P. (2000) *Cultures of ageing: Self, citizen and the body*, Harlow: Prentice Hall.

Gilleard, C. and Higgs, P. (2010) 'Aging without agency: theorizing the fourth age', *Aging & Mental Health*, vol 14, no 2, pp 121–8.

Glaser, K. (2004) 'European association for population studies working group on demographic change and care of older people/Institut National D'Études Démographiques: European networks and projects', *European Journal of Ageing*, vol 1, pp 102–5.

Glaser, K., Tomassini, C. and Grundy, E. (2004) 'Revisiting convergence and divergence: support for older people in Europe', *European Journal of Ageing*, vol 1, pp 64-72.

Glendinning, C. and Moran, N. (2009) *Reforming long-term care: Recent lessons from other countries*, York: Social Policy Research Unit, University of York.

Global Forum for Health Research, www.globalforumhealth.org, accessed 11 July 2011.

Global Health Watch (2005) *Global Health Watch 2005–2006: An alternative world health report*, New York: Zed Books.

Gooberman-Hill, R. and Ebrahim, S. (2006) 'Informal care at times of change in health and mobility: a qualitative study', *Age and Ageing*, vol 35, pp 261–6.

Gorard, D.A. (2006) 'Escalating polypharmacy', *QJM: An International Journal of Medicine*, vol 99, pp 797–800, DOI:10.1093/qjmed/hcl109.

Gorman, M. (2002) 'Global ageing: the non-governmental organization role in the developing world', *International Journal of Epidemiology*, vol 31, pp 782–5.

Gott, M., Small, N., Barnes, S., Payne, S. and Seamark, D. (2008) 'Older people's views of a good death in heart failure: implications for palliative care provision', *Social Science and Medicine*, vol 67, pp 1113–21.

Gough, I. (2001) 'Globalization and regional welfare regimes: the East Asian case', *Global Social Policy*, vol 1, no 2, pp 163–90.

Gragnolati, M., Jorgensen, O.H., Rocha, R. and Fruterro, A. (2011) *Growing old in an older Brazil: Implications of population ageing on growth, poverty, public finance and service delivery*, Washington, DC: World Bank.

Gu, D., Zhang, Z. and Zeng, Y. (2009) 'Access to healthcare services makes a difference in healthy longevity among older Chinese adults', *Social Science & Medicine*, vol 68, pp 210–19.

Gu, D., Sautter, J., Huang, C. and Zeng, Y. (2011) 'Health inputs and cumulative health deficits among the older Chinese', *Social Science & Medicine*, vol 72, pp 806–14.

Guardian (2011) 'Philip Morris sues Australian government over tobacco laws', http://www.guardian.co.uk/world/2011/nov/21/philip-morris-australia-tobacco-laws, 21 November.

Hammarström, G. and Torres, S. (2010) 'Being, feeling and acting: a qualitative study of Swedish home-help care recipients' understandings of dependence and independence', *Journal of Aging Studies*, vol 24, pp 75–87.

Harper, S. (2006) *Ageing societies*, London: Hodder Arnold.

Harrington, C. (2001) 'Regulating nursing homes: residential nursing facilities in the United States', *British Medical Journal*, vol 323, pp 507–10.

Hassim, S. and Razavi, S. (2006) 'Gender and social policy in a global context: uncovering the gendered structure of "the social"', in S. Razavi and S. Hassim (eds) *Gender and social policy in a global context: Uncovering the gendered structure of 'the social'*, Basingstoke: UNRISD, Palgrave Macmillan, pp 1–39.

Hein, W. and Kohlmorgen, L. (2008) 'Global health governance: conflicts on global social rights', *Global Social Policy*, vol 8, no 1, pp 80–108.

Held, V. (2006) *The ethics of care: Personal, political and global*, Oxford: Oxford University Press.

HelpAge International (2005) *Ageing and Emergencies' Ageways*, issue 66, London: HelpAge International.

Heywood, F., Oldman, C. and Means R. (2002) *Housing and home in later life*, Buckingham: Open University Press.

Higgs, P. and Rees-Jones, I. (2009) *Medical sociology and old age: Towards a sociology of health in later life*, Abingdon: Routledge.

Higgs, P., Leontowitsch, M., Stevenson, F. and Rees-Jones, I. (2009) 'Not just old and sick – the "will to health" in later life', *Ageing and Society*, vol 29, no 5, pp 687–707.

Hill, M. and Hupe, P. (2002) *Implementing public policy: governance in theory and practice*, 2nd edn, London: Sage.

Hockey, J. and James, A. (2003) *Social identities across the life course*, Basingstoke: Palgrave.

Howse, K. (2006) *Increasing life expectancy and the compression of morbidity: A critical review of the debate*, Working Paper 206, Oxford: Oxford Institute of Ageing, http:www.ageing.ox.ac.uk.

Hui, E.C. (2010) 'The contemporary crisis of health care in China and the role of medical professionalism', *Journal of Medicine and Philosophy*, vol 35, pp 477–92, DOI:10.1093/jmp/jhq031.

Hyder, A.A. and Morrow, R.H. (2006) 'Measures of health and disease in populations', in M.H. Merson, R.E. Black and A.J. Mills (eds) *International public health: Diseases, programs, systems and policies*, 2nd edn, Sudbury, MA: Jones and Bartlett Publishers, pp 1-42.

Innes, A. (2009) *Dementia studies*, London: Sage.

Izuhara, M. (2010) 'New patterns of family reciprocity? Policy challenges in ageing societies', in M. Izuhara (ed) *Ageing and intergenerational relations: Family reciprocity from a global perspective*, Bristol: The Policy Press, pp 149–59.

James, A. and Hockey, J. (2007) *Embodying health identities*, Basingstoke: Palgrave.

Jawad, M.H., Sibai, A.M. and Chaaya, M. (2009) 'Stressful life events and depressive symptoms in a post-war context: which informal support makes a difference?', *Journal of Cross-Cultural Gerontology*, vol 24, no 1, pp 19–32.

Johnson, K.S., Kuchibhatla, M. and Tulsky, J.A. (2009) 'Racial differences in self-reported exposure to information about hospice care', *Journal of Palliative Medicine*, vol 12, no 10, pp 921–7.

Johnson, M. (forthcoming) 'Biography and generation: spiritual and biographical pain at the end of life', in M. Silverstein and R. Giarruso (eds) *From generation to generation: Continuities and discontinuities in intergenerational relationships*, Baltimore, MD: Johns Hopkins University Press.

Jolanki, O.H. (2009) 'Agency in talk about old age and health', *Journal of Aging Studies*, vol 23, pp 215–226.

Kalache, A. (2009) 'Towards age-friendly societies: from research to policy, from policy to society', *International Journal of Integrated Care*, vol 9, pp 1-2.

Kalache, A. and Keller, I. (1999) 'The WHO perspective on active ageing', *Promotion & Education*, vol 6, no 4, pp 20–3.

Kanchanachitra, C., Lindelow, M., Johnston, T., Hanvoravongchai, P., Lorenzo, F.M., Huong, L.N., Wilopo, S.A. and dela Rosa, J.F. (2011) 'Human resources for health in southeast Asia: shortages, distributional challenges, and international trade in health services', *Lancet*, vol 377, pp 769–81, DOI:10.1016/S0140–6736(10)62035–1.

Katz, A.R. (2009) 'Prospects for a genuine revival of primary health care – through the visible hand of social justice rather than the invisible hand of the market: part 1', *International Journal of Health Services*, vol 39, no 3, pp 567–85.

Katz, S. (2006) 'From chronology to functionality: critical reflections on the gerontology of the body', in J. Baars, D. Dannefer, C. Phillipson and A. Walker (eds) *Aging, globalization and inequality: The new critical gerontology*, New York: Baywood, pp 123–37.

Keating, N. (2005) 'Introduction: perspectives on healthy aging', *Canadian Journal on Aging*, vol 24, no 1, pp 3–4.

Keller, H.H., Dwyer, J.J.M., Edwards, V., Senson, C. and Edward, H.G. (2007) 'Food security in older adults: community service provider perceptions of their roles', *Canadian Journal on Aging*, vol 26, pp 317–28.

Kickbusch, I. (2010) 'Health in all policies: where to from here?', *Health Promotion International*, vol 25, no 3, pp 261–4.

Kinsella, K. and Velkoff, V.A. (2001) *An aging world: 2001*, US Census Bureau, Series P95/01–1, Washington, DC: US Government Printing Office.

Kittay, E.F. (1999) *Love's labor: Essays on women, equality and dependency*, New York: Routledge.

Kittay, E.F., Jennings, B. and Wasunna, A.A. (2005) 'Dependency, difference and the global ethic of longterm care', *Journal of Political Philosophy*, vol 13, no 4, pp 443–69.

Kitwood, T. (1997) *Dementia reconsidered*, Buckingham: Open University Press.

Knapp, M., Comas-Herrera, A., Somani, A. and Banerjee, S. (2007) *Dementia: International comparisons*, A summary report for the Audit Office, London: LSE, PSSRU.

Kofman, E. and Raghuram, P. (2009) *The implications of migration for gender and care regimes in the South*, UNRISD Social Policy and Development Programme Paper Number 41, Geneva: UNRISD.

Kreager, P. and Schröder-Butterfill, E. (2007) 'Gaps in the family networks of older people in three Indonesian communities', *Journal of Cross-Cultural Gerontology*, vol 22, pp 1–25.

Kruk, M.E., Porignon, D., Rockers, P.C. and Van Lerberghe, W. (2010) 'The contribution of primary care to health and health systems in low- and middle-income countries: a critical review of major primary care initiatives', *Social Science and Medicine*, vol 70, pp 904–11.

Kuh, D. and Davey-Smith, G. (2004) 'The life course and adult chronic disease: an historical perspective with particular reference to coronary heart disease', in D. Kuh and Y. Ben-Shlomo (eds) *A lifecourse approach to chronic disease epidemiology*, 2nd edn, Oxford: Oxford University Press, pp 15- 37.

Kuh, D. and Ben-Shlomo, Y. (2004) 'Introduction', in D. Kuh and Y. Ben-Shlomo (eds) *A lifecourse approach to chronic disease epidemiology*, 2nd edn, Oxford: Oxford University Press, pp 3-14.

Kwok, T., Twinn, S. and Yan, E. (2007) 'The attitudes of Chinese family caregivers of older people with dementia towards life sustaining treatments', *Journal of Advanced Nursing*, vol 58, no 3, pp 256–62.

Labonté, R. (2008) 'Global health in public policy: finding the right frame?' *Critical Public Health*, vol 18, no 4, pp 467–82.

Labonté, R. and Schrecker, T. (2009) 'Introduction: globalization's challenge to people's health', in R. Labonte, T. Schrecker, C. Packer and V. Runnels (eds) *Globalization and health: Pathways, evidence and policy*, London: Routledge, pp 1-33.

Labonté, R., Mohindra, K.S. and Lencucha, R. (2011) 'Framing international trade and chronic disease', *Globalization and Health*, http://www.globalizationandhealth.com/content/7/1/21.

Lalonde, M. (1974) *A new perspective on the health of Canadians* (The Lalonde Report), Ottawa: Government of Canada.

Land, H. (1978) 'Who cares for the family?', *Journal of Social Policy*, vol 7, no 3, pp 357–84.

Land, H. and Himmelweit, S. (2010) *Who cares, who pays? A report on personalisation in social care prepared for UNISON*, www.unison.org.uk/million.

Laslett, P. (1989) *A fresh map of life: The emergence of the third age*, Cambridge: MA: Harvard University Press.

Lawton, J. (2000) 'Colonising the future: temporal perceptions and health-relevant behaviours across the adult lifecourse', *Sociology of Health & Illness*, vol 24, no 6, pp 714–33.

Lee, K., Koivusalo, M., Ollila, E., Labonté, R., Schuftan, C. and Woodwards, D. (2009) 'Global governance for health', in R. Labonté, T. Schrecker, C. Packer and V. Runnels (eds) *Globalization and health: Pathways, evidence and policy*, New York: Routledge, pp 289-316.

Leonard, L. (2005) 'Where there is no state: household strategies for the management of illness in Chad', *Social Science & Medicine*, vol 61, pp 229–43.

Lewis, J. and Giullari, S. (2006) 'The adult-worker-model family and gender equality: principles to enable the valuing and sharing of care', in S. Razavi and S. Hassim (eds) *Gender and social policy in a global context: Uncovering the gendered structure of 'the social'*, Basingstoke: UNRISD, Palgrave, pp 173–192..

Lindstrom, B. and Eriksson M. (2006) 'Contextualising salutogenesis and Antonovsky in public health development', *Health Promotion International*, vol 23, no 3,pp 238-244.

Lloyd, L. (2004) 'Mortality and morality: ageing and the ethics of care', *Ageing & Society*, vol 24, no 2, pp 235–56.

Lloyd, L. (2010) 'The individual in social care: the ethics of care and the "personalisation agenda" in services for older people in England', *Ethics and Social Welfare*, vol 4, no 2, pp 188–200.

Lloyd, L., White, K. and Sutton, E. (2011) 'Researching the end-of-life in old age: cultural, ethical and methodological issues', *Ageing & Society*, vol 31, no 3, pp 386–407.

Lloyd-Sherlock, P. (2002) 'Nussbaum, capabilities and older people', *Journal of International Development*, vol 14, pp 1163–73.

Lloyd-Sherlock, P. (2006) 'When social health insurance goes wrong: lessons from Argentina and Mexico', *Social Policy & Administration*, vol 40, no 4, pp 353–68.

Lloyd-Sherlock, P. (2010) *Population ageing and international development: From generalisation to evidence*, Bristol: The Policy Press.

Loewenson, R. (2008) 'Global social policy forum: introduction: tackling health worker migration – addressing the fault lines of policy incoherence', *Global Social Policy*, vol 8, no 1, pp 5–7.

Lopez, A.D., Begg, S. and Bos, E. (2006) 'Demographic and epidemiological characteristics of major regions, 1990–2001', in A.D. Lopez, C.D. Mathers, M. Ezzati, D.T. Jamison and C.J.L. Murray (eds) *Global burden of disease and risk factors*, Washington, DC: The World Bank and Oxford University Press, pp 17–44.

Lumme-Sandt, K., Hervonen, A. and Jylhä, M. (2000) 'Interpretative repertoires of medication among the oldest-old', *Social Science & Medicine*, vol 50, pp 1843–50.

Lund, F. (2006) 'Working people and access to social protection', in S. Razavi and S. Hassim (eds) *Gender and social policy in a global context: Uncovering the gendered structure of 'the social'*, Basingstoke: UNRISD, Palgrave, pp 217–33.

Lupton, D. (1995) *The imperative of health: Public health and the regulated body*, London: Sage.

Lutz, W., Sanderson, W.C. and Scherbov, S. (2008) 'Global and regional population ageing: how certain are we of its dimensions?', *Population Ageing*, vol 1, pp 75–97.

McFarlane, A. and Kelleher, C. (2002) 'Concepts of illness causation and attitudes to health care among older people in the Republic of Ireland', *Social Science & Medicine*, vol 54, pp 1389–400.

McIntyre, D. (2004) 'Health policy and older people in Africa', in P. Lloyd-Sherlock (ed) *Living longer: Ageing development and social protection*, London: Zed Books, pp 160-183.

McKee, K.J. and Samuelsson, G. (2000) 'Macro-social influences on autonomy versus dependency in the oldest old', P. Martin, C. Rott, B. Hagberg and K. Morgan (eds) *Centenarians: Autonomy versus dependence in the oldest old*, New York: Springer, pp 115–27.

McKeown, T. (1976) *The role of medicine*, London: Nuffield Provincial Hospital Trust.

Mackintosh, M. and Tibandebage, P. (2006) 'Gender and health sector reform: perspectives on African experience', in S. Razavi and S. Hassim (eds) *Gender and social policy in a global context: Uncovering the gendered structure of 'the social'*, Basingstoke: UNRISD, Palgrave, pp 237–57.

Mackintosh, M., Chauduri, S and Phares, G.M.M. (2011) ';Can NGOs regulate medicines markets? Social enterprise in wholesaling, and access to essential medicines', *Globalization and Health*, vol 7, no 4, pp 1-13.

McMichael, A. and Beaglehole, R. (2009) 'The global context for public health', in R. Beaglehole and R. Bonita (eds) *Global public health: A new era*, Oxford: Oxford University Press, pp 1-22..

McMunn, A., Nazroo, J. and Breeze, E. (2009) 'Inequalities in health at older ages: a longitudinal investigation of the onset of illness and survival effects in England', *Age and Ageing*, vol 38, pp 181–7.

MacNicol, J. (2006) *Age discrimination: An historical and contemporary analysis*, Cambridge: Cambridge University Press.

Mahon, R. and Robinson, F. (2011a) 'Introduction', in R. Mahon and F. Robinson (eds) *Feminist ethics and social policy: Towards a new global political economy of care*, Vancouver: UBC Press, pp 1–17.

Mahon, R. and Robinson, F. (2011b) 'Conclusion: integrating the ethics and social politics of care', in R. Mahon and F. Robinson (eds) *Feminist ethics and social policy: Towards a new global political economy of care*, Vancouver: UBC Press, pp 178–83.

Manthorpe, J. and Iliffe, S. (2005) *Depression in later life*, London: Jessica Kingsley.

Margrain, T.H. and Boulton, M. (2005) 'Sensory impairment', in M. Johnson (ed) *The Cambridge handbook of age and ageing*, Cambridge: Cambridge University Press, pp 121–30.

Marmot, M. (2005) 'Social determinants of health inequalities', *Lancet*, vol 365, pp 1099–104.

Mathers, C.D., Sadana, R., Salomon, J.A., Murray, C.J.L. and Lopez, A.D. (2001) 'Healthy life expectancy in 191 countries, 1999', *Lancet*, vol 357, pp 1685–91.

Means, R. (2007) '*The re-medicalisation of later life'*, in M. Bernard and T. Scharf (eds) *Critical perspectives on ageing societies*, Bristol: The Policy Press, pp 47-58.

Mechanic, D. (1968) *Medical sociology*, New York: Free Press.

Meinow, B., Parker, M.G., Kåreholt, I. and Thorslund, M. (2006) 'Complex health problems in the oldest old in Sweden 1992–2002', *European Journal of Ageing*, vol 3, pp 98–106.

Mestheneos, E. and Triantafillou, J. (2005) 'Supporting family carers of older people in Europe: a pan-European background', in H. Dohner and C. Kofahl (eds) *Supporting family carers of older people in Europe – empirical evidence, policy trends and future perspectives*, eurofamcare, http://www.uke.uni-hamburg.de/eurofamcare.

Metz, D. and Underwood M. (2005) *Older, richer, fitter: Identifynig the customer needs of Britain's ageing population*, London: Age Concern.

Mini, G.K. (2009) 'Socioeconomic and demographic diversity in the health status of elderly people in a transitional society, Kerala, India', *Journal of Biosocial Science*, vol 41, pp 457–67.

Mkandawire, T. (2001) *Social policy in a development context*, UNRISD Social Policy and Development Programme Paper Number 7, Geneva: UNRISD.

Morgan, A. and Ziglio, E. (2007) 'Revitalising the evidence base for public health: an assets model', *Health Promotion & Education*, vol 14, no 2 (supplement), pp 17–22.

Mudege, N.N. and Ezeh, A.C. (2009) 'Gender, aging, poverty and health: survival strategies of older men and women in Nairobi slums', *Journal of Aging Studies*, vol 23, no 4, pp 245–57.

Murray, J., Banerjee, S., Byng, R., Tylee, A., Bhugra, D. and Macdonald, A. (2005) 'Primary care professionals' perceptions of depression in older people: a qualitative study', *Social Science and Medicine*, vol 63, pp 1363–73.

Mykytyn, C.E. (2008) 'Medicalizing the optimal: anti-aging medicine and the quandary of intervention', *Journal of Aging Studies*, vol 22, no 4, pp 313–21.

Navarro, V. (2007) 'Neoliberalism as a class ideology; or, the political causes of the growth of inequalities', *International Journal of Health Services*, vol 37, no 1, pp 47–62.

Navarro, V. (2008) 'Neoliberalism and its consequences: The world health situation since Alma Ata', *Global Social Policy*, vol 8, no 2, pp 152–5.

Nettleton, S. (2006) *Sociology of health and illness*, 2nd edn, Cambridge: Polity Press.

Nolte, E. and McKee, M. (2008a) *Caring for people with chronic conditions: A health system perspective*, Maidenhead: Open University Press.

Nolte, E. and McKee, M. (2008b) 'Making it happen', *Caring for people with chronic conditions: A health system perspective*, Maidenhead: Open University Press, pp 222-244.

Nussbaum, M. (2000) *Women and human development: The capabilities approach*, Cambridge: Cambridge University Press.

Nyqvist, F., Gustavsson, J. and Gustafson, Y. (2006) 'Social capital and health in the oldest old: the Umeå 85+ study', *International Journal of Ageing and Later Life*, vol 1, no 1, pp 91–114.

Nzegwu, N. (1995) 'Recovering Igbo traditions: a case for indigenous women's organizations in development', in M.C. Nussbaum, and J. Glover (eds), *Women, culture, and development*, Oxford: Clarendon Press, pp 444-465.

Ochiai, E. (2009) 'Care diamonds and welfare regimes in east and south-east Asian societies: bridging family and welfare sociology', *International Journal of Japanese Sociology*, vol 18, pp 60–78.

OECD (2005) *Long-term care for older people*, The OECD Health Project, Paris: OECD.

Ofstedal, M.B., Zimmer, Z., Hermalin, A.I., Chan, A., Chuang, Y.L., Natividad, J. and Tang, Z. (2007) 'Short-term trends in functional limitation and disability among older Asians: a comparison of five Asian settings', *Journal of Cross-Cultural Gerontology*, vol, 22, pp 243–61.

Ogg, J. (2005) *Heatwave: Implications of the 2003 French heatwave for the social care of older people*, Young Foundation Working Paper No 2, London: The Young Foundation.

Oliveira-Cruz, V., Hanson, K. and Mills, A. (2003) 'Approaches to overcoming constraints to effective service delivery: a review of the evidence', *Journal of International Development* vol 15, pp 41-65.

Omran, A.R. (2005) 'The epidemiologic transition: a theory of the epidemiology of population change', *Milbank Quarterly*, vol 83, no 4, pp 731–57.

Orenstein, M.A. (2005) 'The new pension reform as global policy', *Global Social Policy*, vol 5, no 2, pp 175–202.

Oxley, H. (2009) *Policies for healthy ageing: An overview*, OECD Health Working Papers no 42, Paris: OECD.

Palier, B. and Sykes, R. (2001) 'Challenges and change: issues and perspectives in the analysis of globalization and the European welfare state', in R. Sykes, B. Palier and P.M. Prior (eds) *Globalization and European welfare states*, Basingstoke: Palgrave, pp 1-16.

Palloni, A. and McEniry, M. (2007) 'Aging and health status of elderly in Latin America and the Caribbean: preliminary findings', *Journal of Cross-Cultural Gerontology*, vol 22, pp 263–85.

Patel, V., Fisher, A.J. and Cohen, A. (2006) 'Mental health', in M.H. Merson, R.E. Black and A.J. Mills (eds) *International public health: Diseases, programs, systems and policies.* 2nd edn, Sudbury, MA: Jones and Bartlett Publishers, pp 355-83.

Phillipson, C. (2006) 'Aging and globalization: Issues for critical gerontology and political economy', in J. Baars, D. Dannefer, C. Phillipson and A. Walker (eds) *Aging, globalization and inequality*, New York: Baywood Publishing Company.

Plath D. (2009) 'International policy perspectives on independence in old age', *Journal of Aging and Social Policy*, vol 21, no 2, pp 209–23.

Pomerleau, J. Knai, C. and Nolte, E. (2008) 'The burden of chronic disease in Europe', in E. Nolte and M. McKee (eds) *Caring for people with chronic conditions: A health systems perspective*, Maidenhead: Open University Press, pp 15-42.

Pond, B. and McPake, B. (2006) The health migration crisis: the role of four Organisation for Economic Cooperation and Development countries', *Lancet*, vol 367, pp 1448–55, DOI:10.1016/S0140-6736(06)68346–3.

Prince, M., Acosta, D., Albanese, E., Arizaga, R., Ferri, C.P., Guerra, M., Huang, Y., Jacob, K.S., Jimenez-Velazquez, I.Z., Rodriguez, J.L., Salas, A., Sosa, A.L., Sousa, R., Uwakwe, R., van der Poel, R., Williams, J. and Wortmann, M. (2008) 'Ageing and dementia in low and middle income countries – using research to engage with public and policy makers', *International Review of Psychiatry*, vol 20, no 4, pp 332–43.

Prior, L., Chun, P.L. and Huat, S.B. (2002) 'Beliefs and accounts of illness: views from two Cantonese communities in England', in S. Nettleton and U. Gustaffson (eds) *The sociology of health and illness reader*, Cambridge: Polity Press, pp 162 -173.

Prus, S. (2003) 'A lifecourse perspective on the relationship between socioeconomic status and health: testing the divergence hypothesis', *Canadian Journal on Aging*, vol 23 (supplement), pp 145–53.

Putnam, D. (2000) *Bowling alone: The collapse and revival of American community*, New York: Simon & Schuster.

Razavi, S. (2007) *The political and social economy of care in a development context: Conceptual issues, research questions and policy options*, UNRISD Gender and Development Programme Paper Number 3, Geneva: UNRISD.

Redfoot, D.L. and Houser, A.N. (2008) 'The international migration of nurses in long-term care', *Journal of Aging & Social Policy*, vol 20, no 2, pp 259–75.

Rifkin, S.B. and Walt, G. (1986) 'Why health improves: defining the issues concerning "comprehensive primary health care" and "selective primary health care"', *Social Science & Medicine*, vol 23, no 6, pp 559–66.

Ritsatakis, A. (ed) (2008) *Demystifying the myths of ageing*, Copenhagen: WHO Regional Office for Europe.

Robinson, F. (2010) 'After liberalism in world politics: towards an international political theory of care', *Ethics and Social Welfare*, vol 4, no 2 pp 130-44.

Rockwood, K. (2005) 'What would make a definition of frailty successful?', *Age and Ageing*, vol 34, pp 432–4.

Rozario, P.A. and Hong, S.I. (2011) 'Doing it right by your parents: a political economy examination of the Maintenance of Parents Act of 1995', *Critical Social Policy*, vol 20, no 10, pp 1–21.

Ruger, J.P. (2010) *Health and social justice*, Oxford: Oxford University Press.

Rummery, K. (2009) 'A comparative discussion of the gendered implications of cash-for-care schemes: markets, independence and social citizenship in crisis'? *Social Policy and Administration*, vol 43, no 6, pp 643–8, DOI: 10.1111/j.1467–9515.2009.00685.x.

Ryff, C.D. and Singer, B. (1998) 'The contours of positive human health', *Psychological Inquiry*, vol 9, no 1, pp 1–28.

Ryff, C.D., Singer, B.H. and Love, G.D. (2004) 'Positive health: connecting well-being with biology', *Philosophical Transactions of The Royal Society B*, vol 359, pp 1383–94.

Saltman, R.B., Dubois, H.F.W. and Chawla, M. (2006) 'The impact of aging on long-term care in Europe and some policy responses', *International Journal of Health Service*, vol 36, no 4, pp 719–46.

Sanders, C., Donovan, J. and Dieppe, P. (2002) 'The significance and consequences of having painful and disabled joints in older age: co-existing accounts of normal and disrupted biographies', *Sociology of Health and Illness*, vol 24, no 2, pp 227–53.

Schnittker, J. (2005) 'Chronic illness and depressive symptoms in late life', *Social Science & Medicine*, vol 60, pp 13–23.

Schrecker, T., Chapman, A.R., Labonté, R. and De Vogli, R. (2010) 'Advancing health equity in the global marketplace: how human rights can help', *Social Science & Medicine*, vol 71, pp 1520–6.

Seale, C. and van der Geest, S. (2004) 'Good and bad death: introduction', *Social Science and Medicine,* vol 58, no 5, pp 883–5.

Segall, S. (2007) 'Is health care (still) special?', *Journal of Political Philosophy*, vol 15, no 3, pp 342–61.

Sen, A. (1999) *Development as freedom*, New York: Knopf.

Sen, A. (2004) 'Why health equity?', in S. Anand, F. Peter and A. Sen (eds) *Public health, ethics and equity*, Oxford: Oxford University Press, pp 21–34..

Sevenhuijsen, S. (1998) *Citizenship and the ethics of care: Feminist considerations on justice, morality and politics*, London: Routledge.

Seymour, J., Gott, M., Bellamy, G., Ahmedzai, S.H. and Clark, D. (2004) 'Planning for the end-of-life: the views of older people about advance care statements', *Social Science and Medicine*, vol 59, no 1, pp 57–68.

Shakespeare, T. (2006) *Disability rights and wrongs*, Abingdon: Routledge.

Shanmugasundaram, S., Chapman Y. and O'Connor, M. (2006) 'Development of palliative care in India: an overview', *Journal of Nursing Practice*, vol 12, pp 241–6.

Sidorenko, A. and Walker, A. (2004) The Madrid International Plan of Action on Ageing: from conception to implementation', *Ageing and Society*, vol 24, pp 147–65.

Silva, H.T., De Paepe, P., Soors, W., Lanza, O.V., Closon, M.C., Van Dessel, P. and Unger, J.P. (2011) 'Revisiting health policy and the World Bank in Bolivia', *Global Social Policy*, vol 11, no 1, pp 22–44.

Soubbotina, T.P. (2004) *Beyond economic growth: An introduction to sustainable development,* 2nd edn, Washington, DC: The World Bank.

Staehelin, H.B. (2005) 'Promoting health and wellbeing in later life', in M. Johnson (ed) *The Cambridge Handbook of Age and Ageing*, Cambridge: Cambridge University Press, pp 165-179.

Stenner, P., McFarquhar, T. and Bowling, A. (2011) 'Older people and "active ageing": subjective aspects of ageing actively', *Journal of Health Psychology*, vol 16, no 3, pp 467–77.

Sukarsono, A. and Wulandari, F. (2007) 'Indonesia wants fair deal on H5N1 vaccine', Global Health Council news item, 15 February, www.globalhealth.org.

Thomas, C. (2004) 'How is disability understood?' *Disability and Society*, vol 19, no 6, pp 563–8.

Torres, S. and Hammarström, G. (2009) 'Successful aging as an oxymoron: older people – with and without home-help care – talk about what aging well means to them', *International Journal of Ageing and Later Life*, vol 4, no 1, pp 23–54.

Tronto, J. (1993) *Moral boundaries: A political argument for an ethic of care*, New York: Routledge.

Twigg, J. (2002) 'The body in social policy: mapping a territory', *Journal of Social Policy*, vol 31, no 3, pp 421–39.

Twigg, J. (2006) *The body in health and social care*, Basingstoke: Palgrave.

UN (United Nations) (1983) *The Vienna Plan of Action on Ageing*, New York: UN.

UN (2007) *World Economic and Social Survey 2007: Development in an ageing world*, New York: UN.

UN (2008) *The Madrid International Plan of Action on Ageing: Guiding framework and toolkit for practitioners and policy makers*, http://www.un.org/ageing/documents/building_natl_capacity/guiding.pdf.

UN (2009) *Report of expert group meeting: Rights of older persons*, Division of Social Policy and Development, Programme on Ageing, New York: United Nations.

UN (2010a) *World population ageing 2009*, New York: United Nations.

UN (2010b) *Human Development Report 2010. The real wealth of nations: Pathways to human development*, New York: United Nations.

Van der Geest, S. (2004) 'Dying peacefully: considering good death and bad death in Kwahu-Tafo, Ghana', *Social Science and Medicine*, 58:899-911 .

Van Gool, C.H., Kempen, G.I.J.M., Pennix, B.W.J.H., Deeg, D.J.H., Beekman, A.T.F. and van Eijk, J.Th.M. (2005) 'Impact of depression on disablement in late middle aged and older persons: results from the Longitudinal Aging Study Amsterdam', *Social Science and Medicine*, vol 60, pp 25–36.

Vera-Sanso, P. (2006) 'Experiences in old age: a south Indian example of how functional age is socially structured', *Oxford Development Studies Journal*, vol 34, no 4, pp 457–72.

Victor, C.R. (2010) *Ageing health and care*, Bristol: The Policy Press.

Vidovićová, L. (2005) 'To be active or not to be active, that is the question: the preference model of activity in advanced age', *Ageing International*, vol 30, no 4, pp 343–62.

Vincent, J.A. (2003) 'What is at stake in the "war on anti-ageing medicine"?', *Ageing and Society*, vol 23, pp 675–84.

Vincent, J.A. (2006a) 'Globalization and critical theory: political economy of world population issues', in J. Baars, D. Dannefer, C. Phillipson and A. Walker (eds) *Aging, globalization and inequality: The new critical gerontology*, New York: Baywood, pp 245-272.

Vincent, J.A. (2006b) 'Ageing contested: anti-ageing science and the cultural construction of old age', *Sociology*, vol 40, no 4, pp 681–98.

Waerness, K. (2001) 'Social research, political theory and the ethics of care', *Research Review (New Series)*, vol 17, no 1, pp 5–16.

Wahlin, Å., Anstey, K.J., McDonald, S.W.S., Ahmed, S.M., Kivipelto, M., Kunnukattil, K.S.S., Mai, T.T., Nilsson, L.G., Streatfield, P.K., van Boxtel, M.P.J. and Kabir, Z.N. (2008) 'The International Network on Public Health and Aging (INOPA): introducing a life course perspective to the public health agenda', *Journal of Cross-Cultural Gerontology*, vol 23, pp 97–105.

Walker, A. (2009) 'Commentary: the emergence and application of active aging in Europe', *Journal of Aging & Social Policy*, vol 21, no 1, pp 75–93.

Walter, T. (2009) 'Historical and cultural variants on the good death', *British Medical Journal*, vol 327, no 7408, pp 218–20.

Westendorp, R.G.J. and Kirkwood, T.B.L. (2007) 'The biology of ageing', in J. Bond, S. Peace, F. Dittmann-Kohli and J. Westerhof (eds) *Ageing in Society*, 3rd edn, London: Sage.

WHO (World Health Organization) (1978) *Alma Ata 1977, primary health care*, Geneva: UNICEF.

WHO (1981) *Global strategy for health for all by the year 2000*, Geneva: WHO.

WHO (1986) *Ottawa Charter for Health Promotion: First international conference on health promotion, Ottawa, 21 November 1986*, Geneva: WHO.

WHO (1998) *Life in the 21st century: A vision for all*, The World Health Report 1998, Geneva: WHO, chapter 3, 'Health across the lifespan'.

WHO (2001) *Towards a common language for functioning, disability and health: ICF*, Geneva: WHO.

WHO (2002a) *WHO traditional medicines strategy 2002–2005*, Geneva: WHO.

WHO (2002b) *Active ageing: A policy framework*, Geneva: WHO.

WHO (2002c) *The Toronto Declaration on the Global Prevention of Elder Abuse*, Geneva: WHO.

WHO (2002d) *Innovative Care for Chronic Conditions: Building Blocks for Action*, Geneva, WHO.

WHO (2003a) *The World Health Report 2003: Shaping the future*, Geneva: WHO.

WHO (2003b) *What are the main risk factors for disability in old age and how can disability be prevented?*, Health Evidence Network, European Region WHO.

WHO (2004a) *Review of traditional medicine in the South-East Asia region: Report of the regional working group meeting New Delhi, India, 16–17 August 2004*, New Delhi: WHO, Regional Office for South-East Asia.

WHO (2004b) *Towards age-friendly primary health care*, Geneva: WHO.

WHO (2007a) *Women, ageing and health: A framework for action: focus on gender*, Geneva: WHO.

WHO (2007b) *Global age-friendly cities: A guide*, Geneva: WHO.

WHO (2008a) *The World Health Report 2008: Primary health care: now more than ever*, Geneva: WHO.

WHO (2008b) *The Global Burden of Disease: 2004 Update*, Geneva, WHO.

WHO (2008c) *2008–2013 Action plan for the global strategy for the prevention and control of noncommunicable diseases*, Geneva: WHO.

WHO (2009) *Women and health: Today's evidence, tomorrow's agenda*, Geneva: WHO.

WHO (2010) *Health systems financing: The path to universal coverage*, World Health Report, Geneva: WHO.

WHO and International Agency for the Prevention of Blindness (2007) *Global initiative for the elimination of avoidable blindness: Action plan 2006–2011 (Vision 2020: the right to sight)*, Geneva: WHO.

Wilkinson, K., Martin, I.C., Gough, M.J., Stewart, J.A.D., Lucas, S.B., Freeth, H., Bull, B. and Mason, M. (2010) *An age old problem: A review of the care received by elderly patients undergoing surgery*, London: National Confidential Enquiry into Patient Outcome and Death.

Wilkinson, R. and Pickett, K. (2009) *The spirit level: Why more equal societies almost always do better*, London: Allen Lane.

Williams, F. (2010) *Claiming and framing in the making of care policies: The recognition and redistribution of care*, Gender and Development Programme Paper 13, United Nations Research Institute for social Development (UNRISD), Geneva: United Nations.

Williams, R. (1990) *A protestant legacy*, Oxford: Clarendon Press.

Wilson, G. (2006) 'Local culture, globalization and policy outcomes: an example from long-term care', *Global Social Policy*, vol 6, no 3, pp 288–303.

Wimo, A., Winblad, B. and Jonsson, L. (2007) 'An estimate of the total worldwide societal costs of dementia in 2005', *Alzheimer's and Dementia* vol 3, pp 81-91.

World Bank (1993) *World Development Report 1993: Investing in health*, Oxford: Oxford University Press.

World Bank (1994) *Averting the old age crisis,* Oxford: Oxford University Press.

World Bank (2002) *The policy roots of economic crisis and poverty*, Washington, DC: World Bank.

World Bank (2006) *Equity and development*, Washington, DC: World Bank.

World Bank (2010) *The MDGs after the crisis*, Global Monitoring Report, Washington, DC: World Bank.

Wray, S. (2007) 'Women making sense of midlife: ethnic and cultural diversity', *Journal of Aging Studies*, vol 21, pp 31–42.

Yach, D. and Beaglehole, R. (2004) 'Globalization of risks for chronic diseases demands global solutions', *Perspectives on Global Development and Technology*, vol 3, nos 1/2, pp 213–33.

Yach, D., Hawkes, C., Gould, C.L. and Hofman, K.J. (2004) 'The global burden of chronic diseases: overcoming impediments to prevention and control', *Journal of the American Medical Association*, vol 291, no 21, pp 2616–22.

Yach, D., Hawkes, C., Epping-Jordan, J.E. and Steyn, K. (2006) 'Chronic diseases and risks', in M.H. Merson, R.E. Black and A.J. Mills (eds) *International public health: Diseases, programs, systems and policies*, 2nd edn, Sudbury, MA: Jones and Bartlett, pp 273-313.

Yeates, N. (2004) 'Global care chains: critical reflections and lines of inquiry', *International Feminist Journal of Politics*, vol 6, no 3, pp 364–91.

Yeates, N. (2005) '*Globalization' and social policy in a development context: Regional responses*, Social Policy and Development Programme Paper no 18, Geneva: UNRISD.

Yeoh, B.S.A. and Huang, S. (2010) 'Foreign domestic workers and home-based care for elders in Singapore', *Journal of Aging & Social Policy*, vol 22, no 1, pp 69–88.

Yount, K.M., Agree, E.M. and Rebellon, C. (2004) 'Gender and use of health care among older adults in Egypt and Tunisia', *Social Science & Medicine*, vol 59, pp 2479–97.

Zhan, H.J. and Montgomery, R.J.V. (2003) 'Gender and elder care in China: the influence of filial piety and structural constraints', *Gender & Society*, vol 17, no 2, pp 209–29.

Zhang, Z., Gu, D. and Hayward, M.D. (2010) 'Childhood nutritional deprivation and cognitive impairment among older Chinese people', *Social Science and Medicine*, vol 71, pp 941–9.

Index

A

Abe, A.K. 51
Aboderin, I. 122-3, 137
Aboderin, I. et al 41, 98
Abu-Rayya, H.M. 106
Abu-Sharkh, M. and Gough, I. 91
abuse of older people 6, 120-1
access to healthcare 96-7
  age barriers 95-101
  role of NGOs 94
'active ageing' 80-5
  key principles 83
  vs. equity of resource allocations 137-9
  see also healthy ageing
Adeyi, O. et al 53, 69, 90, 107
Advance Directives 116-17
Africa (sub-Saharan)
  childcare provisions by grandparents 7, 40-1, 86-7, 119, 132
  dementia prevalence data 104
  economic data and life expectancy trends 7, 14-15
  morbidity trends 16, 17-18, 127
  population ageing 23
  role of World Bank 60
  trends in family-based care 122
Age Concern England 43
age-based rationing policies 98-101
  'life-span account' approaches 65-6
  values-based approaches 64-6
'age-friendliness' (WHO) 59-60, 70
ageing
  characteristic features 7
  cultural aspects 36-7, 82, 84-5
  definitions and meanings 11-13
  dominant policy discourses 50-1
  healthcare needs of older people 102-3
  influencing factors and determinants 76-9
  life expectancy trends 1-3, 13-15
  lifecourse approaches 7-8, 41-5
  measurement 12-13
  medicalisation processes 28, 89, 100, 108-9, 132

premature 76-7
risk discourses 3, 49-50
social constructions of 49
stereotypes 76
third age/fourth age dichotomy 43-5
see also 'health' conceptualisations
ageism 76, 98-101
agency *see* 'choice' and agency discourses
Agrawal, G. and Arokiasamy, P. 77, 97
Agyei-Mensah, S. and de-Graft Aikins, A. 18
Allet, D. and Crimmins, E. 78
Alma Ata Conference (WHO 1978) 33, 52, 56-7, 72
Anand, S. 2
Anderson, T. 2, 53
anti-ageing medicine 36-7, 101-2
Antonovsky, A. 33-4, 73-4
appearance and health perceptions 36-7
Apt, N.A. 37
'arc of acquiescence' of ageing (Higgs and Rees-Jones) 44-5
Ashton, J. and Seymour, H. 8, 71-2
Asia
  dementia prevalence data 104
  epidemiological changes 16
  family-based care trends 40, 55, 122
  traditional medicines 96
assistive technologies 92
attitudes towards health *see* 'health'
Australia, strategic health plans 56
autonomy
  and 'care' 38-9
  'choice' and agency discourses 1-2, 29, 43-4, 50, 125-6, 136
  losses associated with declining health 4
  vs. equity of resource allocations 137-8
  vs. social nature 4
  see also individualism
Ayis, S. et al 78

B

Baars, J. 50
'baby-boomer' bulge (UK) 24-5
Ballantyne, P.J. et al 108
Banerji, D. 136-7
Bangladesh 84-5
banking crisis (2008) 55-6
Bardage, C. et al 30
'Barker hypothesis' 41
Barrientos, A. 62-3
Batljan, I. and Lagergren, M. 23, 124
Beagle, R. and Bonita, R. 47
Becker, C.M. et al 74
'bed blockers' 99
Bedford, K. 3, 118-19
Bengston, V.L. et al 42-3
Beresford, P. 37, 119
Bern-Klug, M. 118
Bernard, M. 9, 76, 79
Better Ageing Project (Fox et al) 80
Bill and Melinda Gates Foundation 79
Billings, J. and Hashem, F. 34, 73
biomedical approaches to health 28-30
biotechnologies 92
bird flu 94
Birn, A.-E. et al 70, 77
Biswas, P. et al 31
Bito, S. et al 117
Blane, D. 41
Blane, D. et al 33, 113
Blaxter, M. 30-1, 33, 96, 135
Bolivia 54
Bond, J. and Cabrero, G.R. 31, 103-4
Boneham, M.A. and Sixsmith, J.A. 86
'bottom-up' policy directions 59-60
Bourdieu, P. 85
Bowden, P. 38, 41
Bowling, A. 30, 32, 82
Bozorgmehr, K. 50
Bradshaw, H.G. and ter Meulen, R. 102
Brodsky, J. et al 127-8
Buckner, L. and Yeandle, S. 120
Buvinić, M. et al 12-13, 21, 97

C

Cameron, L.J.H. et al 24, 84-5, 98
'capabilities' approaches 62-4
  defined 62
  and healthcare policies 64-6
cardio-vascular disease 15-16, 17, 20, 79,
  89-90, 117
  and socio-economic factors 41-2
'care' conceptualisations 37-41
  and cultural devaluation 38-9
  definitions 38

as process (Tronto) 39-40
as a 'value' (Held) 40
  see also ethics of care; self care
care practices *see* health and care practices
carers (unpaid) 119-22, 126
Carpenter, M. 62-3
Caselli, G. et al 16
cash-for-care schemes 125-6
cataract treatments 103
Cattan, M. et al 78
causes of death 15-17
causes of morbidity 76-9
Chapman, S.A. 84
Charusheela, S. 63
Chazan, M. 86
China
  dementia prevalence data 104
  family-based care provisions 119
  life expectancy 14
  long-term care trends 55, 122-3, 128
  marketisation of care 97
  primary prevention of disease 90
  rise in chronic disease 17
  traditional medical practices 96
'choice' and agency discourses 1-2, 29, 43-4,
  50, 125-6, 136
Chou, R.J.A. 122, 128
chronic (non-communicable) diseases
  delayed onset and the compression of
    morbidity thesis 21-3
  dementia 103-5
  depression 105-6
  epidemiological trends 17-18
  healthcare needs 102-3
  secondary prevention measures 107-8
Colebatch, H.K. 50
Coleman, P. 34
commercialisation of care
  ethical considerations 61-2
  trust issues and concerns 94, 97
  unequal contractual relations 5-6
Commission on Social Determinants of
  Health 56, 61
'compression of morbidity' thesis (Fries) 21-
  3, 26, 45, 69, 75, 109, 111, 131
consumer empowerment 125-6
consumerism 1-2, 135-6
  'anti-ageing' products 36-7
Costa-Font, J. and Toyama, M.G. 98
costs of care *see* health and care costs
Craig, R. and Mindell, J. 32
Crimmins, E.M. 22
cultural approaches
  to Advance Directives 116-17
  to ageing 36-7, 82, 84-5, 99-100
  to dependency/independence 111-13

to family-based care 122-3
to health care seeking 31-2
to lifecourse perspectives 41-3
Cumming, E. and Henry, W.E. 84

D

DALYs (Disability Adjusted Life Years) 12
Daniels, N. 47, 65-6, 136
Daniels, N. et al 77, 89
Dannefer, D. 42
Dannefer, D. and Settersten, R.A. 42
Danyuthasilpe, C. et al 82
Davey-Smith, G. et al 89-90
Davies, E. and Higginson, I.J. 117-18
Day, P. et al 11
Deacon, B. 51, 53
Dean, H. 63, 136
Deeming, C. 84
demand for care, peak ages 25
dementia 19-21, 103-5
  prevalence data 104
demographic data *see* epidemiological data
Department of Health 108
dependency 37-9, 111-15
  and end-of-life care 115-17
  ethics of care 38-9
  and self-care 44, 45, 80-1, 109, 112, 132-3
dependency ratios 3, 7, 11-12, 24-5, 45, 57
depression 105-6
developing countries
  trends in long-term care needs 127-8
  trends in population ageing 23-5
  see also named countries
diabetes, epidemiological trends 17-18, 20
diagnosis and disease defining 29-30
disability, and 'care' discourses 37-41
disability measures 12
  see also dependency ratios
discourses on health and care *see* health and
  care discourses
discrimination and older people *see* ageism
disease mortality data 15-17
  see also epidemiological data
disengagement theory 84
Dixon, T. et al 24
'double burden' of disease 17-18
Downs, M. 115
drug therapies, ethical concerns 94
Dummer, T.J.B. and Cook, I.G. 96
Dyer, S. et al 124-5

E

Earle, I. 70
Ebrahim, S. 100
economic contexts of care 47-8

impact of globalisation 49-50
political and organisational terrains 51-5
see also health and care costs; health and
  care spending
economic productivity of ageing
  populations 25
educational status, and healthcare uptake
  97, 103
Egypt 97
emotions and health 35
employment (paid) 25
end-of-life care
  appropriateness of interventions 100-1
  dependency issues 115-17
  provisions of formal support 117-18
epidemiological data
  causes of death 15-17
  'double burden' of disease 17-18
  life expectancy and mortality trends 13-
  15, 25-6
equity discourses 60-2, 133-9
  the 'capabilities' approach 62-4
  vs. autonomy and individual choice 137-9
  see also socioeconomic inequalities
Estes, C. et al 28, 100
ethics of care
  and dependency 38-9
  equity principles vs. agency and choice
  137-9
  feminist perspectives 121-2, 138
  as a framework for analysis 133-6
  and gerontology 136-9
  international perspectives 5-6
  and lifecourse conceptualisations 38-9
  and policy processes 6-7, 60-2
  theoretical frameworks 4-5
Eurofamcare Consortium 120
European Foresight Monitoring Network/
  Group 91-2, 102
exercise promotion 2-3, 79-82, 84, 104
expert patient 108
eye sight problems and interventions 19-21,
  103

F

family-based care 119-23
  grandparents providing care 7, 40-1, 86-7,
  119, 132
  impact of economic development 25
  international comparisons 40, 55, 119
Fernandez-Ballesteros, R. 86
Ferri, C.P. et al 19, 104
'filial piety' 55, 122
financing arrangements *see* health and care
  spending
Fisher, B. and Tronto, J.C. 38

fitness regimes 37
Fletcher, A.E. 19
Flores, Y.G. et al 123
'fourth age' of ageing 43-5, 116
Fox, K.R. et al 80
frailty 114
Fries, J.F. 22
Fuller, B.G. et al 80
functional abilities, as determinant of health 32-3
'functional age' (Katz) 33, 45
functional health measures 12
funding for healthcare *see* health and care spending

G

gender inequalities in health 21, 97
genetic inheritance of disease 42
Ghana 37
Giles, J. et al 122
Gilleard, C, and Higgs, P. 3, 43-4, 112, 116
Glaser, K. et al 119-20, 124
Glendinning, C. and Moran, N. 55, 120
Global Age-friendly Cities (WHO 2007) 59-60
Global Burden of Disease (GBD) Project 12
  critiques 12-13
'global care chains' 5, 50, 53-4, 118, 128-9
Global Forum for Health Research 1
Global Health Watch 55-6
global healthcare policy discourses 49-50
  cost of care agendas 2-3
  equity of provision 60-2, 133-9
  justice and care principles 6
  impact of oppressive conditions 76-7
  'life-span approaches' 65-6
  limitations of individualism 5, 137-9
  mainstreaming of age-related concerns 57-8
  New Public Health strategies 71-5
  rhetoric vs. reality 55-8
  see also health and care policy processes
'global public good' 61
Gooberman-Hill, R. and Ebrahim, S. 114-15, 119
Gorard, D.A. 29
Gorman, M. 52, 60
Gott, M. et al 117
Gough, I. 54
Gragnolati, M. et al 119-20, 127-8
grandparents providing care 7, 40-1, 85, 86-7, 119, 132
Gu, D. et al 77, 90-1
Guardian newspaper 54

H

Hammarstrom, G. and Torres, S. 115
Harper, S. 23-4, 43, 57-8
Harrington, C. 121
Hassim, S. and Razavi, S. 51
'health' conceptualisations
  as absence of disease 30-2
  biomedical approaches 28-30
  as a commodity 2
  functional/instrumental models 32-3
  as a 'human right' 2, 61-2
  and identity 35-7
  positive approaches 33-5
'Health for All by the Year 2000' (WHO 1981) 72-3
health 'capabilities' *see* 'capabilities' approaches
health and care costs 2-3, 24-5, 92-4
health and care discourses
  general overview 7-8
  'capabilities' approaches 62-4, 64-6
  'care' conceptualisations 37-41
  'health' conceptualisations 28-37
  'health equity' conceptualisations 60-2, 133-9
  'lifecourse' approaches 41-5
health and care policy processes 47-67
  based on dependency forecasts 11-12, 24-5, 25
  by levels of action
    primary preventative 8-9
    restorative 9
    tertiary and later life care 9
  contexts 49-50
  globalisation influences 2-3, 5, 6, 49-50
  in response to epidemiological trends 23-5
  implementation gaps 55-8
  international goals and target-setting 55-8, 70-4
  'path dependencies' 55
  policy 'as' process 48-9
  political and organisational terrains 51-5
  problems and threats 58-60
  quality of life considerations 113-14
  rhetoric vs. practice 55-8
  stakeholder support and engagement 58-60
  use of 'capabilities approaches' 64-6
  see also healthy living policies; preventative health care
health and care practices
  lack of policy focus and attention 5
  long-term care developments 123-8
  regulation needs 59, 127
  see also health services
health and care spending 92-4

distribution considerations 25-6
private sector vs. state funding 1-2, 3
sustainability considerations 3
see also rationing policies
The Health Evidence Network (EU/
WHO) 77-8
health inequalities
and gender 21, 97
and social injustice 2
see also socioeconomic inequalities
health literacy 81, 108
health promotion 70-4
critiques 74-5
and older people's health 76-9
implementation of findings 79-80
promotion of 'active ageing' 80-5
secondary prevention for chronic illnesses
107-8
health security 61
health services 89-91
financing 92-4
impact of population ageing 91-4
healthcare needs of older people 102-3
healthcare rationing policies *see* rationing
policies
healthy ageing 80-5
concept dominance processes 1-3
concept globalisation phenomena 2, 80-1
cultural aspects 36-7, 82, 84-5
epidemiological forecasts 21-3
policy directions 2-3, 79-80
as 'survival' 84-5
see also anti-ageing medicines
healthy living policies
individual behaviours vs. social and
economic 8-9
promotion of 'active ageing' concepts 80-5
in public health discourses 70-87, 101
'self-care' discourses 44, 45, 80-1, 109, 112,
132-3
see also healthy ageing; 'lifecourse'
approaches
heart disease 15-16, 20, 89
and socio-economic factors 41-2
Hein, W. and Kohlmorgen, L. 51-2
Held, V. 4-6, 40, 63, 136
HelpAge International 77
Heywood, F. et al 40
Higgs, P. and Rees-Jones, I. 27, 29, 31, 36-7,
43-5, 99-100, 112, 114
Higgs, P. et al 36-7, 43-4, 81
Hill, M. and Hupe, P. 48, 55
Hockey, J. and James, A. 36
hospital discharges 99
Howse, K. 23
Hui, E.C. 97

human rights and health discourses 2, 6-7,
61-2
Hyder, A.A. and Morrow, R.H. 13

I

iatrogenic disease 29
identity and 'health' concepts 35-7, 114-15
incontinence 99
independence and cultural implications
38-9, 111-13
India
dementia prevalence 104
family-based care 119
health and care financing 93
improving care accessibility 96-7
mortality and morbidity trends 11
onset of functional old age 76-7
palliative and end of life care 117
individualism
'choice' and agency discourses 1-2, 29, 43-
4, 50, 125-6, 136
limitations within global marketplace 5-6
as Western neo-liberal concept 4-5, 134-6
Indonesia 94
Innes, A. 30, 103-5
interdependency of human beings 5
International Agency for Prevention of
Blindness 103
International Network on Public Health
and Ageing 78
Internet use 108
Izuhara, M. 55, 122

J

James, A. and Hockey, J. 35-6
Jawad, M.H. et al 78
Johnson, K.S. et al 115-17
Jolanki, O.H. 112, 115, 117
justice principles and care 6

K

Kalache, A. 59
Kalache, A. and Keller, I. 83
Kanchanachitra, C. et al 95
Katz, A.R. 33, 45, 56, 59, 81
Keating, N. 82
Keller, H.H. et al 77
Kickbusch, I. 56, 58, 60
Kinsella, K. and Velkoff, V.A. 16, 22, 25
Kittay, E.F. 38, 87, 121, 134
Kittay, E.F. et al 3-5, 135
Kitwood, T. 40
Knapp, M. et al 105
Kofman, E. and Raghuram, P. 38

Kreager, P. and Schröder-Butterfill, E. 116, 121-2
Kruk, M.E. et al 95
Kuh, D. and Ben Schlomo, Y. 27, 41-2, 69
Kuh, D. and Davey Smith, G. 77
Kwok, T. et al 117

L

Labonté, R. 2, 54, 60-1
Labonté, R. and Schrecker, T. 75, 79
Labonté, R. et al 54
'laissez-faire' approaches (policy-making) 58-9
Lalonde, M. 71-2
Land, H. 27
Land, H. and Himmelweit, S. 40, 125, 135
Laslett, P. 7-8, 43
Lawton, J. 44
Lee, K. et al 53
Leonard, L. 90-1
Lewis, J. and Giullari, S. 63, 136
liberalism, as dominant policy discourse 50
life expectancy trends 1, 13-15, 25-6
   as indicators of inequality 2, 64-5
   threshold extension 64-5
   use of 'functional ageing' as predictor 33, 45
'life-span account' (Daniels) 65-6
'lifecourse' approaches 41-5
   concept described 7-8
   key principles 42-3
   third age/fourth age dichotomy 43-5
'lifestyle' diseases 17-18
Lindström, B. and Eriksson, M. 72
literacy 63-4
living wills 116-17
Lloyd, L. et al 101, 116-17, 124, 126
Lloyd-Sherlock, P. 11, 21, 39, 49, 52, 58-9, 63, 91, 95-6, 98-9, 103, 127
Loewenson, R. 94-5
long-term care
   accountability 127
   policy developments 123-8
   private sector organisations 126-9
   regulation 59, 121, 127
Lopez, A.D. et al 15
Lumme-Sandt, K. et al 29
Lund, F. 129
Lupton, D. 29-30
Lutz, W. et al 12, 14

M

McFarlane, A. and Kelleher, C. 30-1
McKee, K.J. and Samuelsson, G. 78
McKeown, T. 89

Mackintosh, M. and Tibandebage, P. 40-1, 85
Mackintosh, M. et al 94
McMichael, A. and Beaglehole, R. 72
MacNicol, J. 65
Madrid Action Plan on Ageing (MAPAA) 57-8, 82-3
Mahon, R. and Robinson, F. 4-5, 127-8, 135
Manthorpe, J. and Illiffe, S. 105-6
Margrain, T.H. and Boulton, M. 19, 103
Marmot, M. 21, 28
Means, R. 100
measurement tools for health and disease 12
Mechanic, D. 30-1
medical interventions 89-91
   cf. primary prevention strategies 90-1
   new technologies 92
medicalisation of old age 28, 89, 100, 108-9, 132
Meinow, B. et al 108
Mestheneos, E. and Triantafillou, J. 120
Metz, D. and Underwood, M. 43
migration of healthcare workers 94-5
   global chains of care 128-9
   screening and regulation 128
Millennium Development Goals 55
mind—body interconnectedness 35
Mini, G.K. 11
MIPAA *see* Madrid Action Plan on Ageing (MAPAA)
Mkandawire, T. 48
models of health and care
   biomedical 28-30
   functional/instrumental 32-3
   positive/salutogenic 33-5, 69-70, 73-5, 87, 102, 132, 134
   'tertiary prevention model' 8
morality and healthcare behaviours 31, 80-5
   age discrimination practices 98-101
   see also ethics of care
morbidity data 15-23, 26
   and disability 19-23
   and the 'double burden' 17-18
   and gender 21
Morgan, A. and Ziglio, E. 34, 73
mortality causes 15-17
mortality rates 13-15
Mudege, N.N. and Ezeh, A.C. 85-6, 98
Murray, J. et al 106
Mykytn, C.E. 100, 102

N

Nairobi, care by grandparents 85
Navarro, V. 2, 52

'the negotiated body' (James and Hockey) 35-6

'nested dependencies' (Kittay) 38-9, 138

Nettleton, S. 32-3, 74-5

New Public Health Movement 71-4
  critiques 74-5

NGOs (non-governmental organisations)
  impact on access to medicines 94
  impact on global policy-making 60

Nolte, E. and McKee, M. 18-19, 54-5, 103, 107-8

Nussbaum, M. 62-3

Nyqvist, F. et al 86

Nzegwu, N. 64

O

obesity 23

Ochiai, E. 122-3

OECD 111, 119, 120-1, 123-6

Ogg, J. 77

Older, Richer, Fitter (Metz and Underwood) 43-4

Oliveira-Cruz, V. et al 91

Omran, A.R. 16

Open Method of Co-ordination (social protection/social inclusion) (EU 2004) 54-5

'optimal health' 102

Orenstein, M.A. 53

osteoporosis, genetic inheritance 42

Ottawa Charter (WHO 1986) 72-4

out-of-pocket payments 98

Oxley, H. 81, 107, 120-1, 135

P

Palier, B. and Sykes, R. 54

palliative care 117-18

Palloni, A. and McEniry, M. 16-17, 80

patient 'experts' 107-8

personalised care packages 123-4

Petersen, A. and Lupton, D. 75, 77, 81

pharmaceutical industries 94

Phillipson, C. 3, 49

physical exercise promotion 2-3, 79-82, 84, 104

Plath, D. 111-12

policy making for health and care *see* health and care policy processes; healthy living policies

political contexts of care policy-making 51-5

polypharmacy 29-30

Pomerleau, J. et al 90

Pond, B. and McPake, B. 95

population ageing
  epidemiological trends 13-17
  and healthcare systems 91-4
  and social support systems 23-5

positive ageing *see* healthy ageing

premature ageing 76-7

preventative health care 8, 69-87
  key models 8
  moral agendas and 'active ageing' 80-5
  public health and health promotion 70-4
    critiques 74-5
    influence of strategies on age-related discourses 76-9
    putting into practice and implementation 79-80
  secondary prevention 107-8
  socioeconomic determinants and social capital 85-7

primary healthcare
  'age-friendly' policies 59, 72-4, 82
  cf. 'primary care' 56-7
  mainstreaming of older people's needs 95-6

primary prevention *see* preventative health care

Prince, M. et al 104-5

Prior, L. et al 34

private equity firms 50

private (for profit) sector healthcare 1, 50
  as global model for care 50-1, 51-3
  idealised market rhetoric vs. 'real' world market relations 5-6
  merging with public sector institutions 51-2
  see also commercialisation of care

'prudential life-span account' (Daniels) 65

Prus, S. 22-3

public health
  commitments to 2
  definitions 70
  and health promotion 70-4
  role and remit 71-4
  value 76-9
  see also primary healthcare

public–private partnerships 51-5

Putnam, D. 86

R

rationing policies
  and ageism 98-101
  'life-span account' approaches 65-6
  values-based approaches 64-6

Razavi, S. 51

Redfoot, D.L. and Houser, A.N. 128-9

regulation of long-term care providers 59, 121, 127

relational autonomy 137-8
resource allocation
    and ageism 98-100
    and the ethics of care 136-7, 137-9
    use of capabilities approaches 64-6
Rifkin, S.B. and Walt, G. 71-2, 79
'rights' discourses 2, 6-7, 61-2, 78, 136-7
risk discourses 3, 49-50
Ritsatakis, A. 80-1
Robinson, F. 138
Rockwood, K. 114
Rozario, P.A. and Hong, S.I. 40
Ruger, J.P. 64-6, 136
Rummery, K. 126
Ryff, C.D. and Singer, B. 27, 32, 34-5, 75,
    123
Ryff, C.D., Singer, B. and Love, G.D. 34-5

S

Saltman, R.B. et al 25, 119
salutogenic approaches 33-5, 69-70, 73-5,
    87, 102, 132, 134
    see also 'upstream actions'
Sanders, C. et al 113-14
Schnittker, J. 105-6, 114
Schrecker, T. et al 61-2
screening programmes 81-2
Seale, C. and van der Geest, S. 116-17
secondary prevention 89-94
Segall, S. 2
self-care 44, 45, 80-1, 109, 112, 132-3
self-identity and 'health' concepts 35-7,
    114-15
Sen, A. 2, 62
Sevenhuijsen, S. 4, 38, 134
Seymour, J. et al 116-17
Shakespeare, T. 27
Shanmugasundaram, S. et al 117
Sidorenko, A. and Walker, A. 57
sight problems 19-21, 103
Silva, H.T. et al 54
smoking, global trade 54
social capital 85-7
    community vs. individual 86
social identity and health 35-7
social support policies, in response to
    epidemiological trends 23-5
socioeconomic determinants, and social
    capital 85-7
socioeconomic inequalities
    and health rights 56-8
    impact on access to services 95-101, 103
    impact of oppressive employment regimes
        76-7
    international goals and targets 55-8
Soubbotina, T.P. 51

Southern Cross (UK) 50, 127
Spain, social capital of ageing 86
spiritual health 34-5
Staehelin, H.B. 30, 45
statins 89-90
Stenner, P. et al 83
stereotyping 76
Structural Adjustment Programmes 55
sub-Saharan Africa *see* Africa (sub-Saharan)
Sukarsono, A. and Wulandari, F. 94
support measure policies *see* health and care
    policy processes
support practices *see* health and care
    practices
surveillance and public health measures
    81-2
symptom management 30-2

T

technological advances 92
'tertiary prevention model' of health and
    care 8
Thailand 82, 96
'third age' dichotomies 43-5
Thomas, C. 27
tobacco companies 54
Toronto Declaration on the Global
    Prevention of Elder Abuse (WHO 2002)
    6, 62
Torres, S. and Hammarstrom, G. 82
trade treaties 54-5
traditional medicine practices 96
Tronto, J. 4, 6, 39-40, 56, 134-6
Tunisia 97
Turkey 56
Twigg, J. 3, 36, 39, 44, 99, 112, 115

U

UN 11, 13-14, 21, 50-1, 57, 62, 79, 133
UN Declaration of Human Rights 6
unpaid care 119-22, 126
'upstream actions' 69-87
    concept description 8-9
    critiques 75

V

value-based policy-making discourses 60-2
van der Geest, S. 116-17
van Gool, C.H. et al 106
Vera-Sanso, P. 76
Victor, C.R. 32
Vidovićová, L. 83-4
Vienna Plan (UN 1983) 57, 122

Vincent, J.A. 36, 49, 102
vulnerability 114

W

Waerness, K. 124
Wahlin, A. et al 78
Walker, A. 83, 137
Walter, T. 115
Westendorp, R.G.J. and Kirkwood, T.B.L.
  22, 42
WHO 1, 6, 8, 13-15, 17, 19-21, 32, 33-4,
  52, 56, 58-9, 70-3, 77, 79-80, 82-3, 92-6,
  99, 101, 103, 107, 117, 134-5
Wilkinson, K. et al 99
Wilkinson, R. and Pickett, K. 48
Williams, F. 27, 118, 124
Williams, R. 30, 32
Wilson, G. 55
Wimo, A. et al 12
World Bank 8, 48, 52
  role in healthcare policy-making 51-5
World Development Report 52-3
World Economic and Social Survey (UN
  2007) 133
World Health Assembly 55
World Health Reports 56, 98, 106
Wray, S. 28

Y

Yach, D. and Beaglehole, R. 17
Yach, D. et al 80, 107
Yeates, N. 50, 53-4, 128
Yeoh, B.S.A. and Huang, S. 40
Yount, K.M. et al 97
youth cultures 36-7

Z

Zhan, H.J. and Montgomery, R.J.V. 55
Zhang, Z. et al 41